# TARÍACURI'S LEGACY

THE CIVILIZATION OF
THE AMERICAN INDIAN
SERIES

# Tariacuri's Legacy

## The Prehispanic Tarascan State

**By Helen Perlstein Pollard**
**Introduction By Shirley Gorenstein**

University of Oklahoma Press : Norman and London

Unless indicated otherwise, all photographs, including those of objects in museums, were taken by Helen P. Pollard. All maps and drawings are by Helen P. Pollard. The following maps first appeared in other publications, and are reprinted with permission. Map 1.2: Helen P. Pollard, "The Construction of Ideology in the Emergence of the Prehispanic Tarascan State," *Ancient Mesoamerica* (New York: Cambridge University Press, 1991), fig. 1, 168. Maps 2.1, 2.2, 2.3, 2.4: Helen P. Pollard, "An Analysis of Urban Zoning and Planning at Prehispanic Tzintzuntzan," *Proceedings of the American Philosophical Society* 121, no. 1 (1977), 47, 50, 56, 58. Maps 3.1, 3.2, 3.4: Shirley Gorenstein and Helen P. Pollard, *The Tarascan Civilization*, Vanderbilt University Publications in Anthropology, no. 28 (1983), 8, 56, 79. Maps 3.5, 3.6: Shirley Gorenstein and Helen P. Pollard, "Xanhari: Protohistoric Tarascan Routes," in *Ancient Road Networks and Settlement Hierarchies in the New World* (New York: Cambridge University Press, 1991), 171–72. Maps 4.3, 4.4: Helen P. Pollard, "Ethnicity and Political Control in a Complex Society: The Tarascan State of Prehispanic Mexico," in *Factional Competition and Political Development in the New World* (New York: Cambridge University Press, in press), figs. 2, 5. Map 5.1: Helen P. Pollard, "Ecological Variation and Economic Exchange in the Tarascan State," 262. Reproduced by permission of the American Anthropological Association from: *American Ethnologist* 9:2 (May 1982). Not for sale or further reproduction.

**Library of Congress Cataloging-in-Publication Data**

Pollard, Helen Perlstein.
    Taríacuri's legacy : the prehispanic Tarascan state / by Helen Perlstein Pollard ; introduction by Shirley Gorenstein. — 1st ed.
       p.     cm. — (The Civilization of the American Indian series ; v. 209)
    Includes bibliographical references (p.    ) and index.
    ISBN 0-8061-2497-0 (alk. paper)
    1. Tarasco Indians—History. 2. Tarasco Indians—Antiquities. 3. Mexico—Antiquities. I. Title. II. Series.
F1219.8.T37P65   1993
972'.01—dc20                                     92-37080
                                                   CIP

*Taríacuri's Legacy: The Prehispanic Tarascan State* is volume 209 in The Civilization of the American Indian Series.

1     2     3     4     5     6     7     8     9     10

# CONTENTS

# FIGURES

# MAPS

# TABLES

# PREFACE

THIS study of the Tarascan State is the product of more than two decades of my research into the prehistory of west Mexico. As a graduate student at Columbia University in the late 1960s I took a seminar on archaeology and ethnography taught by the late Edward Lanning. After spending weeks learning about Tarascan ethnography I was prepared to apply my knowledge to Tarascan prehistory. Unfortunately, with only one month remaining in the course I discovered just how little in the way of field research, and even less in the publication of fieldwork, had been done in the region. Before the semester was over my dissertation topic was chosen, a study of the prehistoric Tarascan capital as an urban center. As the years have passed I have continued to focus on questions posed in that first seminar paper and to raise new questions I had not imagined when I first learned about the "New Archaeology."

Over the course of these decades I have incurred many personal and intellectual debts. My dissertation committee guided that first work, and I wish to thank my chair, Shirley Gorenstein, and Pedro Carrasco, who have remained colleagues. The other members included the late Edward Lanning, Robert Stigler, and Gordon Ekholm. Pedro Armillas advised me on that first fieldwork, and INAH provided research and export permits. As an archaeologist who has been unusually dependent on historical documents, I owe eternal gratitude to J. Benedict Warren for locating, transcribing, and making generally available the primary sixteenth-century documents pertaining to the Tarascans. To Ben and Pat I owe great friendship. My other intellectual debts will be apparent in the text; my financial support for field research over the years has come from the Wenner-Gren Foundation for Anthropological Research, the Latin American Institute of Columbia University, the National Science Foundation, the National Endowment for the Humanities, and, for travel and teaching release associated with this book, Michigan State University.

Finally, I wish to dedicate this book to my children, Jason and Riva, for understanding my passion for archaeology and Michoacán; and to the Purépecha, in the hope that understanding their past can help them to empower their future.

HELEN PERLSTEIN POLLARD

*East Lansing, Michigan*

# INTRODUCTION
## BY SHIRLEY GORENSTEIN

IT is astonishing that the prehispanic Tarascans, famous among the Aztecs and well known to their Spanish conquistadores, have been little studied and poorly understood—until recently.

Within days of the Spanish conquest of Tenochtitlán, the Aztec capital, Cortés wrote to Charles V that there was a lord of a very great province called Michoacán, which extended to the Pacific Ocean. For their part, having heard about the conquest of the Mexicans, the Tarascans sent emissaries to the Spaniards (*Relación de Michoacán* 1956; Warren 1985). At first, both parties engaged in the same kinds of discourse: gift exchange and military display. Cortés offered the emissaries "jewels" as well as a theatrical skirmish by some of his horsemen. Only a few Spaniards returned with the Tarascans to their capital, Tzintzuntzan, where their king, Tangáxuan II, responded with a military display of his own. His warriors, in full hunt regalia, displayed their skill with the bow and arrow by killing a large number of deer. They presented the Spaniards with five deer. In return the Spaniards gave them green feathers, pigs, and a dog. While the green feathers were highly valued, the pigs were utterly disdained. Indeed, the latter gifts were later looked upon as an ominous sign.

Meanwhile, two Spaniards traveled across Michoacán and reached the Pacific Ocean. They returned to Tenochtitlán with natives from the coast and samples of gold. This feat whetted Cortés's interest in Michoacán as a route to the coast and a source of precious metals.

The Tarascan party that returned to Cortés included two members of the royal elite and brought even finer gifts. Cortés responded with an escalated military display, this time a parade and skirmish of horsemen, a formation of foot soldiers, the firing of weapons by the harquebusiers, the attack of a tower with artillery, and most important, a tour of the destroyed and razed Aztec capital. He sent the Tarascans back with impressions of Spanish power and with gifts for their king.

It is not clear what jockeying for position took place in the ensuing months. Certainly there were other exchanges, including a Spanish visit to Tzintzuntzan and perhaps a Spanish-Tarascan alliance against Colima. But by the summer of 1522, not quite a year after the fall of the Aztec capital,

Cortés knew some interesting things about the Tarascan kingdom: it had myriad objects of precious metals, it had silver and gold mines, and it had access to the Pacific Ocean. It also had a king, or *cazonci*, who had a tight control over the kingdom. Cortés decided to send an expeditionary force into Michoacán; its leader was Cristóbal de Olid. Following the Aztec route to the Tarascan territory, Olid and his forces of about two hundred Spaniards and several thousand native allies arrived at the great fortification of Taximaroa. But the Tarascans did not or could not mount their traditional military effort. The Tarascan king was still in the throes of the politics of a difficult interregnum and apparently could not launch a military campaign at the frontier, the Tarascans' first line of defense. The forces at Taximaroa, and also the divisions from the nearby fortifications already in the field, were not mobilized. Olid and his forces traveled from the frontier through Tarascan territory to the capital city. The king, much of the Tarascan nobility, and an army of several thousand—and perhaps as many as one hundred thousand—faced Olid and his forces half a league outside Tzintzuntzan on the well-traveled road to Tenochtitlán. They chose not to fight.

During the next years the Tarascan kingdom was under two civil governments: the *cazonci*'s Tarascan rule and Cortés's Spanish administration. Olid and his army did not conquer Tzintzuntzan the way Cortés conquered Tenochtitlán. Olid's forces were not engaged in battle, nor did they engage; rather they spent their time hunting for treasure and dismantling religious shrines (López Sarralangue 1965; Warren 1985). Nevertheless, the towns of the Tarascan kingdom acknowledged the Spanish presence and rights. How did this happen? The Tarascan state, powerful enough to build an empire, was strong enough to hold the kingdom together while the *cazonci* considered his relationship to the Spaniards. So, while Cortés believed Michoacán was conquered, the *cazonci* believed he still had an empire. Although the encomienda system was put into place and tribute went to the Spaniards, the Tarascans continued to give the *cazonci* at least part if not all of his traditional portion. Such fealty gave the *cazonci* considerable economic support. In addition, paradoxically, he maintained much of his political power. The administrators who governed in the provinces continued to spend time in court. They were appointed by the *cazonci*, were loyal to him, and otherwise had little direct obligation to their towns. Thus, there was no commanding local native authority for the Spanish encomenderos to coopt.

It was through a strange and fortuitous alliance between Nuño de Guzmán, president of the First Audiencia of New Spain, and Don Pedro Panza (or Cuinierángari), a Tarascan noble adopted as a brother by the *cazonci* and a close advisor and player for both sides in the conquest drama, that the existence of an apparent state as well as a hidden state was resolved. The Spaniards had the *cazonci* executed (*Relación de Nuño de Guzmán* 1526; Warren 1985).

The history of the conquest of Michoacán gives certain information about the Tarascan state. It shows the centralization of political power, the sense of kingdom defined by boundaries and traversed by a tribute network. It portrays the *cazonci* as both politically inept and adept, but certainly as the holder of a charismatic position. It describes a large, well-run Tarascan army that was well equipped, even by Spanish standards, and highly successful, capable of achieving the political goal of expanding the Tarascan kingdom from the small Lake Pátzcuaro Basin, of less than 1,000 sq km, to an empire of more than 75,000 sq km.

The recognition of the important and powerful Tarascan state was part of prehispanic native history. The wars between the Tarascans and the Aztecs in the fifteenth and sixteenth centuries were chronicled in native accounts and told to the Spaniards. The descriptions emphasize the large number of Tarascan soldiers brought into each battle, their elaborate dress, their effective weapons, their professional strategies and tactics, and finally the decisiveness of their victories. Durán, admittedly with some exaggeration, wrote of the twenty thousand warriors—Aztecs, Texcocans, Tecpanecs, and Otomí, among others—who had died in one campaign (Gorenstein 1985). In the seventeenth century, Spaniards wrote that the remains of the warriors could still be seen along several kilometers of the frontier (Beaumont 1932). And even today, Mexicans say that the bones of the dead could be found at Taximaroa.

Political, economic, social, military, and material complexity notwithstanding, the Tarascans were not an important subject of later ethnohistorical or archaeological investigation. The reason lies, at least in part, in the history and sociology of knowledge of the Mesoamerican scholarly, and particularly the archaeological, community.

In the sixteenth and seventeenth centuries, the Spanish chroniclers produced accounts of history and of daily life with some description of material culture, including descriptions of places and objects. There were official chroniclers, chroniclers among the religious, chroniclers who had participated in the conquest, and travelers. For Michoacán, there were comparatively few recorders, although they did include Fray Jerónimo de Alcalá, the author of *Relación de las ceremonias y ritos y población y gobierno de los indios de la provincia de Michoacán* (RM 1956), Diego Muñoz, Diego Basalenque, Alonso Ponce, Juan de Grijalva, Alonso de la Rea, and into the eighteenth century, Isidro Félix de Espinosa and Pablo de la Purísima Concepción Beaumont (Brand 1943).

But Michoacán did not have the chroniclers or visitors that came to central Mexico, the heart of Spanish administration. The famous writers, or perhaps, those who became famous because of their attention to central Mexico, recognized but did not detail Tarascan life and history as they did Mexican. Michoacán had only the passing attention of such influential writers as Fray Bernardino de Sahagún, who wrote simply that the king of Michoacán was no less than the king of Mexico (Sahagún 1950–1969). Herrera, focusing on the Mexicans, noted the Tarascans because of their interaction with the Mexicans, and discussed to some extent their pacification. Torquemada, whose visits to Michoacán were unofficial, that is, outside of his responsibilities to his order, concentrated on the native peoples of central Mexico.

Ethnohistorians—archaeologists of the nineteenth century—were primarily interested in describing prehispanic material culture. This meant architecture for the most part, but also artifacts. The most spectacular sites were in the Maya area and in central Mexico. The Lake Pátzcuaro Basin sites, with their limited number of public monuments, did not attract the attention that Teotihuacan, Tula, Copan, Palenque and other Mayan sites did. So the neglect of Tarascan studies due to the limited coverage in early ethnohistorical documents was exacerbated by the particular interests of nineteenth- and early twentieth-century archaeologists and ethnohistorians. Among this group, Eduard Seler was almost alone in his interest in the Tarascans (1908). His work is best known for illuminating the regions where he put his greatest effort, namely, the Maya, central Mexico, Mixtec, Tlaxcala, and Oaxaca.

It was in the mid-twentieth century that an intellectual process catapulted the Basin of Mexico to the center of archaeological study. After the initial decades of discovery and description, there was a push toward the development of paradigms. A powerful paradigm was appropriated by a number of anthropologists: evolution. The most influential evolutionist paradigm for archaeologists was the theory of multilinear evolution, formulated by Julian H. Steward. In this formulation Steward chose the Basin of Mexico to exemplify the development of civilization in the New World. The influence of that work profoundly affected the design of research and the course of funding. Several great projects were launched, including the Teotihuacan Mapping Project and the Basin of Mexico Survey Project.

But Steward's work created a theoretical problem. Steward was attempting to model civilization. He chose the Aztec example. Possibly in his mind, but certainly in the minds of those who used his model, example and model became one. Thus, Aztec culture and society became the prototype of civilization. The Tarascan state, different in character from the Aztec state, was not elevated to the stage or category of civilization. Without a supportive paradigm and with comparatively little extant data about it, Tarascan society was a backwater of Middle American studies.

Indeed, the lack of interest in the Tarascans was exacerbated by another problem, that of West Mexico, not commonly considered by archaeologists as part of the area of high culture called Mesoamerica. West Mexico appeared not to have the requisites of high cultures: widespread monumental material remains; a high degree of specialization and stratification in economic, social, and political organization; and urban centers.

In the second half of the twentieth century, a few archaeologists began to wonder if West Mexico was in fact without these requisites, or if it was simply without intense investigation. These scholars built on the 1930–1940s research, sponsored by the University of California at Berkeley, of Donald Brand, Edward Gifford, Isabel Kelly, and Carl Sauer. Then the University of California, Los Angeles, launched a series of research projects from the 1950s until 1970. These included work at Amapa, Nayarit; sites on the central Pacific coast, including the Barra de Navidad, the Morett site, and the Melchor Ocampo site; and the Magdalena Lake Basin. In addition, other comparatively small-scale projects were launched (Chadwick 1971).

In the western Mesa Central, the work on the chamber tomb complex revealed an early religious system that had origins in or connections to South America. Some insight into the larger cultural context of the tomb complex was found in Phil C. Weigand's studies in the Jalisco highland lake system (Weigand 1985). Weigand noted the existence of independent ceremonial centers, but most important, he described the growing complexity of society in this region. He described a Teuchitlán tradition in which there was increased population density and the economic development of the district as a key locus for the surrounding region. Architecture was elaborated and included ball courts. After the tomb complex subsided, social and political systems were stratified, and centralization of administration began to be developed.

Coastal Mexico profited from the attentions of Joseph Mountjoy and the archaeologists of the Marismas Nacionales of Western Mexico Project, who showed the organization of the exploitation of coastal microenvironments from southern Sinaloa to Colima. Clement Meighan revealed the complexity of the Postclassic Amapa site with its ceremonial areas of mounds and plazas (Chadwick 1971; Mountjoy and Torres 1985).

Some of the monumental sites of the Balsas-Tepalcatepec Basin were located by the Instituto Nacional de Antropología e Historia Project and by Louise Iseult Paradis, working in the Mezcala subregion (Cabrera Castro 1986; Chadwick 1971; González Crespo 1979).

In Sonora, archaeologists investigated the "statelets" of the Rio Sonora district. Others identified the Trincheras cultural tradition. The archaeologists working in this region revealed the complex economic relationship between it and the United States Southwest. They revealed that the region most closely connected with the United States Southwest was the Sierra Madre Occidental and the western Mesa Central. Here flourished the Chalchihuites cultural tradition of Zacatecas and Durango. J. Charles Kelley noted the stronghold sites of Cruz de la Boca and Cerro de Gualterio and the ceremonial centers of Cerro de Moctehuma and Cerro de los Viveras. Phil Weigand described the elaborate mining industry and its role in the complex trade structure that included not only the United States Southwest, but also central Mexico. Alta Vista was identified as a processing center and a staging area for trading expeditions (Weigand 1982a, 1982b).

In these last decades the trade structure and trade networks of West Mexico have been examined, helping to define the characteristics of civilization as they appear in West Mexico. Another particular aspect of West Mexican culture that became the subject of study was the development of metallurgy. The recent work of Dorothy Hosler, among others, put its appearance in Jalisco, Michoacán, and Nayarit at A.D. 800 and placed its origins in Ecuador, Colombia, and lower Central America, raising the question of long-distance maritime trade (Hosler 1988a, 1988b). The work showed that metallurgy in West Mexico began as a far more vital activity than it did elsewhere in Mesoamerica, and its influence was more powerful.

Yet, even as these West Mexican studies were being pursued successfully, many Mesoamericanists were either unaware of, or, having their minds occupied by contrary scholarly ideologies, could not incorporate the new data and interpretations into their research conclusions. Even in the 1970s and 1980s, Mesoamerican studies were filled with the inexplicable, rueful comments of scholars who believed that West Mexican archaeology and ethnohistory were poorly cultivated fields.

By 1974 there was a considerable body of work on West Mexico, and Betty Bell tried to close the gap between the widespread misperception of it as an unknown region of undeveloped culture and the results of current research, which showed the contrary. She wrote, "In contrast to the old view of West Mexico as a poor country-cousin with a meager cultural equipment borrowed belatedly from its betters elsewhere, what we are now beginning to see is a distinctive sub-area of Mesoamerica, with a cultural complexity and time-depth unsuspected until only a few years ago." In 1985, Michael S. Foster and Phil C. Weigand served as editors of the compendium, *The Archaeology of West and Northwest Mesoamerica*. They wrote: "Research in the last two decades has indicated that the evolution and adaptations of the indigenous cultures of the region parallel those found elsewhere in Mesoamerica." And Weigand, who had been revealing and interpreting the complexities of West Mexican culture in Jalisco and Zacatecas, put the major theoretical issue on the table with a quote from Octavio Paz: "[I]t is a mistake to study from the Nahua perspective (and more so from the later Aztec) the totality of Mesoamerican civilization, which is a reality that is richer, more diverse, and older."

Tarascan studies have been a major part of enfolding West Mexican studies. In the last decades much has been revealed about the Tarascans, in good part as a result of the efforts of Helen Perlstein Pollard. Although the great monumental structures at Tzintzuntzan had been excavated, the other parts of Tzintzuntzan had not been investigated with comparable interest. Pollard's work, surveying Tzintzuntzan, led her to some new conclusions about the nature of that settlement. She was able to identify five specialized zones and define its urban character. She concluded that Tzintzuntzan was an administrative city. Later, she expanded her interest in Tarascan settlements to include three other Lake Pátzcuaro Basin communities, namely Ihuatzio, Pátzcuaro and Erongarícuaro, and critical communities in the territory. She has also written on the economic capacity of the Tarascan core, the Lake Pátzcuaro Basin, and its dependence on the resources of the territory.

Pollard's continuing interest in the connection between the political and economic systems of the Tarascan state led her to a close study of the economy of the Tarascan kingdom, in which she examined the roles of the market, the tribute system, and the government agencies. She analyzed in detail the geographical source of goods, the mechanisms by which goods became available for consumption, and the question of who utilized the goods and services. She has worked particularly on Tarascan metallurgy, determining that it is a significant marker of elite social status as well as a major source of wealth for the ruling dynasty.

In writing this book, Pollard offers a full and informed description and interpretation of prehispanic Tarascan culture and society for the first time in the history of Tarascan studies. The book is especially illuminating because of its rich context. Pollard understands the effect of the natural environment and the messages and meaning of the built environment. She plumbs the ecology for its connection to and its influence on social institutions. She infers societal organization from her own deep familiarity with the physical remains of the capital city. She shows the intricate connectedness between the Tarascan economic and political systems and their unique forms. She reveals Tarascan knowledge and ideology, including religious ideas that she shows served to support the Tarascan state. Finally, and importantly, with a clear sense of both Tarascan history and development, she places Tarascan civilization in two arenas of study: Mesoamerica and the nature of the state. In doing this, she expands Mesoamerican history and changes our understanding of that rare form of political organization.

# TARÍACURI'S LEGACY

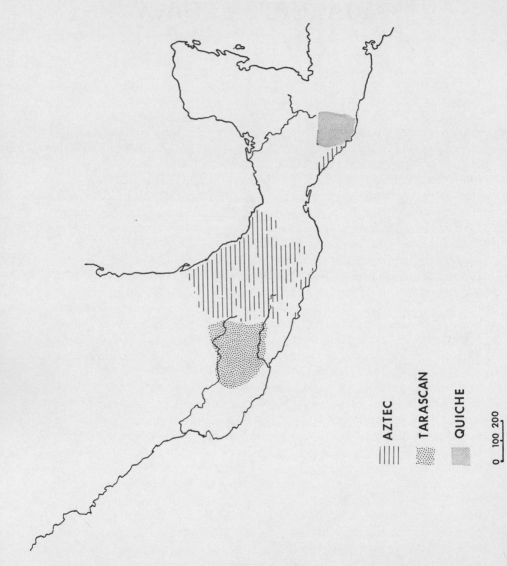

AZTEC

TARASCAN

QUICHE

0  100 200

KM

# CHAPTER 1

# PROTOHISTORIC MESOAMERICA AND THE TARASCANS

IN the early sixteenth century, much of West Mexico was under the political control of the kingdom of Tzintzuntzan, Irechecua Tzintzuntzani, known to Europeans as the Tarascan kingdom (map 1.1). As the second largest and most powerful Mesoamerican empire, the Tarascan kingdom was a valued target, first of Aztec, later of Spanish aggression. Indeed, on February 23, 1521, the first Spaniard entered Tarascan-controlled territory, and by the following summer Cortés sent out an expedition of Spanish soldiers to establish a colony and to seize effective control (Warren 1985:29, 42). In the centuries following European contact, the political conquest, completed by 1530, was accompanied by a cultural conquest that continues to this day. Taríacuri, the great culture-hero and legendary founder of the Tarascan state, is no longer seen as the link between the people and their destiny. Rather, he was replaced by Bishop Vasco de Quiroga, "Tata Vasco," colonial administrator and cleric from 1538 to 1565, who is extolled as the creator of the new social order. More recently, this founder of the colonial world is being increasingly replaced by Lázaro Cárdenas, ex-governor of the state of Michoacán, ex-president of the Mexican Republic, and hero of the latest new order, the modern Mexican state. As Taríacuri's legacy was dismantled, it was devalued by scholars and forgotten by his descendants.

A resurgence of interest in Tarascan civilization began in the 1970s, as modern ethnic Tarascans, or *purépecha*, sought to come to terms with their identity in the Mexican state, and as scholars recognized the significance of Tarascan prehistory. In many profound ways, the Tarascan state differed from other contemporary Mesoamerican states. An analysis of this civilization therefore not only provides information about prehistoric Mexico and the world in which the more famous Aztec empire functioned, but it also provides a model of one form of variation that archaic states exhibit. In addition, as the only empire to emerge in prehistoric western Mexico, the Tarascan case offers us an opportunity to evaluate the conditions under which centralized states emerge in regions that have interacted with, but have not been dominated by, states. Finally, the Tarascan kingdom is the late prehistoric society described in the *Relación de Michoacán*, recorded in 1541, and acknowledged to be one of the finest documents ever written about a prehistoric Native American civilization.

## THE TARASCAN HERITAGE

Despite the resurgence of scholarly interest in Tarascan civilization, the cultural heritage from which the Tarascans emerged is only poorly understood. Archaeological research in the territory once controlled by the Tarascan kingdom, the modern state of Michoacán and adjacent parts of Guanajuato, Jalisco, and Guerrero, has been sporadic and site-oriented (map 1.2; see Schondube 1987). Moreover, much of this work has been directed to sites occupied during the florescence of Tarascan culture (see discussion of Tarascan archaeology). Only three projects have been regional in scope and pre-Tarascan in focus: the Mexican salvage programs along the Balsas River (El Infiernillo and La Villita) during the 1960s, conducted by the Instituto Nacional de Antropología e Historia (INAH); the INAH salvage programs along the Gasoducto line, crossing Michoacán from Lake Cuitzeo to Lázaro Cárdenas in the early 1980s, with the associated Cuitzeo Basin Project; and the recently completed Proyecto Zacapu in the Zacapu Basin by the Centre d'Etudes Mexicaines et Centramericaines (CEMCA). Of these, only the Balsas and Zacapu projects included excavations with carbon-dated remains. All of this means that table 1.1, a summary of cultural development, is highly abstracted from limited information, and therefore quite tentative.

Table 1.1   General Cultural Sequence

| Mesoamerican Periods | Central Michoacán | Toluca Basin | Basin of Mexico |
|---|---|---|---|
| A.D. 1500 Protohistoric | Tarascan | Aztec | Aztec |
| A.D. 1400 Late Postclassic | Milpillas* | Matlatzinca | |
| A.D. 1200 Middle Postclassic | | | |
| | Urichu* | | |
| | Palacio* | | |
| A.D.  900 Early Postclassic | ——— | | Toltec |
| | Tingambato | Teotenango | |
| A.D.  700 Late Classic | | | |
| | Jarácuaro* | | |
| A.D.  400 Middle Classic | ——— | | Teotihuacan |
| A.D.    1 Early Classic | Loma Alta* | | |
| B.C.  400 Late Preclassic | Chupícuaro* | | Cuicuilco |
| B.C. 1200 Middle Preclassic | El Opeño* | | Zacatenco |
| | Capacha* | | |
| B.C. 2500 Early Preclassic | | | Zohapilco |

Note: Table adapted from Weaver 1981. Toluca and Mexico Basin chronologies are given only for orientation and are incomplete. Michoacán sequence emphasizes central Michoacán (see text).

*Indicates at least one radiocarbon date.

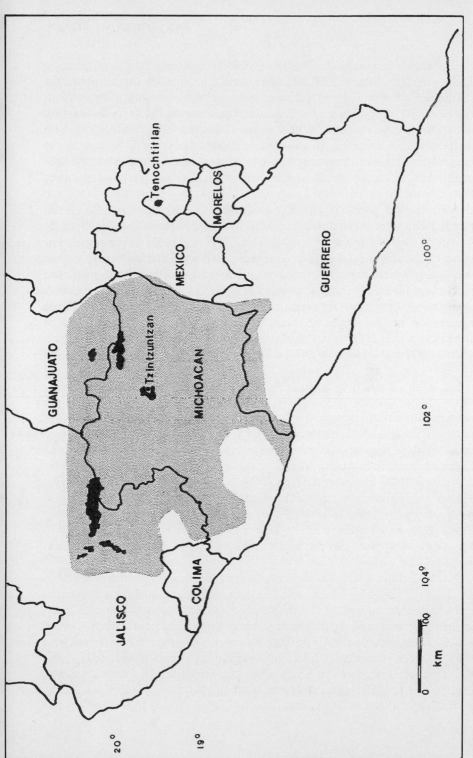

Map 1.2. Western Mesoamerica and the Tarascan State

The earliest occupation of this zone took place during the Paleo-Indian or Lithic period (before 2500 B.C.) by small groups of hunter-gatherers (Schondube 1987). The evidence for these earliest inhabitants is limited to fluted projectile points and other stone implements found in association with Pleistocene mammoths and bison (Oliveros 1975). While the best documentation comes from the Lake Chapala Basin, it is reasonable to suggest that similar occupations were taking place along other late Pleistocene lakes, such as Sayula in the west, Cuitzeo, Zacapu, and possibly Pátzcuaro.

The Archaic period is virtually unknown, but by the Early Preclassic populations were located in agriculturally based villages, known from El Opeño in the west and the Balsas Basin on the south. From the remains of these earliest known ceramic-producing societies it is clear that the region was occupied by many localized cultures, each with distinct histories, patterns of interaction with adjacent zones, and patterns of interaction with each other. This diversity remains characteristic of Michoacán until the emergence of the Tarascan state. El Opeño, the best documented of formative societies, consists of eleven excavated shaft tombs dating from 1500 to 800 B.C. (Noguera 1931; Oliveros 1975; Weaver 1981; Schondube 1987; Oliveros, personal communication 1991). The burial cult revealed by these tombs, including ceramic vessels, figurines, and the shafts themselves, suggests cultural interaction along the Santiago-Lerma River system with cultures to the west in Jalisco and Nayarit, as well as linkages to the east. Further south, in the middle and lower Balsas Basin, El Infiernillo small village sites containing ceramics suggest ties to the Capacha culture of Colima and the Pacific coast from Nayarit to Guerrero (Cabrera Castro 1986; Chadwick 1971; González Crespo 1979; Maldonado 1980; Muller 1979). Pollen cores from the Lake Pátzcuaro Basin reveal domesticated maize pollen from approximately 1500 B.C. (Hutchinson, Patrick, and Deevey 1956; Watts and Bradbury 1982). This suggests that human settlement was far more widespread than can be documented by the current archaeological evidence.

By the Late Preclassic there were at least three regional cultures found in Michoacán (map 1.3). These included the Chupícuaro culture of the northern and central zones, the Chumbícuaro culture of the Tepalcatepec Basin in the southwest, and the Balsas/Mezcala culture of the central Balsas to the south. Each zone was characterized by small-scale agrarian societies, and each has been identified primarily by variation in burial-associated ceramics. The best known is the Chupícuaro culture (fig. 1.1), found along the middle Lerma drainage in southern Guanajuato, the Lake Cuitzeo Basin, and, with localized variants, near Morelia (Santa María) and in the Zacapu and Pátzcuaro basins (Arnauld 1987; Chadwick 1971; Gorenstein 1985; Macías Goytia 1988; Michelet 1986, 1988a; Michelet, Arnauld, and Berthelot 1989; Moedano 1946; Moguel Cos 1987; Oliveros 1975; Weaver 1981). Chupícuaro communities appear to have been primarily adapted to lacustrine ecosystems, locating their villages on islands within marshes or along lakeshores or rivers (e.g., Chupícuaro, Acámbaro, Zacapu-Loma Alta, Lake Pátzcuaro, and the many Lake Cuitzeo sites). During the Early Classic period, local changes in ceramic style and more elaborate public architecture is found at the site of Santa María, near Morelia (Piña Chan 1977), and Chehuayo, in the Cuitzeo Basin (Macías Goytia 1989). This evidence plus more widely known variations in burial artifacts suggest that by the first centuries A.D. social ranking may have existed at the larger settlements (see Schondube 1987). Nevertheless, the location of settlements on the floor of lake basins and the general absence of settlements in defensible positions indicate minimal local aggression and/or movements of peoples. Chupícuaro artifacts or stylistically similar artifacts are found along the upper Lerma in the Toluca Basin, and further east into the Basin of Mexico and Tlaxcala, indicating significant, if indirect, social interaction between northern Michoacán and central Mexico at this time. The Chumbícuaro culture is known primarily from the plain of Apatzingán (Kelly 1947) and is dated from 100 B.C. to A.D. 100, while the Balsas/Mezcala culture is located along the central Balsas (Cabrera Castro 1986; Maldonado 1980; Muller 1979). While regionally distinct, they each appear to be related to adjacent zones to the south and west (Schondube 1987).

A major cultural transformation took place between A.D. 400 and 900. After centuries of autonomous village societies, distinguishable by stylistic variation in artifacts and local economic adaptations, a new form of settlement, the ceremonial center, appeared in Michoacán. The ceremonial centers known from this period, including El Otero (near Jiquilpan), Tres Cerritos (near Cuitzeo, C-53 in the Gasoducto survey), with possibly minor centers at Queréndaro and/or Zinapécuaro (Lake Cuitzeo Basin) and Tingambato (near the Pátzcuaro Basin), are widely dispersed in central Michoacán. They are separated by regions occupied by populations essentially continuing regional traditions, although in interaction with these new centers. The centers themselves contain architectural forms and artifacts indicating direct contact with Teotihuacan culture of the Basin of Mexico. At El Otero this includes a ball court; plazas and pyramids; stucco painting; and large group tombs, one of which held forty-two individuals, jade, rock crystal, pyrites, and turquoise (Noguera 1944; Oliveros 1975). At Tres Cerritos, a site that continued to be occupied until Spanish contact, this includes three large mounds and two sunken plazas. The earliest architecture

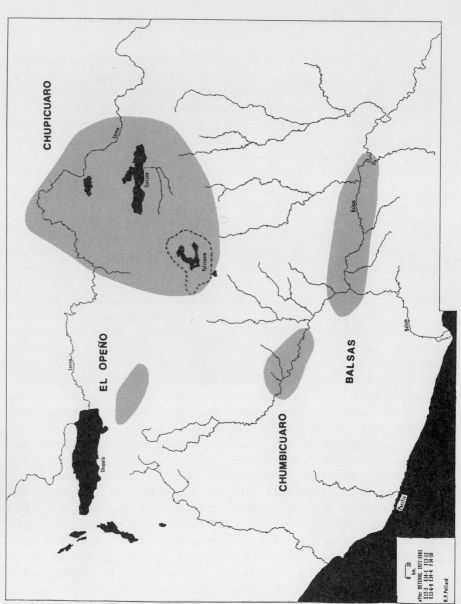

Map 1.3. Preclassic Michoacán

Fig. 1.1. Chupícuaro figurine, height 15 cm. (From Ferdinand Anton, *Women in Precolumbian America*, Abner Schram Publisher, New York, 1973, plate 15.)

at the site includes talud-tablero (a particular form of terraced platform characteristic of Classic-period Teotihuacan) and at least two large tombs, one of which contained more than thirty individuals, 120 vessels, marine shell, jade, turquoise, rock crystal, and an alabaster Teotihuacan mask (Macías Goytia 1988). At Tingambato there are a series of plazas, altars, a central pyramid (fig. 1.2), a ball court, and a large tomb containing the remains of at least thirty-two people (Piña Chan and Oí 1982). Among the artifacts are a cloisonné decorated vessel, marine shell and mosaic disks inlayed with pyrites, jadeite, jade, and turquoise. For the first time, there is evidence of dental mutilation in six of the Tingambato male burials, exhibiting A-2, A-4, and B-4 patterns (Romero Molina 1986). The talud-tablero architecture on the pyramid (fig. 1.3) and plazas reveals links to central Mexico, although all but a few ceramics are local. Outside these centers, from the Lerma River and Lake Cuitzeo Basin to the middle Balsas, a few sites in each zone contain thin orange pottery, cloisonné decoration, mosaic disks, Teotihuacan-like figurines, and occasionally talud-tablero architecture (Cabrera Castro 1986; Maldonado 1980; Oliveros 1975). In all cases the number of such artifacts is low, often a handful, and they represent only a small proportion of material goods associated with central Mexican

Fig. 1.2. Tingambato pyramid.

Classic-period culture. Thus, for example, while dental mutilation appears for the first time at Tingambato, it represents only a limited variety of such mutilation found at this time, and includes practices known elsewhere since the Middle Preclassic; dental incrustation (Romero's types E and G) is never found in Michoacán.

The meaning of these new centers and Teotihuacan-style artifacts is extremely unclear. Due to the salvage nature of most research, none of the deposits at the larger centers has been dated to anything more precise than A.D. 400–900. This means that they, and the more dispersed artifacts, may date to the Middle Classic and reflect populations interacting with the extensive Teotihuacan economic network; or they may date to the Epiclassic (A.D. 700–900) and reflect small groups of elite/priests/artisans who migrated out of the Basin of Mexico following the collapse of Teotihuacan, bringing some aspects of their heritage with them. A third possibility remains, that the archaeological evidence reflects a complex mixture of both processes, plus the added impact of the independent emergence of complex societies in Jalisco during the Classic period (Weigand 1985). There are

Fig. 1.3. Tingambato sunken plaza. Note talud-tablero architecture and entrance to tomb.

strong adherents to all alternatives, although the current evidence suggests Teotihuacan interaction along the Balsas during the Middle Classic, while central Mexican interaction with central and northern Michoacán was after A.D. 600 (Michelet 1988a, 1988b).

The effect of these contacts was to increase the process of social differentiation already taking place and stimulate the emergence of territorially discrete and competing polities. What they, or more precisely their elites, were competing over is unclear, but may have included access to interregional and intraregional trade to the east and west. The high proportion of Zinapécuaro obsidian utilized at Tula, Hidalgo, from A.D. 800 to 1000 (Diehl 1974; Healan 1989) suggests that by A.D. 800 portions of northeastern Michoacán were interacting more directly with Central Mexico than they had since the Middle Preclassic.

In the Zacapu Basin the period between A.D. 400 and 900 saw significant population growth, reflected in the increase of archaeological sites from thirteen to fifty-eight (Michelet, Arnauld, and Berthelot 1989). By A.D. 900 the effects of these changes resulted in major shifts in settlement patterns. In the Cuitzeo and Zacapu basins, the best known areas for this time period, but also along the Lerma and Balsas rivers, there are indications of population nucleation at defensible locations. In many zones this is the beginning of a pattern that grows until the emergence of the Tarascan state. Along with these settlement changes come the widespread adoption of red-on-cream ceramics, which are integrated with local ceramic traditions. Such shifts in style are known from a wide region of north and central Michoacán, including Zinapécuaro, Cuitzeo, Tiristarán, Morelia, Teremendo, Zacapu, Lake Pátzcuaro, Carapan, Zamora, and Tangamendapio. The coincident appearance of metallurgy in Michoacán, possibly earlier in Nayarit and Jalisco (Hosler 1988a; Mountjoy 1969; Mountjoy and Torres 1985), and in the lower Balsas Basin (Maldonado 1980) suggests that cultural exchange and/or population movements linked Michoacán directly to societies to the north and west. Again, the Santiago-Lerma River and Balsas-Tepalcatepec rivers appear to have been the primary routes of change. Hosler (1988b) suggests that the introduction of metallurgy was made by means of merchants plying the coastal canoe trade from southern Ecuador up the West Mexican coast. Oliveros has noted that at the time of Spanish contact canoe traders along that coast would put in at the port of Zacatula, at the mouth of the Balsas River, for up to six months before their return voyage was possible (Oliveros 1975). Hosler's suggestion is based upon technical analyses of the metal objects themselves. During the Early Postclassic the metal objects, known almost exclusively from burials, were made of copper and copper-silver by means of cold hammering, annealing, and lost-wax casting in styles and types of objects known earlier from coastal Ecuador.

By the Middle/Late Postclassic (A.D. 1200), societies throughout the region had little direct interaction with central Mexico but were instead participating in regional cultures, sharing traits and beliefs that later were characteristic of the Tarascans. Some of these traits appear to have diffused from further west in Mexico, particularly along the Santiago-Lerma River system; others were products of local cultural change. Specific traditions appearing now include more complex metallurgy, abundant ceramic pipes and occupation of sites later of sacred significance to the Tarascans, large-scale rubble-filled mounds clustered into plazas and located on hillslopes or *malpaís*, and petroglyphs later associated with the Tarascan sun-hunting deity Curicaueri. Hosler (1988b) notes that a number of metallurgical techniques and styles were introduced at this time into West Mexico. The source of these innovations appears to be south coastal Peru trade with coastal Ecuador, and then trade from Ecuador to West Mexico. Among the new features were loop-eye needles, axe money (of sheet metal), and wirework bells, which, in addition to previously made forms, were worked hot. New bronze alloys were produced during the Late Postclassic, including copper-arsenic, copper-tin, and copper-arsenic-tin.

The current archaeological evidence suggests that during the Middle/ Late Postclassic, local elites competed for communities, marking their relative success with polychrome pottery, metal goods, and patron deities. The absence of regional authority and decision-making in the face of what appear to have been increasing populations led to the formation of highly nucleated populations in some areas. The best documented example is that of Zacapu, with an estimated occupation of the *malpaís* (known as El Palacio in the literature) of 11 sq km and upwards of twenty thousand people (Michelet 1988b; Michelet, Arnauld, and Berthelot 1989; Michelet, Ichon, and Migeon n.d.), while the lake-marsh below was abandoned.

According to the *Relación de Michoacán* (abbreviated RM), during the Late Postclassic there were a series of migrations of peoples into central Michoacán. These included groups referred to as *chichimecs*, *nauhuas*, and the ancestors of the Tarascan royal dynasty known as *uacúsecha* (eagles). They are said to have been hunters and gatherers, especially deer hunters, who migrated from the north and settled in discrete communities within and adjacent to the Lake Pátzcuaro Basin, joining the already existing Tarascan-speaking population. Current evidence indicates that the numbers of migrants were very small or that they had assimilated local cultural traditions before actually entering central Michoacán. While there are clear ties between some Late Postclassic traits and the Lerma River Basin, there is no evidence of movement of Chichimecs, in the sense of hunter-gatherer Uto-Aztecans from north of the Mesoamerican frontier. To what extent this origin legend is myth or history will probably always be uncertain, but unlike the Postclassic period in the Basin of Mexico, which saw the spread of the Nahuatl language associated with population movements from the north, Tarascan remained the language of the Michoacán central plateau.

Nevertheless, even if the number of migrants was relatively small, in the context of the Late Postclassic their effects may have been great. While there were several different language-ethnic groups in the Pátzcuaro Basin by A.D. 1200, their relative sizes must have varied greatly. For example, the Nahuatl speakers of Xaráquaro (Jarácuaro) indicated in the RM, "We are many more than they, for there are not many Chichimecs," referring to the *uacúsecha* of Pátzcuaro (RM 1980:64ff.). The subsequent competition between their elites for access to basic resources is given as the cause for a succession of wars in which political and economic power was concentrated in the *uacúsecha* elite. According to official Tarascan history, the warrior-leader Taríacuri united the several independent polities of the Pátzcuaro Basin into a unified state during the first half of the fourteenth century (table 1.2). Following his death, his son and nephews extended the state beyond the Pátzcuaro Basin and began the political and economic changes that saw the emergence of a new Mesoamerican civilization. Until considerably more archaeological research is targeted to these centuries of transformation, the process by which the Protohistoric (A.D. 1450–1530) kingdom came into being will remain in the realm of myth and legend.

Table 1.2    Genealogy of the Tarascan Kings

| Ruler | Seat of Power | Reign |
|-------|---------------|-------|
| *Colonial* | | |
| Don Antonio Huitziméngari | Governor of Michoacán | 1545–1562 |
| Don Francisco Taríacuri | Governor of Michoacán | 1543–1545 |
| Don Pedro de Arellano assumed control as corregidor of Michoacán following the execution of Tangáxuan II and acted as regent for the king's sons, 1530–1543. | | |
| *Protohistoric* | | |
| Tangáxuan II (Tzintzicha Don Francisco) | Tzintzuntzan | 1520–1530 |
| Zuangua | Tzintzuntzan | 1479–1520 |
| Tzitzispandáquare | Tzintzuntzan | 1454–1479 |
| *Late Postclassic* | | |
| Tangáxuan I | Tzintzuntzan | ?–1454 |
| Hirepan | Ihuatzio | |
| Hiquingaje (younger son) | Pátzcuaro | ca. 1350–? |
| Taríacuri | Pátzcuaro | ca. 1300–1350 |
| Interrupted by brief rule by Curatame II, his older son. | | |
| Pauacume II | Pátzcuaro | |
| *Early Postclassic* | | |
| Uapeani II | Uayameo | |
| Curatame I | Uayameo | |
| Uapeani I | Uayameo | |
| Pauacume I | Uayameo | |
| Sicuirancha | Uayameo | |
| Thicatame (Hireti-ticatame) | Zacapu, then Zichaxuquaro | |

Note: This table is adapted from the RM (1980:f. 139), with paleography by Francisco Miranda; the RM (1956:xxxiii), introductory essay by Paul Kirchhoff; and data in *The Conquest of Michoacán* (Warren 1985) and *Historia sucinta de Michoacán* (Bravo Ugarte 1962). All Postclassic-period dates are estimates, given for general orientation only. Protohistoric-period dates are derived from either post-conquest Spanish documents or correlation with Aztec events (primarily battles).

## THE TARASCAN LANGUAGE (PURÉPECHA)

While ethnohistoric documents refer to native speech as either "lengua de Cintzuntza" (language of Tzintzuntzan) (Lagunas 1983:146) or *purépecha* (language of the people/commoners) (*Relaciones geográficas* 1987:81), the dominant language of the Tarascan state is generally referred to as Tarascan. The modern language has been studied by linguists and anthropologists over the last century (León 1888; Velasquez 1978; Nansen Díaz 1985; Mary Foster and Paul Friedrich; see Suárez 1983). Basing his research primarily upon the sixteenth-century Gilberti dictionary (1975) and his own modern studies, Swadesh attempted an analysis of protohistoric Tarascan (1969). More recently, J. Benedict Warren has supervised the editing and reprinting of the 1574 Lagunas grammar and dictionary (1983), the 1558 Gilberti grammar (1987), and the 1559 Gilberti dictionary (1990), and has transcribed a third dictionary housed in the Latin American Library, Tulane University (*Diccionario grande de la lengua de Michoacán*, 1991). While dialect divergence within Tarascan is often believed to be relatively recent, Lagunas made it clear that he was basing his dictionary and grammar on Tarascan as spoken in the Pátzcuaro Basin. This version he viewed as the "courtly, cultured and universal language of Michoacán, to be preferred to the incongruous, barbarous and badly pronounced language that they use in some towns, inasmuch as the language of Michoacán is all one" (Warren 1983:343).

Tarascan has long been recognized as a linguistic isolate within Mesoamerica (Swadesh 1969), and for many basic features, it stands out from the patterns of other Mesoamerican languages. Thus, for example, there is no word compounding, although "Tarascan is the language with the largest inventory of affixes (all in fact suffixes); there are more than 160 frequently used affixes, so most words are polymorphic" (Suárez 1983:65). Only Tarascan and Huave lack a glottal stop. Tarascan has the richest system of aspect and tense (thirteen tenses and six modes) (Suárez 1983:72), similar to Southern Tepehuan. Only Copainala Zoque, Tarascan, Huichol (partially), and Yaqui have morphological case systems (Suárez 1983:87). Attempts to classify amerindian languages have resulted in widely differing placements of Tarascan. Swadesh (1969:25) considered Zuni and Quechua to be most similar, although proposing at least four to five thousand years since Tarascan became a distinct linguistic community. The most recent regional classification is that of Greenberg (1987), where Tarascan and neighboring Cuitlatec are each considered separate language groups of the Chibchan languages, distributed outside of Mesoamerica in much of lower Central America and (modern) Colombia. While he does not attempt to estimate the time of divergence, comparison to his other language groups indicates that the divergence of the Tarascan linguistic community occurred no later than the Archaic period (ca. 7000–2000 B.C.). The difficulty of dealing with such ancient evolutionary relationships has led most linguists to treat Tarascan as an unrelated Mesoamerican language, with only distant historical relationships to other amerindian languages (see Suárez 1983 and Friedrich 1984).

Within Mesoamerica, Tarascan can be evaluated by the degree of sharing of basic phonological, morphological, and syntactic traits with other native languages of the region. In a recent study of Mesoamerica as a linguistic unit, a series of Mesoamerican and non-Mesoamerican languages were evaluated for the presence or absence of thirty-one features (Campbell, Kaufman, and Smith-Stark 1986). The degree to which these languages share the selected features is believed to reflect interaction between communities of speakers over long periods of time. Thus, the similarities are not seen as genetic, due to the origin and differentiation of languages, but as reflecting diffusion across linguistic boundaries due to social interaction.

Of the twenty-seven features which were compared to Tarascan, between twelve and nineteen were shared between each Mesoamerican language and Tarascan. Some of the similarities are probably due to geographical proximity, such as the relatively high sharing with Cora (sixteen) and Huichol in neighboring Nayarit, and the higher sharing with Tlapanec (nineteen) and Mazatec (sixteen) among the Otomanguean languages in Guerrero. Other sharing may reflect important routes of communication and long-term social interaction. The similarity to Totonac (nineteen) may reflect such processes operating along the northern border of Mesoamerica from the Lerma-Santiago River Basin (Cora and Huichol) across the Bajío into the Panuco River system. Nevertheless, evidence from study of the Tarascan language supports the more general conclusion about Mesoamerican languages: "Several facts point to a situation in which linguistic contacts were primarily among the upper classes and that their potential effects reached lower groups only sparingly" (Suárez 1983:159).

## THE PEOPLE

While the Tarascan language is an isolate in central and western Mexico, the anthropological study of the modern peoples reveals their biological links to Mesoamerica. Based upon studies of blood systems, anthropometry of living population, and craneometric characteristics, Sacchetti (1983) has defined a demotype B, within which Tarascan populations cluster. His classification of modern Tarascans is based upon the work of several physical anthropologists, some going back to the turn of the century, and all from communities considered *purépecha*. In addition to Tarascans, the B demotype includes Otomí, Mazahua, and Nahua from Hidalgo and Jalisco, among others—in other words, the central and western portion of the central plateau. The populations of southern Mexico, the Mayan region, and Central America are clearly distinguishable, despite four centuries of demographic change.

## STUDYING THE PROTOHISTORIC STATE

### THE DOCUMENTARY RECORD

One of the great advantages of studying societies in existence at the time of European contact is the documentary record left by colonial explorers, missionaries, and administrators describing a prehistoric world. In the case of the Tarascans this is especially valuable because they kept no written records themselves, despite their knowledge of such documents in other parts of Mesoamerica. There are a small number of pictorial manuscripts, including the *Lienzo de Jucutacuto*, which may or may not predate Spanish contact, but they are of limited coverage and subject to widely varying interpretation (see Gorenstein and Pollard 1983:13ff. for a discussion of these sources). The most significant documents for the purpose of interpreting the Protohistoric period are those that are explicitly describing "how things were in the past" and those dating from before 1550. Later documents must be used with care because, depending upon the subject, major sociocultural changes were well under way by the late sixteenth century.

The preeminent source is the *Relación de las ceremonias y problación y gobierno de los indios de la provincia de Michoacán*, recorded in 1540–1541 in the Tarascan capital, Tzintzuntzan. A Franciscan priest, believed to be Fray Jerónimo de Alcalá, translated and transcribed narratives of a group of Tarascan noblemen (Warren 1971). The *Relación de Michoacán*, as it is commonly known, contains 140 folios and 44 illustrations. It contains three parts, focusing on the Tarascan state religion, Tarascan society, and official state history, including the Spanish conquest. Unfortunately all but one folio of the first section has been lost. Several editions of the RM have been published, based upon the manuscript in El Escorial, Madrid, or later copies in the Library of Congress, Washington, D.C., and Morelia, Michoacán (see Warren 1985:328). The most detailed edition was produced in 1956, and more recently, a new transcription, also based upon the Madrid document, was published in 1980. An English edition, based upon the Morelia copy, appeared in 1970, and a recent translation into French has been published. Most of our information about the development of the Tarascan state comes from a large section of the RM dictated to the Spanish friar, based upon the "official history" of the Tarascan people. Each year the chief priest and the king would hear legal disputes and "administer justice" for twenty days (one Mesoamerican month). At the close of this time the feast of Ecuata Conscuaro would be celebrated (the Great Gathering, June 27). As part of these celebrations the chief priest (*petámuti*) would recite the Tarascan "official history" (fig. 1.4) (RM 1980:17–19).

Supplementing the RM are several documents written within the Tarascan region as part of early colonial administration. These include the *Relaciones geográficas* (abbreviated RG) of 1579–1580 (1958, 1985, 1987), the Caravajal Visitation of 1523–1524 (Warren 1977, 1985), the early encomienda grants of 1523–1525 (Simpson 1934; Warren 1985), the Ortega Visita of 1528 (Warren 1977), and the *Suma de visitas de pueblos* of 1547–1550 (1905). The *Minas de cobre* of 1533 (Warren 1968, reprinted 1989) and various court documents filed during the sixteenth century contain direct testimony about prehispanic land rights, tribute, transportation, mining, and ethnicity. These are located in the Archivo General de Indias, Seville; the Archivo General de la Nación, Mexico City; and the Municipal Archives of Pátzcuaro, now available in the library of the Museo Nacional de Antropología, Mexico. Excellent summaries of these documentary sources can be found in Brand 1943, Gerhard 1972, Paredes 1976, and Warren 1977 and 1985. Later documents, such as those by Ponce (1586, published 1968), Ramírez (1585 in Miranda edition of RM 1980), Beaumont (1776–1780, published 1932), *Inspección ocular en Michoacán* of 1799 (Bravo Ugarte 1960), Martínez de Lejarza of 1822 (1974), and Romero (1862) are of particular value in tracing place names and ecological changes and summarizing earlier manuscripts now lost. Pictorials accompanying these documents are occasionally copies of sixteenth-century maps, also lost. The history and use of these maps is detailed in Gorenstein and Pollard (1983:ii).

In addition to these explicitly historical documents, we have a corpus of sixteenth-century dictionaries and grammars of the Tarascan language written by Franciscan friars as part of their missionary goals (Warren 1983). At least three dictionaries and two grammars are now known, including the 1558 grammar by Maturino Gilberti (1987); the 1559 dictionary, also by Gilberti (1975, 1990); and the 1574 dictionary and grammar by Juan Baptista de Lagunas (Lagunas 1983). The two grammars and the dictionary by Lagunas had long been inaccessible to most scholars until recent publication in facsimile by J. Benedict Warren. A third dictionary, mistakenly thought to be a copy of Gilberti's, has recently also been transcribed and published by Warren (Anonymous, 1991). The word lists, etymologies, and grammatical rules provide significant information about Tarascan kinship, social classes, beliefs, and worldview at a time early enough to be useful for understanding the Protohistoric period.

Fig. 1.4. "Speeches and reasoning of the chief priest regarding the history of their ancestors." (From *The Chronicles of Michoacan*, translated and edited by Eugene R. Craine and Reginald C. Reindorp, Copyright © 1970 by the University of Oklahoma Press, plate 41.) "De la plática y razonamiento que hacía el sacerdote mayor a todos los señores y gente de la provincia" (RM 1956:lamina xxiv).

Finally, relevant historical documents also include those written in other parts of Mesoamerica, especially the Basin of Mexico, that describe how non-Tarascans viewed the Tarascan kingdom. Foremost of this type of source is Sahagún's *Florentine Codex* of 1569 (1950–1969), but it also includes Zorita's *Relación* (Carrasco 1986) and the various Aztec codices that refer to Tarascan-Aztec military campaigns (see Hassig 1988; and Herrejón Peredo 1978).

## THE ARCHAEOLOGICAL EVIDENCE

As I have already indicated, archaeological research in Michoacán has been limited and sporadic, although much of what has been done relates to the Tarascan state. The greatest amount of research has been carried out at the Tarascan capital, primarily under the auspices of the Instituto Nacional de Antropología e Historia, Mexico. In 1930, when modern archaeological research began, Alfonso Caso and Eduardo Noguera placed test-pit excavations in two of the ethnohistorically known Tarascan centers (Tzintzuntzan and Ihuatzio) in an effort to provide collections for the National Museum (Caso 1930; Noguera 1931). Caso returned in 1937 and 1938 to begin mapping and excavations on the Great Platform at Tzintzuntzan (Acosta

1939). In 1940, 1942–1944, and 1946 these were continued under Rubín de la Borbolla, along with reconstruction of several pyramid bases (Acosta 1939; Gali 1946; Moedano 1941, 1946; Rubín de la Borbolla 1939, 1941, 1944). In 1956 limited excavations were continued under Orellana. In 1962, 1964, and 1968 Román Piña Chan continued this work on the Great Platform at Tzintzuntzan (Castro-Leal 1986). The tenth and latest season of work by the Instituto Nacional de Antropología e Historia at the ceremonial core of Tzintzuntzan was carried out by Cabrera Castro (1987) in 1978–1979 with current work by Efraín Cárdenas under way (1992–94). In 1970 I conducted an intensive surface survey of the urban extent of Tzintzuntzan (Pollard 1972, 1977).

On the regional level, a study of the Protohistoric-period political system of the Lake Pátzcuaro Basin by Gorenstein and Pollard (1976–1980) led to the identification of ninety-one settlements occupied during the apex of the Tarascan state (Gorenstein and Pollard 1983). In 1981–1982, eighty-three sites were recorded in the eastern half of the Lake Pátzcuaro Basin as part of the Proyecto Arqueológico Gasoducto (Tramo Yuríria-Urapan), under the direction of Carlos Silva Rhoads, INAH Salvamento Arqueológico (Moguel Cos 1987), of which more than thirty were tentatively assigned to the Protohistoric. The following year (1983), a surface survey of the western half of the lake basin added sixty sites to the basin total, forty-four of which were assigned to the Protohistoric. Similar surveys in the Zirahuén and Cuitzeo lake basins have documented the abundance of Tarascan-associated sites, although the speed and incompleteness of these salvage surveys have provided very limited data. The far more detailed surveys in the Balsas River Basin undertaken before the construction of dams in the zones of Infiernillo (1963) and La Villita–Palos Altos (1967–1968) provide archaeological documentation of Tarascan presence in this important southern zone of the empire (González Crespo 1979; Maldonado Cárdenas 1980; Cabrera Castro 1986).

Outside of the Lake Pátzcuaro Basin only two projects have focused on the period of Tarascan domination. The first, carried out from 1971 to 1974 under the direction of Shirley Gorenstein, was a study of the Tarascan-Aztec military frontier. Several of the Tarascan fortified sites were located and surveyed, with major excavations focused on Cerro del Chivo, Acámbaro (Gorenstein 1985). The second, carried out from 1983 to 1987 (with analyses still under way) by CEMCA under the direction of Dominique Michelet, entailed excavations and mapping at the Tarascan center of Zacapu, a regional survey of the Zacapu Basin, and study of the obsidian quarries in the region of Zináparo (Michelet 1986, 1988a, 1988b; Arnauld 1987).

In addition to the research within the Pátzcuaro Basin, the regional surveys, and targeted study of Tarascan archaeology, many other archaeological projects carried out within the territory once held by the Tarascan state have provided some information. These have been summarized by Chadwick (1971) for the period through 1970 and appear as salvage reports, rarely published, for the period since 1970 (e.g., Contreras Ramírez 1987; and Macías Goytia and Cuevas García 1988). The Cuitzeo Basin project, under the direction of Macías Goytia, INAH, has included excavations at Huandacareo, an administrative center founded after Tarascan conquest of the basin, and Tres Cerritos (Cuitzeo), an earlier center, which continued in use under the Tarascans (Macías Goytia 1988, 1989). Finally, technical analyses of Tarascan artifacts from museum collections provide information about raw materials, technology, style, and economic interaction (Bray 1984; Castro-Leal 1986; Flores de Aguirrezabal and Quijada López 1980; Grinberg 1988; Hosler 1985, 1988a, 1988b).

## HUMAN PALEOECOLOGY

To understand the relationship between population, economic resources, and political power in the emergence and maintenance of a prehistoric empire, one must have basic information about the human ecosystem. This information includes such topics as the distribution and composition of land-use zones, the location of water and mineral resources, and the size and distribution of human settlements in relation to these resources. For the Tarascan territory, an increasing number of analyses provide such information for the modern and prehistoric periods.

The first large-scale study was by Robert West (1948) in his cultural geography of central Michoacán. He used United States Army Air Force aerial photographs taken in 1942 and published the most accurate maps of the time. A number of smaller-scale studies were also carried out in the Tarascan sierra and lake basins, especially Lake Pátzcuaro. These included studies of lake biodynamics (Osorio Tafall 1944), geomorphology (Ancona 1940), and composition (De Buen 1944); mineral resources (Blasques and Lozano García 1946); economic geography (Foglio Miramontes 1936); and wildlife (Leopold 1959). Only one study was explicitly paleoecological; it involved taking pollen cores in Lake Pátzcuaro (Hutchinson, Patrick, and Deevey 1956).

By the 1960s the need to have more accurate information for planning economic development programs produced another burst of studies. These included descriptions of soil types (Gil Flores 1966; Aguilera and Aceves 1973), vegetation zones (Correa Pérez and Reyna 1973), and land use (Plan Lerma Asistencia Técnica 1968), which paralleled similar publications at the national level (e.g., Flores Mata et al. 1971; and García 1973).

In the 1970s the need for accurate topographic maps for the entire nation resulted in the CETENAL (later DETENAL) aerial photography program.

By 1975 these aerial photographs, at 1:50,000, were available for scholarly use. The topographic maps made from this series of photographs were available beginning in 1978 for some parts of Michoacán, and for the entire Tarascan territory by 1982. Meanwhile another pollen core was taken in Lake Pátzcuaro (Watts and Bradbury 1982), and a program in highland lake paleoecology was begun by the Oxford University Tropical Paleoenvironments Research Group (Metcalfe and Harrison 1983; Metcalfe, et al. 1987; Street-Perrott, Perrott, and Harkness 1989). In 1977 a project in *purépecha* ethnoecology was begun under the direction of Manuel Toledo of the Instituto de Biología, Universidad Nacional Autónoma de México, with collaboration of the Dirección General de Culturas Populares, Secretaría de Educación Publica, and the Universidad Michoacana, Morelia (Mapes, Guzmán, and Caballero 1981; Toledo and Barrera-Bassols 1984). These data have been combined with information from the documentary record, archaeology, and ethnography to determine the Protohistoric Tarascan ecosystem and the dynamic interaction between population, resources, and political power (Gorenstein and Pollard 1983; Pollard 1979, 1982a, 1983, 1987; Pollard and Gorenstein 1980).

## MODERN ETHNOGRAPHY

The role of ethnography in the analysis of the prehispanic Tarascan kingdom is largely restricted to the construction of ethnographic analogies, that is, the description of behavior that may aid in the interpretation of archaeological and/or ethnohistoric data. Many such analogies pertain to technology and resources that have persisted since European conquest, such as the use of the atlatl on Lake Pátzcuaro (Stirling 1960) or the construction and efficiency of traditional fishing nets (Smith 1965). However, ethnographic information often has proven to be of wider applicability, supplying data on, for example, relative travel time by canoe and by foot (West 1948); nutritional values of traditional diets (Brand 1951); identification of local place names; and relationships between regional settlement systems, marketing networks, and localized resources (Gorenstein and Pollard 1980).

The Tarascan region of central Michoacán, home to the modern *purépecha*, or ethnic Tarascans, has been the locus of intense ethnographic study (map 1.4). Beginning at the turn of the century with the monumental research of Nicolás León (1888, 1903) and the shorter reports of Lumholtz (1902) and Seler (1908), modern anthropology exploded in Michoacán with the creation of the Tarascan Project in 1940. Under the inspiration of Lázaro Cárdenas a joint United States (Smithsonian Institution) and Mexican (Instituto Politécnico Nacional and the Departamento de Asuntos Indígenas)

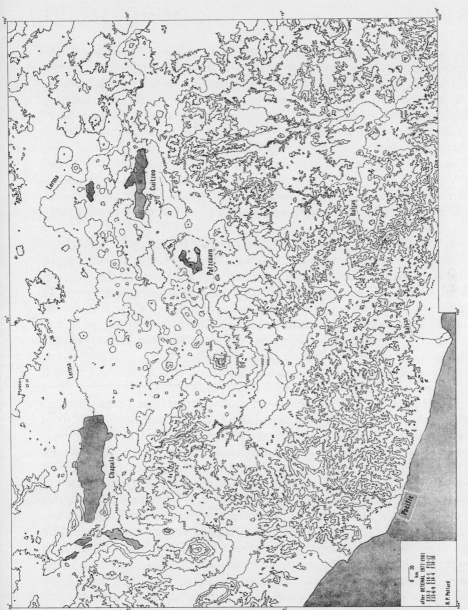

Map 1.4. Topographic Map of the Tarascan Domain

Lerma

Cuitzeo

Patzcuaro

Balsas

Balsas

Lerma

Chapala

Pacific

0    10
     km
after DETENAL 1977-1981
E13-3  E14-1  F13-12
E13-6-9 E14-4 F14-10

H.P. Pollard

group of anthropologists focused on the Tarascan zone. Their work in the Sierra and Pátzcuaro and Cuitzeo lake basins included detailed descriptions of settlements, technology, and economy that are particularly valuable to the archaeologist (e.g., Beals and Carrasco 1944; Beals, Carrasco, and McCorkle 1944; Brand 1951; Foster 1948; Stanislawski 1950).

More recently, anthropologists have augmented this work, adding to the variety of ecological zones and local adaptations studied (e.g., Belshaw 1967; Dinerman 1972; Gortaire Iturralde 1971; Moore 1973; Nelson 1971; Smith 1965; Van Zantwijk 1967). To these data must be added the study of the modern Tarascan language (e.g., Friedrich 1984; Velasquez Gallardo 1978), particularly as it facilitates the interpretation of sixteenth-century texts.

## THE LANDS OF THE LORD OF TZINTZUNTZAN

The Tarascan domain spanned the lands between two of Mexico's greatest rivers, the Lerma-Santiago to the north and the Balsas to the south. In doing so, the Tarascans controlled four major geographic regions and an enormous variety of resources. The brief description of these regions that follows has been drawn primarily from the recent geographical synthesis of this territory (INEGI 1985) but also includes material from West (1948) and Gorenstein and Pollard (1983:appendix 1). This summary is not intended as an exhaustive statement of modern Tarascan ecology, and greater detail will be introduced later in the text when appropriate.

The Tarascan central plateau is a high volcanic region that constitutes the western extention of the central Mexican Mesa Central (fig. 1.5). It is dominated by Cenozoic volcanic mountains and small lake basins above 2,000 m. There are more than three thousand volcanic cinder cones within Michoacán, the most recent of which is Paricutín, which erupted on February 20, 1943, and over the next decade grew to more than 500 m above the plateau. The highest peak is Tancítaro, at 3,845 m. The bedrock of this region is accordingly dominated by basalts, andesites, rhyolites, and lava flows. The climate is temperate (Cw), with a mean annual temperature of 18° C in the valleys and 12.5° C in the mountains. Frosts are common from twenty to eighty days each year, and rainfall, strongly season in the summer months, varies from an average of 646 mm a year in the north to 1,642 mm a year in the south. The dominant soils are young, volcanic Andosols, which are deep, black, and reddish; Luvisols, which are high in organics, clayey, and easily eroded; and Acrisols, which are acidic, red clays of low fertility. These soils support pine, pine-oak, and at the higher elevations, fir forests. There are seven major pine species, at least eight species of oak, and a variety of other deciduous species common in the lower elevations and lake basins, including madroño, hawthorne, and alder.

Fig. 1.5. Arantza, Michoacán, in the Tarascan central plateau.

Human occupation of this region has focused on the lake basins, such as Pátzcuaro (fig. 1.6), and the marshes, such as Zacapu. The absence of large surface streams and rivers has led to a dispersal of settlements adjacent to springs in the remainder of the region. Nevertheless the central plateau offers abundant forest resources and temperate agriculture with few recorded droughts.

The semitropical rims of the central plateau contain volcanic mountains and plains decreasing in elevation from 2,000 m to 1,200 m, occurring to the north and south of the central plateau. The climate is warmer (mean temperature 18.1° C–21.9° C), with frosts common only one to twenty days each year. Rainfall ranges from 720 mm along the northern rim to 1,699 mm in parts of the southern rim.

The northern rim includes the Lerma River Basin, Lake Chapala, Lake Cuitzeo, and Lake Yuríria. The dominant soils are alluvial volcanics and include Vertisols, which are highly fertile black soils; Feozems; Luvisols; and some Andosols on the mountains. These soils support pine-oak forests in the higher elevations and madroño-oak forest at lower elevations. Much of the plains are under continuous cultivation, interspersed with subtropical matorral vegetation. In the northeast and northwest are thermal springs, obsidian flows (Zinapécuaro-Ucareo in the northeast and Zináparo in the northwest), and, in the northeast, small deposits of silver and gold.

Fig. 1.6. Lake Pátzcuaro Basin, looking north.

The southern rim, often referred to as the southern escarpment, is also characterized by fertile, black Vertisols that have attracted human settlement, and mountain Andosols that support pine-oak forests (fig. 1.7). The vegetation of the zone is, however, extremely variable, constituting a transition from the pine forests of the central plateau to the tropical scrub of the Balsas Depression. Dominant trees vary from pine and oak, to copal, brazil, and tepehuate. A large variety of subtropical domesticated plants, including fruits, vegetables, and cotton can be grown there.

South of the escarpment lie the Balsas Depression and the southern Sierra Madre, often treated as one. These two regions are composed of complex Mesozoic deposits, including igneous, metamorphic, and sedimentary bedrock. Directly south of the central plateau is the Balsas Depression, including the middle and lower Balsas Basin and the tributary Tepalcatepec Basin, both below 500 m. These basins are dry and semi-dry lowlands (BS). The mean annual temperature of the dry portions is 27.1° C and the average annual rainfall is 546 mm per year. The semi-dry portions are warmer (mean temperature 28° C) but wetter (mean rainfall 725 mm). The soils tend to be young, shallow Regosols and acidic Acrisols. They support a low deciduous or scrub forest. The complex geomorphology

Fig. 1.7. The southern escarpment just north of La Huacana.

includes a number of resources of particular value to human occupation, including marble deposits in the southwest Tepalcatepec Basin, and copper, gold, silver, iron pyrites and lead deposits in the eastern and central Balsas Basin.

The southern Sierra Madre is located largely southwest of the Tepalcatepec Basin. It is composed of volcanic mountains and small intermontane valleys, mixed with metamorphic and sedimentary deposits. This zone stretches from 1,500 m to 500 m in elevation. The tropical climate (Aw) averages 23° C in temperature and 989 mm in rainfall, concentrated from June to October. The soils are predominantly red, clay Luvisols and young rocky Lithosols. These soils support a low deciduous oak forest mixed with scrub vegetation dominated by cactus. Mineral deposits of copper, gold, and silver are found in the southeast portion of this region near Huetamo and the southwest portion near Coalcoman. Human settlement has always been dispersed and primarily focused on the mineral resources.

Thus, the lands of the lord of Tzintzuntzan spanned more than 3,000 m in elevation, from sea level to the volcanic peaks of the central plateau, and included temperate, subtropical, and tropical climates allowing for the production of a wide range of domesticated and wild resources. Nevertheless, the demographic, social, economic, and political heartland of the Tarascans was in the central plateau among the pine-oak forest, lake basins, and marshes. It was here that the state was formed, in the Lake Pátzcuaro Basin, and from here that their great lord, the cazonci, ruled in their capital, Tzintzuntzan.

# CHAPTER 2

# THE TARASCAN CAPITAL
## TZINTZUNTZAN

TARÍACURI'S most visible legacy was the capital city, Tzintzuntzan (map 2.1). As the locus of most of the archaeological research on the Tarascans and the place where the *Relación de Michoacán* was recorded, Protohistoric Tzintzuntzan reveals more fully and directly the nature of Tarascan society than any other place in the Tarascan domain.

The settlement that was ceded to the Spaniards in 1522 had flourished during the Protohistoric period (A.D. 1450–1520) as the imperial capital, and before that as the largest center of the Tarascan state (A.D. 1350–1450) (fig. 2.1). As they are currently indistinguishable archaeologically, I have referred to these two centuries as the Taríacuri phase at Tzintzuntzan (Pollard 1972, 1977, 1980). This same time period, the Late Postclassic, has also been termed the Upper Lacustrine (Rubín de la Borbolla), the Tarascan Empire (Willey), and the Chila (Piña Chan) in the literature (Pollard 1972:50). An earlier community certainly existed within part of what later became the city, probably by A.D. 1000 (Pollard 1980:683), but it is undocumented (or unpublished) at the present and will not be referred to in this chapter. The following description of this capital is based upon the ten seasons of excavation and reconstruction by INAH (1930–1978), my detailed surface survey (1970–1972), and the relevant ethnohistoric documents.

## THE TARASCAN CAPITAL AS AN URBAN CENTER

The prehispanic settlement was located on the south shore of the northern arm of Lake Pátzcuaro. It extended from the lakeshore to Cerrito Colorado, some 4 km to the south, and between the slopes of Cerro Taríacuri (variously Taráqueri or Tariácueri) on the west and Cerro Yaguarato (variously Yahuarato or Yaguaro) on the east. Except for the land immediately along the lakeshore, the surface is not level; from the south to the north there is a gradual drop of more than 200 m, and the mountains to the east and west rise 400–600 m at their peaks (fig. 2.2).

The bedrock surrounding the settlement is basalt and andesite. A small cave is located on the north (lakeshore) slope of Cerro Taríacuri. There are several deposits of red and white clays along the slopes of Cerro Taríacuri

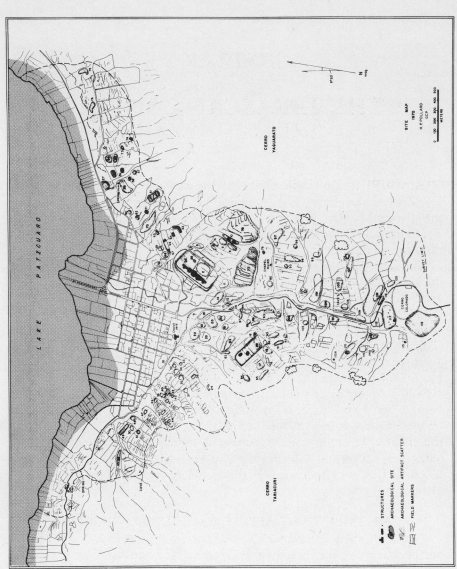

Map 2.1. Tzintzuntzan Archaeological Survey Zone

Fig. 2.1. Aerial photograph of Tzintzuntzan, 1942 (Defense Intelligence Agency, National Archives, Washington, D.C.).

and Cerro Colorado, still being used for ceramic production. The lands within the ancient city fell within two environmental zones in the Proto-historic period, the lakeshore zone and the lower sierra slopes (see chapter 3). Most of the soil is a volcanic andosol called *charanda* (red earth) in Tarascan. While moderately fertile, it has a very high clay content (sometimes over 40 percent), and once the vegetation cover has been removed it is extremely susceptible to erosion (Gorenstein and Pollard 1983:136). There are several springs within the limits of the prehispanic settlement, and two major arroyos drain the hillslopes.

Fig. 2.2. Tzintzuntzan, looking north. Note main ceremonial platform on slopes of Cerro Tariácuri.

## SETTLEMENT SIZE AND POPULATION

Protohistoric Tzintzuntzan is estimated to have measured at least 6.74 sq km (674 ha), a size probably reached shortly before European contact. The settlement area was determined by surface survey and analysis of artifact samples (see appendix 1).

The population is estimated to have been between 25,000 and 35,000 people. Previous estimates have been based on the work of Mendizábal (Pollard 1972:60), who placed the prehispanic population of Michoacán at 280,000, and Romero (1862:78), who estimated the population of Tzintzuntzan at 40,000. In 1963 Borah and Cook published the first revision of these estimates, placing the 1519 population of Michoacán at 1.3 million people.

Much of the variation in population estimates for Tzintzuntzan has resulted from the use of historic documents, which varied in what was meant by "the city of Michoacán." Depending on the decade or century, "the city of Michoacán" referred to Tzintzuntzan, Pátzcuaro, the entire lake basin, or, occasionally, the modern state capital of Morelia. Based upon the population figures given in the *Suma de visitas* (1547–1551), Lebrón (1544), *Tasaciones* (1560), *Pueblos* (1570), *Relaciones* (1571), and the RG for

Pátzcuaro (1581), Borah and Cook reconstructed the 1565 population of Tzintzuntzan at 35,759 (1963). It is clear, however, that this population figure refers to the entire lake basin. Romero's earlier figure of 40,000 had been based upon taking the 1565 estimate of tributaries and multiplying it by four, thus arriving at a figure similar to Borah and Cook's.

The documentary evidence, when adjusted for size of household and proportion of tributaries, suggests the following figures for the Pátzcuaro Basin: 1550: 46,200; 1565: 35,500; and 1580: 16,500 (Pollard 1972:62ff.). Depending upon whether you use the Borah and Cook ratios of 1565 population to 1520 population (Borah and Cook 1960:48; Borah and Cook 1963:87) or Sanders's (1970) critique, the 1520 estimate for the basin is 210,000 (Borah and Cook) or 95,000–106,000 (Sanders). As will be indicated in chapter 3, the Sanders figures agrees with basin estimates based upon settlement number and size.

Archaeological approaches to population estimates are more helpful regarding Tzintzuntzan itself. The area of the settlement believed to have been residential measured approximately 4 sq km (3.97 sq km), which is 50 percent of the survey zone and 60 percent of the settlement. Comparison to modern Ihuatzio, a nucleated Tarascan village for which house census data are known (Van Zantwijk 1967), gives a minimal estimate of 26,400 people. The RM lists more than 3,000 laborers and twelve craft groups associated with the royal palace, and an upper class of at least 5,000 is reasonable. This brings the estimate to at least 30,000 people.

Another approach comes from the statements in the RM that when marching in military campaigns the people from Tzintzuntzan carried 200 banners, those from Ihuatzio 40, and those from Pátzcuaro 40 (1956:192). If each banner or flag represented the basic administrative unit of the settlement (the *ocámbecha* unit, or ward), which in 1520 contained twenty-five households, and each household contained four to six persons (Cook and Borah 1972:125, 128), then the city population is estimated at 20,000–30,000. Again, the high concentration of elite households and craft specialists associated directly with the royal palace was probably not reflected in the number of military units. Adding a minimal 5,000 persons gives an estimate of 25,000–35,000 for the population of the Protohistoric capital.

This estimate accords well with the area of the settlement in proportion to the area of all settlements in the Pátzcuaro Basin in 1520 (see chapter 3). It also accords well with the population of Tzintzuntzan seen as a proportion of the better-documented size of the basin population in 1520. Based on this estimate, the population density for Tzintzuntzan would have been 4,452 people per sq km, and 7,500 people per sq km within the residential zones.

## URBAN LAND USE

The study of land use within Tzintzuntzan involved the determination of nonrandom variability among the sites surveyed with regard to artifact distribution, structures, and features; the use of ethnohistoric and historic data to suggest the interpretation of this variability and to document the presence of other structures and features not discerned archaeologically; and the assignment of individual sites to land-use zones. A site was defined by concentrations of artifacts spatially isolable; these concentrations were the smallest units of data collection. Data pertaining to the distribution of artifact types and modes, structures, and features were gathered from the analyses of survey collections (Pollard 1972) and published results of the Instituto Nacional de Antropología e Historia work. In total, 120 sites were surveyed, of which 89 included artifact collections.

These data have allowed the isolation of three categories of zones within Tzintzuntzan: residential zones, manufacturing zones, and public zones. The defining features of each zone will be briefly summarized along with any ethnohistoric correlations and functional interpretations. The full descriptions of the archaeological sites and artifact categories can be found in appendixes 1, 2, and 3. The tabulations of number of artifacts per category per site can be found in Pollard 1972.

### RESIDENTIAL ZONES

Residential zones were defined by the presence of stone and ceramic material indicative of food preparation, serving, and storage, including graters, coarse wares, jars, bowls, flakes, blades, manos, and metates. Many sites have concentrations of basalt stone, perhaps house foundation remnants. In the 1977–1978 excavations of a house compound by Cabrera Castro (1987), designated Edificio F and Tz-79 in the surface survey, such a concentration of basalt stone was found to represent house foundations (60 cm high) and a contiguous paved patio.

These identifications are confirmed by illustrations found in the RM showing various prepared foods placed in shallow bowls (RM 1956:226) and maguey wine in everted rim jars (RM 1956:131). Another illustration (RM 1956:200) shows a house with what appears to be a stone foundation. The houses themselves were probably of wood or adobe (Brand 1951:51; Beals, Carrasco, and McCorkle 1944:33). The roof was of straw, as described in the RM (1956:227) and stated by Sahagún (Beals, Carrasco, and McCorkle 1944:33). Several illustrations in the RM show what appear to be thatch roofs.

Type i residential zones are believed to have been low-status or commoner wards within the city. They are located on the northeast slope of Cerro

Tariácuri behind the modern town to the west of the churchyard, on the northwest slope of Cerro Yaguarato east of the main platform (Tz-25), on the slopes of Cerro Tariácuri and Cerro Yaguarato south of Tz-29 (Santa Ana) and north of Cerro Colorado, and southwest of Cerro Colorado (map 2.2) at fifty-three sites (see Pollard 1972:74 for a complete listing).

Commoner households are associated with lithic tools of gray obsidian or basalt and ceramics dominated by coarse wares, with a high ratio of jars to bowls, and few or no miniature bowls, plates, or spouted vessels. The ceramics have no pink, white, or gray slip, and sherds are generally only monochrome or bichrome. There are few decorative motifs and only simple pipestem forms.

This association of artifacts with urban commoners is found in an illustration in the RM (1956:213) with the caption "De la manera que se casaba la gente baja" ("On the marriage of commoners") (fig. 2.3). The illustration shows everted rim jars and convex wall bowls associated with the lower class but does not show any of the more elaborate ceramic forms often found in other illustrations in the RM. Their absence here reflects the reality of commoner household goods. Lithic material from all these sites indicates some stone tool manufacture and use within the residential zone. Indeed, the RM (1956:177) states that bows and arrows were in such demand that they were made by the people of the city each day.

Type ii residential zones are believed to have been occupied by the highest social group in Tzintzuntzan, including the king, referred to as *cazonci* in Tarascan, and his family. They cluster in two units (encompassing twelve sites) located southwest of the main platform (at Tz-12 and Tz-13) and including and adjacent to the Santa Ana platform (Tz-29) (see map 2.2).

The material remains associated with type ii zones include the basic ceramic and lithic assemblage described for type i residential zones, but with the addition of a wide range of goods imported into the lake basin or produced by full-time craft specialists for elite consumption. These include red and green obsidian, ear and lip plug fragments, unusual ceramic vessel forms (out-sloping wall, everted rim, incurved rim, and composite silhouette bowls, plates, and spouted vessels), and highly decorated pottery with pink, white, and gray slip, polychrome decoration, negative decoration, and unusual motifs (double spiral, hatching, checkerboard, dots and X, Z, and S motifs) (fig. 2.4).

An illustration from the RM (1956:207) with the caption "De la manera que se casaban los señores" ("On the marriage of lords") (fig. 2.5) contains three groups of ceramics—everted rim jars, convex wall bowls, and spouted vessels with loop handles. The similar scene in the companion picture of the commoners contained no spouted vessels. Other illustrations with spouted

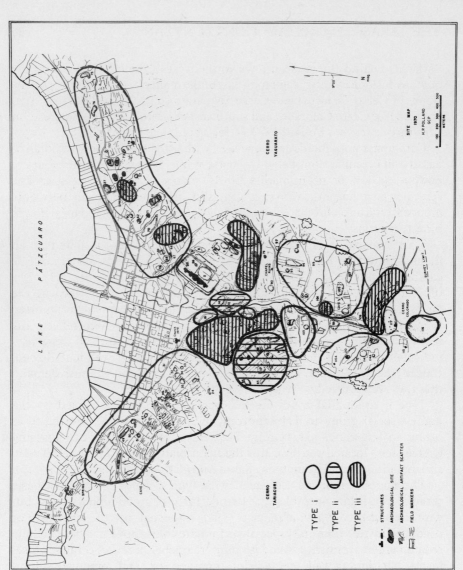

Map 2.2. Tzintzuntzan Residential Zones

Fig. 2.3. "On the marriage of commoners." (From *The Chronicles of Michoacan*, translated and edited by Eugene R. Craine and Reginald C. Reindorp, Copyright © 1970 by the University of Oklahoma Press, plate 12.) "De la manera que se casaba la gente baja" (RM 1956:213).

vessels dealt with the burial of the dead king and goods from the king's house (RM 1956:218, 251).

Among the officials of the administration described in the RM was one who oversaw the plate-makers. Plates, unlike bowls, are restricted in distribution to type ii sites.

Within the RM are statements of the material accompaniments of high status, and among these are lip and ear plugs (1956:203, 195, 157, 124). Burials of high-status individuals took place within and near the *yácatas*, ceremonial pyramids on the main public platform. Excavations by Rubín de la Borbolla (1944) near Yácata 5 (Tz-25) revealed two sets of burials, five male and nine female. Associated with the male burials were clay pipes and obsidian ear and lip plugs. Associated with the females were large numbers of polychrome ceramics. In addition other excavations near the *yácatas* have revealed large numbers of miniature bowls, negative decoration, and other examples of the unusual motifs listed above (Rubín de la Borbolla 1939, 1941, 1944; Castro-Leal 1986). Among the burials studied was a high incidence of dental mutilation, for both men and women, of types A-1 and

Fig. 2.4. Tzintzuntzan ceramic (Museo Nacional de Antropología, Mexico).

A-2 (Romero Molina 1986) and cranial deformation. Cranial deformation is explicitly referred to as an elite characteristic in the RM (1980:187).

While both clusters of type ii sites are believed to represent elite residential zones, I believe that Tz-29, also called the Santa Ana platform, was the main residence of the king and his family. Unlike the main platform (Tz-25), which has considerable evidence of primary religious functions (see "Public Zones," below), the area around Tz-29 appears essentially residential. Unfortunately, the surface of the platform itself has been cleared of artifacts, and the first Catholic chapel in Michoacán was built on this site in 1525–1526 (Warren 1985:89). Nevertheless, there is a clear distinction in the RM illustrations between temples and residences. In one (1956:171), the king sits in front of a large house with the artisans of his court. Numerous references appear to a large patio of the king located "delante sus casas" (in front of his houses) (1956:13, 219). In an illustration of the king's son returning home, there are several houses, one of which has

Fig. 2.5. "On the marriage of lords." (From *The Chronicles of Michoacan*, translated and edited by Eugene R. Craine and Reginald C. Reindorp, Copyright © 1970 by the University of Oklahoma Press, plate 11.) "De la manera que se casaban los señores" (RM 1956:207).

a short stair leading to it and contains a stool or throne. These buildings, of residential, not temple, design appear to be on a raised platform. The only other patio referred to in the RM text is that of the five temples (Tz-25).

In addition to these ethnohistorical clues, there is an unusually low proportion of pipes and pipe fragments at type ii sites, despite large samples and local pothunting, which focuses on the finer pottery. Among all site samples the pipe fragments make up 15 percent of the ceramic collections. At sites associated with religious activity the pipe fragments comprise 27 percent of the ceramic collections. Tobacco and smoking tend to be associated with religious ritual in the RM (fig. 2.6) (Porter 1948). The chief priest, for example, carried tobacco in the gourd worn on his back (RM 1956:181). Among the sites designated as residential type ii, with the exception of Tz-12, discussed below, the proportion of pipe fragments is 4 percent or less of the ceramic collections. Thus the area around the Santa Ana platform does not seem to conform to an interpretation of this platform as primarily religious in focus. If, however, Tz-29 was the focus of the king's residence, then it served multiple functions of political, administrative, residential, and some religious functions.

There is a certain amount of variation within sites designated "high-status residential." Tz-12 has a high proportion of pipes and pipe fragments (30 percent) and obsidian prismatic blades, probably due to its proximity to the main platform (Tz-25). Rituals associated with these *yacatas* may have taken place in the residences of Tz-12. Tz-18, adjacent to the Santa Ana platform (Tz-29), contains unusually high proportions of polychrome plates (60 percent of all plates collected) and produced four of the six nonlocal sherds in the survey, including Aztec Black-on-red and Cholula Polychrome. Twice in the RM, foreign emissaries are received at the king's residence, first those from Moctezuma and second those from Cortés (1956:237, 246). Tz-18 may reflect this function.

Type iii residential-zone sites are interpreted as middle-status residences, although "middle" is not to be confused with the concept of a middle class. They probably represent the lower branches of the high-status group in the social structure of Tzintzuntzan. The RM discusses several levels of high status, including *señores* (of the royal lineage), *principales* (nobles), and *caciques* (village chiefs) (López Sarralangue 1965:37). In describing the marriage of *señores* the RM refers to other "lower *principales*" (1956:210). It is probable that certain occupational specialists occupied higher status positions than "la gente baja," but the artifact assemblages appear most consistent with the first interpretation. The association of small ceremonial units adjacent to several of these sites reinforces this view.

Type iii residential zones are located between the two platforms (Tz-25 and Tz-29) and south of the modern church; adjacent to the spring at Ojo de Agua; immediately northeast, south, and southeast of the main platform; midway between Tz-29 and Cerrito Colorado; and adjacent to the north side of Cerrito Colorado (see map 2.2) at twenty-eight sites.

These sites contain some, but not all, of the lithic and ceramic artifacts found at the high-status sites. While there are polychrome ceramics, there are few or no miniature bowls or plates. Decorative motifs include dots, lines, and bands but lack double spirals, hatching, and checkerboard patterns. White, pink, and gray slip is rare or absent. Small supports (probably associated with minibowls) are found, some spouted vessel sherds, and some negative and red and white painting. Obsidian is gray; red and green are rare or absent. The assemblages appear in many ways between the extremes of high- and low-status sites. For example, low-status sites lack small supports, but high-status sites do contain such supports, most of

Fig. 2.6. Tarascan pipes (American Museum of Natural History, New York).

which are painted. The sites included here contain the supports, but they are rarely painted.

Random variation may have caused this apparent difference, although two factors lessen this possibility. First, in the sampling procedure an effort was made to locate polychrome sherds and unusual vessel forms. Second, previous nonrandom sampling (looting) is best known from the area of high-status sites. If skewing occurred, it is more likely in the underrepresentation of the high-status sites, rather than type iii sites.

The excavations by Cabrera Castro at Edificio F or Tz-79, referred to earlier in this chapter, occurred at one of these sites along the slopes of Cerro Yaguarato. Within an area of about 27 m by 24 m were located two stone terraces containing four rooms and a patio (Cabrera Castro 1987). From the patio descended a small access ramp, facing west, or downslope. The rooms were contiguous, although it appears that room 4 was constructed first, and shortly after three rooms were added along a right angle to the first as the terrace and patio area was expanded. The final result is a habitation with three small rooms ( 6 m by 4 m, 7 m by 4 m, 6.5 m by 4.5 m), one larger room (at least 7 m by 7 m), a paved patio in front of the rooms, and a hearth or altar (90 cm by 72 cm by 20 cm high). A black polished jar was found in the retaining wall of one terrace, and one primary but incomplete burial was found adjacent to the step of room 3. In the RM, residences of the commoners are always shown as single-room houses, while elite houses are often drawn as multiple-room dwellings with one large room at a right angle to the rest (see Tudela's introduction to the RM 1956 edition, page xi). Much of the variation in house forms shown in the RM is in the roof types and decoration, not found in the excavations.

A type iv residential zone is located on the northwest slope of Cerro Yaguarato and clusters between the modern barrio of Ojo de Agua and the main platform (the zone is not indicated on map 6). This zone coincides with type i and iii residence zones in the same area and may possibly represent an ethnically non-Tarascan population residing in the city.

The sole criterion for this zone is the presence of Querenda Ware ceramics. This ware differs in paste, firing, vessel forms, and decorative motifs from the rest of the ceramics in the Taríacuri phase and is described in appendix 2. Its distribution within Tzintzuntzan is highly concentrated: only twenty-two sites of eighty-nine sampled in the survey contained Querenda Ware, and only six had more than one sherd. More specifically, 88 percent of the sherds were located northeast of the main platform in what is now the modern barrio of Ojo de Agua, 39 percent from site Tz-59, and 20 percent from Tz-70. In site Tz-59 and Tz-70 this ware represents almost half the total ceramic samples, although it represents less than 4 percent of the ceramic sample from Tzintzuntzan as a whole.

When the survey was completed it was felt that this ware, with its unusual features and distribution, was the result of temporal or ethnic variation within the city. Since that time, research by Shirley Gorenstein and the author along the Tarascan political frontier seemed to confirm the latter interpretation (Gorenstein 1985; Pollard 1976). Querenda Ware ceramics have been located from the frontier sites of Taximaroa, Michoacán; Zitácuaro, Michoacán; and Cerro Chivo at Acámbaro, Guanajuato. Stratigraphic excavations at Cerro Chivo place the ware in the Late Postclassic, synchronous with the Taríacuri phase. A survey by the author in the Lerma River Basin near Cerro Chivo has established the strong presence of this ware, along with types not found at Tzintzuntzan, in the settlements inside the Tarascan political domain but along its borders.

Current excavations by the author (1990–92) at Urichu on the southwest shore of Lake Pátzcuaro have also recovered Querenda Ware ceramics dating to the Postclassic. They may date to the Early Postclassic and represent a widely distributed ceramic type dating before the emergence of the Tarascan State. Until additional work is done in the Lake Pátzcuaro Basin, the interpretation accepted here is that individuals representing populations living along the politically sensitive northeast Tarascan boundaries resided in zone iv. It is possible that they represented one of the several ethnically distinct groups within the Tarascan state (such as Otomí or Matlatzincas). Whether the group performed political or economic functions within the urban system cannot be determined at this time.

## MANUFACTURING ZONES

The primary function of the five type 1 lithic workshops (map 2.3) was the production of lithic tools, particularly prismatic blades. The sites are characterized by a high proportion of lithic artifacts, primarily unretouched prismatic blades (21 percent of all primatic blades in the samples are from these five sites). Also found are high proportions of polyhedral blade cores and blades with ground platforms still attached. Generally there are few ceramics, especially polychrome and decorative motifs, although Tz-75 and Tz-99 contain minibowls and spouted vessels, respectively.

The variability in the assemblages, including those primarily residential sites with lithic manufacture (see residential type i), suggests basic generalized tools produced and used within residential units. The RM (1956:172) indicates, however, that there were specialists, *navajeros* (knife makers), producing prismatic blades according to the techniques described by Crabtree (1968). The absence of large quantities of chipping debris and relatively small numbers of crude blades and flakes/blades with cortex suggests that the obsidian was acquired by specialists and households as small nodules or even macrocores, with primary reduction taking place adjacent to the obsidian quarries. Recent trace-element analysis of 381 obsidian artifacts from the city indicates that 95 percent of the gray-black obsidian was imported from the Zinapécuaro-Ucareo quarries of northeast Michoacán (fig. 2.7).

The primary function of the four type 2 lithic workshops was the manufacture of various other artifacts (map 2.3). Characteristic of this type is a "pavement" of chipping debris with high proportions of red and green obsidian (53 percent of all red and green obsidian), crude blades, flakes, notched tools, pointed tools, and unfinished or broken ground obsidian pieces (ear and lip plugs, cylinders, and disks). There are relatively few ceramic artifacts, especially polychrome sherds. Only simple convex-wall bowls and everted rim jars are found at these sites.

There is much lower variability between these sites than between type 1 sites. All ceramic assemblages are small and simple, suggesting minimal residence at the sites. The lithic assemblages suggest the manufacture of nonutilitarian objects associated with high-status residential zones. The absence of large polyhedral cores and the small size of flakes of red and green obsidian suggest these obsidians were acquired as small nodules.

The primary activities of type 3 lithic workshops involved the use of large scrapers. Only two such zones were located in the survey (map 7).

There is a high proportion of lithic material in type 3 workshops, most of which includes large unifacial scrapers, especially end and bilateral scrapers (see Pollard 1972). There are few ceramic remains, and these are generally

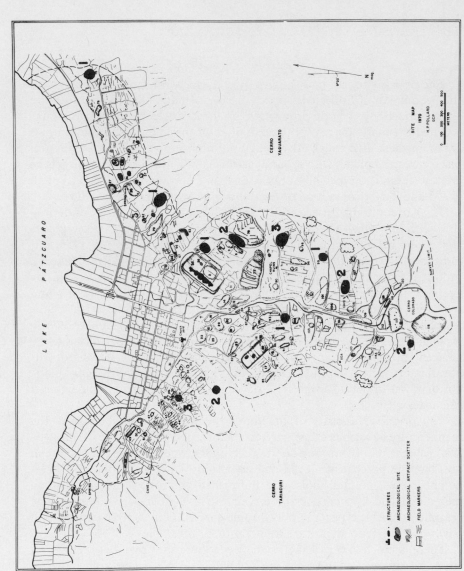

Map 2.3. Tzintzuntzan Lithic Workshops

Fig. 2.7. Tarascan stone knives and spear points, produced by specialists and associated with ceremonial/public ritual (Museo del Estado, Morelia).

undecorated. About 30 percent of all scrapers collected in the survey were from these two sites, including 50 percent of the end and bilateral scrapers.

The lack of chipping debris suggests use, rather than manufacture, of scrapers. Any activities requiring large scrapers, such as cleaning and preparing skins, woodworking, scraping maguey in the preparation of pulque, and the like could have been performed here.

The RM also mentions more than twenty-eight specialist groups, including tanners, leatherworkers, sandal-makers, potters, flower-workers, masons, silverworkers, featherworkers, carpenters, gourdplate painters, and painters (1956:176–82). Unfortunately, there is no mention of the localization of the manufacture or residence of these groups, although some may have been housed directly within the king's residence (1956:171, 172).

## PUBLIC ZONES

The primary public zone of Tzintzuntzan was located on the northwest slopes of Cerro Yaguarato, centered on the main platform (Tz-25), and included at least two smaller areas, Tz-10 and Tz-66 (map 2.4).

Tz-25 is commonly called the main platform or central plaza of Tzintzuntzan (map 2.5). It constitutes the Zona Arqueológica of the Instituto

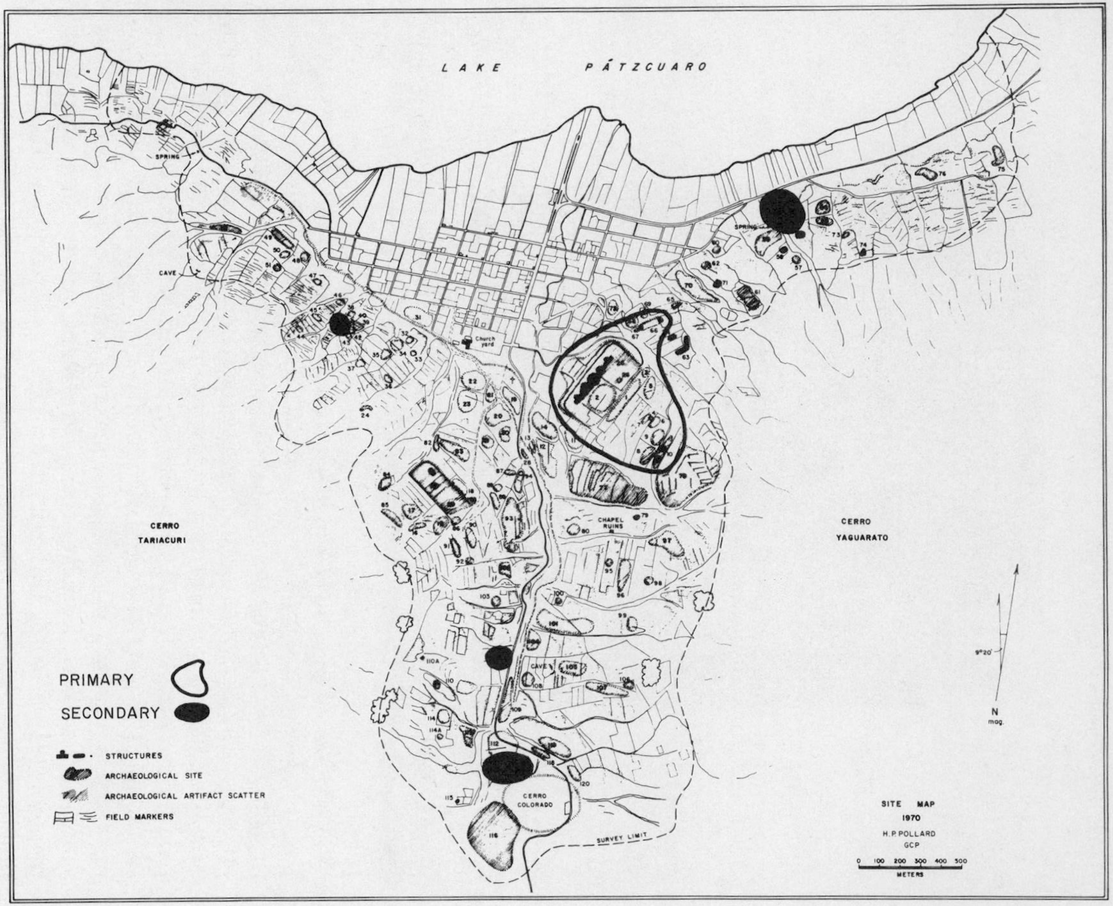

Map 2.4. Tzintzuntzan Public Zones

Nacional de Antropología e Historia of Mexico. The works of Noguera (1931), Acosta (1939), Rubín de la Borbolla (1939, 1941), Gali (1946), Piña Chan (1963, 1977), and Cabrera Castro (1987) should be consulted for detailed descriptions of the site and excavations there (see appendix 1). A brief description with photographs from the last century can be found in León (1888).

In general, the main temple complex consists of a large artificial platform, 450 by 250 m, built on the lower slope of Cerro Yaguarato (fig. 2.8). The platform has a rubble core and is faced with stacked tabular basalt. The front and probably also the sides were stepped. From the center front of the platform a ramp extends in a series of sloping terraces toward the northwest. Several small structures were located at the top of the ramp.

There are five stone platforms, or *yácatas*, located along the east side of the platform surface. They are rubble-core mounds faced with dressed basalt slabs, which are often covered with petroglyphs. The *yácatas* have an unusual shape, consisting of rectangles with circular extensions. At least four and maybe five superpositions are visible on Yácata 5, one of the four *yácatas* reconstructed by the Instituto Nacional de Antropología e Historia.

On the rest of the main platform are located several burial chambers (fifty-eight or sixty-one burials have been excavated in the INAH research), a series of rooms termed Edificio B, and several mounds along the back (southeast) edge, off the platform. One of these mounds was excavated in 1977–1978 and revealed five rooms believed to have been storerooms for ritual paraphernalia (Cabrera Castro 1987:549). An ossuary was located just off the northeast side of the platform.

Above the main platform on the slopes of Cerro Yaguarato are located two square basalt stone mounds set in the center of a large terrace (Tz-10). These are Yácatas 6 and 7, described by Ramón Gali (1946:57–59). Of similar size, shape, and construction are two mounds located within 100 m of the northern edge of the main platform (Tz-66). Both of these sites are assumed to be religious in function and to be associated with the main platform. A map published by Beaumont (1932:25–26) contains temple structures located in similar positions with respect to the main platform.

According to the RM, religious ceremonies took place on the main platform. The five large structures, called *cues* in the RM, were dedicated to the god Curicaueri and his four brothers (1956:255). These structures were also used for burials of high-status individuals (1956:221ff.; Rubín de la Borbolla 1944). When the Spaniards first arrived in Tzintzuntzan they visited the king's residence and later returned to the "patio of the five large temples, and lodged in the houses of the priests" (1956:255–56). Structure B, located on the west end of the platform, may be one of the priests' houses.

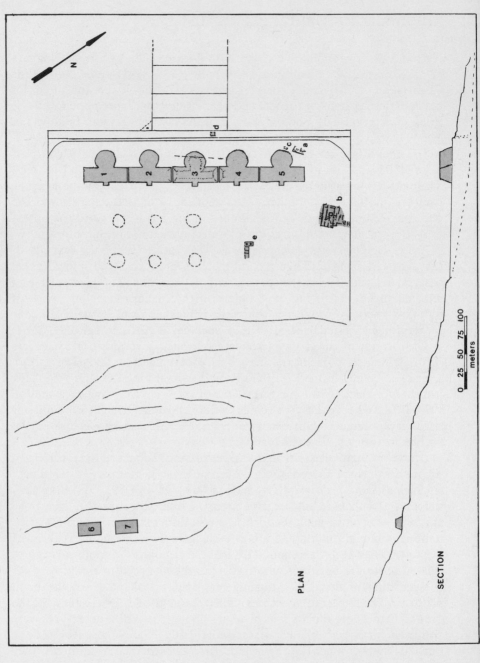

PLAN

SECTION

0 25 50 75 100
meters

N

Fig. 2.8. *Yácatas*, main platform, Tzintzuntzan, looking southwest.

A skull rack described in the RM, as well as large sacrificial stones, were probably also located on the platform (1956:182). Along the rear edge of the platform (east edge), one of several structures was excavated in 1977–1978. As previously indicated it consisted of a series of five rooms, which the excavator, Cabrera Castro, believes to have been storerooms for ritual materials (1987).

Four sites are designated secondary public zones (see map 2.4). They are characterized by the remains of rubble-filled stone structures and/or a high proportion of pipes and pipe fragments (27 percent or more of the ceramic artifacts). In addition they contain middle-status habitation assemblages, and all are associated with (looted) burials.

These sites are viewed as local religious centers within the various residential zones of the settlement. In modern Ihuatzio, a Tarascan settlement south of Tzintzuntzan along the lake shore, a distinction is made between *yácata*, a temple containing tombs, particularly royal tombs, and *echecuahta*, other temples (Van Zantwijk 1967:270). The secondary temples at Tzintzuntzan are assumed to have been the latter, although the Spaniards generalized the term *yácata* to all temples. The RM states that there were several temples (*cues*) in the settlement dedicated to gods other than Curicaueri (1956):197).

Several structures labeled "Yacatas del Rey" on the Beaumont map of Tzin-tzuntzan (dated to the 1540s; Gorenstein and Pollard 1983:14–17) and two structures at the base of a small hill on the Seler map (late 1540s; Gorenstein and Pollard 1983:16–17) may represent the secondary group of ceremonial structures located at Tz-117 near the southern end of the settlement. A single temple structure on the Seler map is approximately in the location at Tz-41.

In the RM illustration of marriage among the common people there is a small temple or altar to which wood is being brought (see fig. 2.3). As this appears to be taking place in a residential area it is probably not unreasonable to view these sites as religious zones within residential zones.

Further support for the above interpretation comes from the fact that three of the four sites of this type are said to have been the general locations of Colonial chapels, one of which still remains at Ojo de Agua (site Tz-27). It was not unusual for Spanish priests to usurp the religious authority of prehispanic religions by occupying their temple foundations.

The RM indicates that two altars existed at the entrance to the city (1956:190) but they have not been found.

There are no sites or areas to which a primarily political or administrative function can be assigned. The houses of the king were the locus of political activity as described in the RM and for type ii residential zones. For example, the hearing and judging of civil and criminal offenses took place in the "patio of the king" (Tz-29) (1956:13). The houses were multipurpose, incorporating residential, political, and probably some religious functions (for example, on page 186 of the RM there is a decription of a small temple within the "casas del Cazonci"). In addition, certain manufacturing activities may have taken place here.

Other public zones include specialized structures described in the RM but for which there is no locational data:

Casa de las águilas: Possibly a form of men's house or hospital associated with the healing of wounds received in battle. These structures are mentioned often in the text, but only one statement, referring to their use by wounded soldiers, indicates anything about their function (1956:36). The Gilberti dictionary lists *pamenchécuaro* as a hospital for the sick, although whether this refers to the same kind of structure of another is unclear (Sepúlveda y H. 1988).

Jail: There are numerous references to a jail in which those who had broken laws were placed. The jail was for residents of Tzintzuntzan and the surrounding towns (RM 1956:11, 12).

Zoo: This was probably located within the palace structures. In the zoo were eagles and other birds, "lions and tigers," jackals, and wolves (RM 1956:178).

Storehouses: One kind of storehouse was for crops, cotton mantles, and other items of tribute used by the state. The other kind of storehouse served as a treasury for storing the personal wealth of the king, including precious metals and feathers. The treasury is illustrated in the RM as a rectangular building containing a small altar surrounded by chests containing gems, feathers, gold, and silver (1956:152). It was probably located within the palace buildings, although specific mention is made of other treasuries located on various islands within the lake. According to the RM, the treasury within the palace contained forty chests, called *chuperi*. Half were filled with gold and half with silver (1956:257).

Ball court: The only ball court mentioned in the RM is in connection with the movement of the priests of the goddess Xarátanga (a patron goddess of Tzintzuntzan) to Sipiho. At Sipiho, located south of Tzintzuntzan near the lakeshore, was built a ball court, a bath, and some temples (RM 1956:26). This is undoubtedly the area of Ihuatzio known as Querétaro ("place where the ball game is played," Gilberti 1975:98). There is no knowledge of any ball courts within the city itself.

Baths: Several statements in the RM indicate the presence of baths, including one within the houses of the king (1956:185). While they are described as hot baths, it is not clear whether they were sweat baths, or *temascales*, such as found in other parts of Mesoamerica. Baths in thermal springs, such as those in the Cuitzeo Basin at Araró, Zinapécuaro, and Chucándiro were part of Tarascan medicinal treatment (Sepúlveda y H. 1988).

Commercial zones: The direct documentary evidence for a market at Tzintzuntzan comes from Spanish observations that the market in existence in the early Colonial period had existed earlier and was continuing its Protohistoric functions (Gorenstein and Pollard 1983:64). Details about what was sold and who attended markets are found in the RM, but they pertain to markets in other settlements (Pollard 1982a). On two occasions, the death of the king and the appearance of Spaniards in Tzintzuntzan, marketing activity was forbidden (RM 1956:256, 223). Because both events took place in the capital, they can reasonably be taken as indirect evidence of a market, probably daily, in Tzintzuntzan.

There is, however, no evidence of the location of the marketplace. The most likely place for a market would have been in the flat area under the modern town, within easy reach of canoe traffic and the main road leaving the basin to the east or the south. According to Foster, this area was the locus of a weekly market until the early years of this century (1948:131). On the Beaumont map of Tzintzuntzan, this area, adjacent to the lakeshore, is shown without houses but within the city.

Defensive zones: There is no evidence of any fortifications within the settlement or walls, moats, or guardhouses surrounding the city. Nor are any structures known to have been fortified. The very location of the settlement between the mountains Tariácuri and Yaguarato may have served a defensive function.

Cemeteries: There is no evidence of any zone set aside primarily for burials. Burials—urn, flexed, and extended—have been excavated from the main platform (Tz-25) (Rubín de la Borbolla 1939; Castro-Leal 1986) and are described in the RM (1956:221ff.). Looted burials were found at several sites designated as secondary religious zones, and isolated burials were probably placed within residential terraces, such as the one excavated in 1977–1978 (Cabrera Castro 1987).

Based on the above analysis of zoning in Protohistoric Tzintzuntzan, it is possible to state that the urban settlement exhibits a moderate degree of zoning. Most zones are multipurpose, although clear distinctions can be made. These zones and their interpreted functions include:

I. Residential (with some lithic manufacture and use; possibly some ethnic variation)
   A. Low status
   B. Middle status
   C. High status (with some political, administrative, and religious functions)
II. Manufacturing (with some residence)
   A. Blade manufacture
   B. Nonutilitarian-object manufacture
   C. Scraper-use activity
   D. Other: featherworking, potting, tanning, sandal-making, flower-working, masonry, carpentry, metalworking
III. Public Zones
   A. Religious (with some residence, burial activity)
      1. Primary
      2. Secondary
   B. Political-administrative (combined with high-status residential)
IV. Commercial

Planning in a settlement reflects conscious decision-making with respect to the location of its physical components. As such decisions are made at several levels, planning can be judged on the basis of individual structures, sectors of settlements, and entire settlements.

The primary excavated structures at Tzintzuntzan include those located on the main platform (Tz-25). The spacing of the five *yácatas*, and their identical and unusual shape, including several superpositions, attest to careful planning. Edificio B on the main platform and the several other structures in the primary religious zone also indicate planning on the individual level. Illustrations of residential structures in the RM show single-room dwellings associated with low-status groups and single-room and multiroom dwellings associated with high-status individuals. Both seem fairly standardized, although minimal planning would be necessary. In general, individual structures were planned, although this planning did not involve any great technological or intellectual complexity (such as involving astronomical orientations or complex architectural feats).

The only sectors of Tzintzuntzan that exhibit deliberate planning are the religious/political zones, including the two large artificial platforms (Tz-25 and Tz-29) and the structures at Tz-117. The relationship between the main platform, the structures on it, and the terrace behind it containing the structures of Tz-10 are too nonrandom in their distribution not to have been planned. The main platform faces 45° west of astronomical north and appears to have been determined largely by the slope of the mountain overlooking the settlement and the lakeshore. I noted that the platform can be seen from all parts of the prehispanic settlement, an arrangement that may or may not have been planned. The slope and orientation of the slopes also seem to have determined the relationship between the two large platforms.

Because of the great amount of soil erosion and lack of structural remains, it is impossible to ascertain the relationship between structures in the residential zones. Judging from the meager remains and illustrations in the RM and Colonial maps, it is unlikely that there was any overall zonal planning.

Presently, the entire surface area within the survey zone on the slopes of Cerro Tariácuri or Cerro Yaguarato is terraced. These rock-embanked, noncontour terraces are built laterally across the sloping surface of the mountains. They are used to slow soil erosion, allow for greater retention of rainwater, and provide flatter surfaces for cropping. As evidenced by the two large platforms, the prehispanic occupants of Tzintzuntzan were experienced in terracing. Artifacts and stone concentrations appear to be associated with these terraces. In several cases, burials (looted) were found in the rear walls of terraces. Therefore, while it cannot be absolutely determined at present, there is a good possibility that the terraces were for habitation and garden plots. In any case, they are related to the contour of the hillslope, with no overall plan evident.

There is no evidence of any planning on a settlement level. While transport and communication networks often form the basis of settlement planning, there is no evidence of thoroughfares of any sort through the settlement. It is probable that the remains of a cobblestone road connecting Tzintzuntzan with Ihuatzio and Pátzcuaro, located along the north-south depression that runs between Cerro Tariacuri and Cerro Yaguarato, may be prehispanic in date. The earliest Colonial maps show no other routes except the Spanish grid plan.

In sum, Tzintzuntzan exhibits planning of individual structures and planning of some activity zones, but no planning of the total settlement.

## TARASCAN SOCIETY IN THE CAPITAL

The direct relationship between the spatial expression of zoning and planning, and the structure and functioning of such behavior, can now be utilized to construct the basic urban system in Tzintzuntzan.

With respect to the economic structure of Protohistoric Tzintzuntzan, there is a small but suggestive amount of information available. A significant part of the economic systems of urban settlements generally involves the production of goods and services. The evidence presented above indicates clearly that lithic implements were produced within the settlement at workshops and included prismatic blades, flakes, and scrapers. In addition, obsidian and basalt implements, including flakes, blades, and projectile points, were produced in residential zones. Various nonutilitarian objects were also produced in the settlement in workshops (type 2). Specialized artisan groups described in the RM (1956:176–82) and believed to be located near the king's residence also produced utilitarian and nonutilitarian objects relating to bow-making, carpentry, woodworking, painting, featherworking, leatherworking, fishing, hunting, masonry, pottery-making, flower-working, sandal-making, stair-making, tanning, banner-making, metal-working, canoe-making, and cotton-jacket-making. To some unspecifiable extent all the products of these activities were produced or in some stage of processing in Tzintzuntzan. In the agricultural zone adjacent to the settlement and in garden plots within the settlement limits, the following products were probably grown: maize (red, white, and variegated), amaranth, kidney and scarlet runner beans, red and green chile, capulin, gourds, maguey, nopal, chayote, tobacco, tomato, zapote blanco, and yucca (RM 1956:24, 96, 175–77, 181–87). The primary services produced in the settlement were those activities of the bureaucratic functionaries of the political and religious hierarchies, doctors, herbalists, custodians of the palace, storytellers, merchants, spies, messengers, and couriers (RM 1956:170–90).

There is some evidence for the spatial clustering of some productive units in the lithic workshops within the settlement, but it is not possible to correlate these with family, lineage, or nonkin based units. Ethnohistoric and ethnographic evidence suggests that occupation groups were spatially localized in wards or barrios (Van Zantwijk 1967:42, 69, 93–94). However, basically there are few data relevant to the structure and membership of productive units.

The evidence of planning and zoning in the city reflects in part the technology of economic exchange. The lack of formal street patterns would have made intrasettlement exchange slow and cumbersome. If there was a major north-south route through the center, it would have provided valuable contact between the lakeshore and southern extents of the city. The placement of the marketplace and the lack of standardized internal transport networks probably attests to the importance of the lake as a means of transport, communication, and distribution of goods and services.

The economic means of distribution probably involved both market systems and redistribution networks. The market system is documented several times in the RM and probably existed within the settlement (1956:39, 83, 91, 144, 213). The lack of a direct reference to its presence at Tzintzuntzan in the RM suggests that it was not as significant in the economic structure of the city as in other like settlements of Mesoamerica at this time. Redistributive networks, however, with the king at the center, are well documented in the RM for Tzintzuntzan (1956:151, 170, 173, 174, 177, 213). Tribute was collected within the city and from other settlements in the Tarascan state in the form of local goods (foods, clothing, precious metals, and feathers), services to the state (military and labor), and the maintenance of political appointees and temple lands. Within the city this tribute was collected and deposited in grandaries, chests in the palace, and residences of special deputies. The smallest unit of collection was twenty-five families in 1525. Goods were redistributed by the king and his administration in the form of religious offerings, support for the army, major feasts, gifts to foreign emissaries, and support for his household.

## THE HOUSEHOLD: KINSHIP, FAMILY, AND LINEAGE

Although the social structure of the city is more evident from the previous analyses than is the economic system, there is little direct evidence about the structure or role of kinship. However, we can suggest the presence of territorial groupings with some kinship functions.

All persons living within the same house were considered a family (RM 1956:173). This was clearly a variable unit, sometimes including an extended family, sometimes, for example, a married couple or a mother and son (RM 1956:173–74). The average family size for the Tarascan region was five to six persons (Cook and Borah 1972), although this too must have varied. The recognized forms of marriage are described in some detail in the RM. They included monogamy and several forms of polygamy, including mother-and-daughter polygamy (RM 1956:211–16). There is mention of one king who had at least sixteen wives, seven of whom were buried with him (RM 1956:184, 220). It is likely that polygamous households were concentrated among the elite because references to polygamy always refer to the nobility. Sororate and levirate marriages were also practiced (RM 1956:211–16).

Residence was generally virilocal, although since it was on land provided by the husband's father, it might be termed patrilocal. Within the RM there are examples of independent nuclear families, independent polygamous families, and patrilocal extended families, although from the documents there is no way to discern the frequency of any pattern.

The archaeological evidence for household structure is quite limited. Apart from the one excavation of a residence in Tzintzuntzan (Edificio F, or Tz-79), which I believe to represent a middle-status household, the remaining data are restricted to the size of residential terraces at Tzintzuntzan, the drawings in the RM of houses in the capital, and excavations in residential zones of Zacapu. The latter are the most extensive set of data on Tarascan urban residential zones, although they pertain to a community northeast of the Pátzcuaro Basin and date to the period immediately preceding the expansion of the Tarascan Empire. The largest number of houses excavated from the area known as Las Milpillas, thirty-seven, consisted of single-room rectangular structures, commonly measuring 16–32 sq m (Michelet, Ichon, and Migeon n.d.). They contained stone foundations and paved patios just outside the single entrance, similar to the house excavated at Tzintzuntzan. Above the foundations it is assumed that wood and thatch were used, as is depicted in the RM. Within the rooms are small rectangular hearths, often found with three stones, known to support cooking vessels. Several structures have adjacent granaries, both rectangular and circular.

Kin-based units above the level of the household may have functioned to regulate marriage and descent. An analysis of kinship terms from the sixteenth century (Gilberto 1987:201f.) suggests that within the family, age and gender were significant in structuring social relationships. Specifically the kin terms reveal that in reference to children ($-1$) and grandchildren ($-2$), relative generation was most significant; in reference to parents ($+1$) and grandparents ($+2$), both gender and generation were significant; the gender of the brother or sister through whom you were related was more important than either your gender or generation; and the gender of the speaker was primarily important in the speaker's generation (table 2.1).

Table 2.1    Sixteenth-Century Tarascan Kinship Terminology* (Gilberti 1987)

| Male Speaker or Both | | Female Speaker |
|---|---|---|
| *sirucua* | lineage    from *siruri* (head) | |
| *mahcaiuriri* | from *iuriri* (blood) | |
| *tata* | father | |
| *nana* | mother | |
| *cura* | grandfather (fafa and mofa) | |
| *cucu* | grandmother (famo and momo) | |
| *uuache* | child (m and f) (L. *uuatsite*) | |
| *nimatecua* | grandchild (m and f) | |
| *minguarecata* | spouse (wife) | *minguarehpeti* (husband) |
| *herache* | my brother | *mimi* my brother |
| *ureca* | my older brother | |
| *teruhuacuri* | the one in the middle (Anon. 1991 *teruuacuri*) | |
| *uuenganheri* | my younger brother | |
| *xauiru* | the youngest brother | |
| *pirenche* | my sister | |
| *uuece* | my younger sister | *pipi* my older sister |
| *uuache* | nephew or niece by a brother (*auitaecuaro uuache*) cousin through a brother | |
| *ihtza* | nephew or niece by a sister cousin through a sister | |
| *auita* | uncle by my father (fa bro), also *tata* | |
| *papa* | uncle by my mother (mo bro) | |
| *uaua* | aunt by my father (fa sis) | |
| *tzitzi* | aunt by my mother (mo sis), also *nana* | |
| *cura* | grandparents' brother (greatuncle) | |
| *cucu* | grandparents' sister (greataunt) | |
| *itsicue* | brother-in-law | *iuscue* |
| *iuscue* | sister-in-law | *tuuiscue* |
| *tarascue* | son-in-law daughter-in-law father-in-law mother-in-law | |

Table 2.1   *Continued*

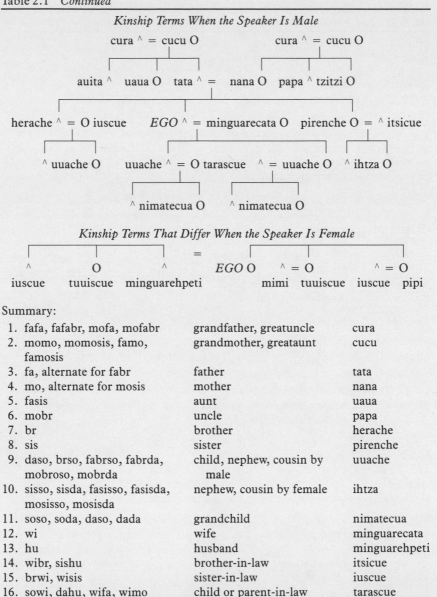

*Kinship Terms When the Speaker Is Male*

cura ^ = cucu O                              cura ^ = cucu O

auita ^   uaua O   tata ^ =   nana O   papa ^ tzitzi O

herache ^ = O iuscue      *EGO* ^ = minguarecata O   pirenche O = ^ itsicue

^ uuache O      uuache ^ = O tarascue   ^ = uuache O   ^ ihtza O

^ nimatecua O      ^ nimatecua O

*Kinship Terms That Differ When the Speaker Is Female*

^            O            ^         =         *EGO* O   ^ = O      ^ = O

iuscue   tuuiscue   minguarehpeti         mimi   tuuiscue   iuscue   pipi

Summary:

| | | |
|---|---|---|
| 1. fafa, fafabr, mofa, mofabr | grandfather, greatuncle | cura |
| 2. momo, momosis, famo, famosis | grandmother, greataunt | cucu |
| 3. fa, alternate for fabr | father | tata |
| 4. mo, alternate for mosis | mother | nana |
| 5. fasis | aunt | uaua |
| 6. mobr | uncle | papa |
| 7. br | brother | herache |
| 8. sis | sister | pirenche |
| 9. daso, brso, fabrso, fabrda, mobroso, mobrda | child, nephew, cousin by male | uuache |
| 10. sisso, sisda, fasisso, fasisda, mosisso, mosisda | nephew, cousin by female | ihtza |
| 11. soso, soda, daso, dada | grandchild | nimatecua |
| 12. wi | wife | minguarecata |
| 13. hu | husband | minguarehpeti |
| 14. wibr, sishu | brother-in-law | itsicue |
| 15. brwi, wisis | sister-in-law | iuscue |
| 16. sowi, dahu, wifa, wimo | child or parent-in-law | tarascue |

*To conform to modern orthography and reflect the sounds of the Tarascan language, all "v" used for initial "u" have been written as "u," all "y" for initial "i" are written as "i," and all "q" are written as "c."

In general the terms suggest bilateral kinship prevailed, with bilineality indicated to some extent in grouping children, nephews, nieces, and cousins of brothers together.

When describing the marriage of the nobility, the RM (1956:213) states that "they always marry their relatives, and take wives of the stock they came from, and they do not mix the lineages" ("se casaban siempre con sus parientes, y tomaban mujeres de la cepa donde venían, y no se mezclaban los linajes"). Succession of administrative positions always went to sons, brothers, and nephews of the dead man (RM 1956:203), and the RM is replete with references to the superior lineages of the Tarascan nobility.

What these data suggest is that kin groupings, probably patrilineages, did have some marriage- and descent-regulating functions, at least among the upper class. However, based upon the kinship terminology and the ethnohistorical documents, there is no evidence for strong matrilineal or patrilineal institutions.

## THE WARD OR DISTRICT

There is considerable evidence for the presence of wards or barrios within Protohistoric Tzintzuntzan, and there is evidence that these territorial units had marriage-regulating and religious and ceremonial functions in the center. For both upper- and lower-class residents, marriage was officially recognized only if it took place within the same ward (RM 1956:211, 216). In 1593 Tzintzuntzan had fifteen functioning wards, each with a chapel (Van Zantwijk 1967:226). In 1945 the inhabitants could remember thirteen and locate eleven (Foster 1948:26). It is not possible to locate these wards in the prehispanic city limits because of the confusion of names and places over the last 350 years. However, four Colonial chapels were located in the survey, and three were adjacent to secondary religious zones. They included Tz-27 in the modern barrio of San Bartolo; Tz-29 in barrio Santa Ana; Tz-111, with no barrio name; and Tz-80 in barrio Santiago. Another such site, Tz-117, is located where informants reported barrio San Juan was once found. These sites were interpreted as local religious centers within the residential zones of the city. I suggest that these sites represented small religious centers, such as temples, within each ward and, like ethnographically recorded *uapanecua* or *wapanekwa* (Van Zantwijk 1967:81–95), formed part of the structure of intrasettlement religious ceremonies. Tzintzuntzan would have had fifteen or more endogamous, territorial units with ceremonial functions. Occupational specialists may have been located within separate wards. However, within Tzintzuntzan these wards had no land-regulating function; that was done on a settlement-wide basis (RM 1956:185).

The RM indicates that there was a second level of territorial grouping within the settlement. This unit consisted of twenty-five households and was used for tribute collection, labor for public works, and taking censuses (1956:173). An official of the government, the *ocámbecha*, was appointed to oversee each of these units. It is likely to have been a subdivision of a ward, presently called a *manzana* in Michoacán. There is no archaeological evidence for this unit, and it may have been a later addition to the administrative organization of the city.

Based on the population estimate for the city, the number of people per household, the number of wards, and the size of subwards (Pollard 1972), a rough estimate is 1,600–2,300 persons in each ward, ten to nineteen subwards per ward, and 125–150 persons in each subward.

## SOCIAL CLASSES

The zoning of residential units within the settlement can best be viewed as the territorial expression of status groups. Based on the evaluation of urban zoning, at least three social groups can be recognized. In the RM (1956), four social classes are distinguished: the king (*irecha, cazonci*) and lords (*señores*), located in residence zones ii; the nobles (*principales*), located in residence zones iii; the commoners (*la gente baja, purépecha*), located in residence zones i; and slaves, who were probably located in the residences of the king, lords, and nobles. Each class was distinguished by dress, household structure, marriage, wealth, responsibilities and privileges, and access to occupations. There was minimal movement between these classes. Based on the archaeological evidence it is possible that some ethnic divisions existed in the city (residence type iv). The ethnic unit discussed in type iv occupied both low- and middle-status residence zones. However, it is difficult to say how these ethnic units articulated with the social classes of the population.

## THE IMPERIAL CAPITAL

Political and religious functions were central to the nature and growth of Tzintzuntzan, but economic activity was heavily embedded within other systems or peripheral to the basic power structure. The distribution of population within the city, the location of major public buildings, and the choice of buildings to receive significant investment of labor and materials all reflect the centrality of political, not economic, activities. Thus, for example, the political and religious centers (Tz-25 and Tz-29) were centrally located, separately zoned activity areas of relatively large size, marked by a high degree of planned structures, features, and areas. The commercial and manufacturing zones, on the other hand, were spatially dispersed and peripherally located, and no conscious planning was associated with any of them.

While religious activity was clearly distinct in the zoning of functions as revealed in structures, features, and artifacts, the political system was heavily embedded in the social structure of the upper classes. There were no separate buildings for judicial, administrative, or legislative functions. All were part of the multipurpose residence zones of the king and lords.

From the RM it is clear that the king and lords, the upper social class, occupied the dominant positions within the political administration as their primary status and were only secondarily considered priests capable of performing certain important ceremonies such as ritual sacrifice (see chapters 6 and 7). The political system dominated the religious hierarchy, utilizing the ideological system to reinforce political power and legitimacy. The two prominent archaeological features of the settlement, the two large artificial platforms, were associated with these two powerful components of the city—the king's palace and the temples of Curicaueri. Irrespective of past roles, at the time of Spanish conquest, the political organization was the dominant function of the urban settlement. The Spaniards may even have recognized this in the placement of the first chapel on the platform of the king's palace (Santa Ana). In fact, despite the turning of Tzintzuntzan into the center of Catholic missionizing after 1525, the temple platform was never destroyed, only abandoned.

It is possible that in describing the territorial social units of the settlement, one mechanism for this highly centralized integration of the settlement has been detailed. The archaeologically visible unit, the ward or barrio, has been associated with ceremonial and marriage regulation activities. Both of these functions were controlled by the religious structure of the settlement. A second, smaller unit, or subward, was described in the RM. This unit, controlled by the *ocámbecha*, a political functionary, was associated with tribute collection, labor groups, and census units, and was possibly used for the formation of army units (Pollard 1972:65). All of these are functions of a state. This suggests that as far as the political organization of the settlement was concerned, the ward was a weak unit, and the real administrative levels of Tzintzuntzan were the subward and the entire settlement, the latter controlled by the king. I believe that the subward level was created by the administration for the purpose of circumventing the ward structure, which was already controlled by the religious hierarchy, thereby increasing the central control of the political system.

The initial growth of Tzintzuntzan as an urban settlement appears to have been generated by political and not economic factors. This is in sharp contrast to other Mesoamerican centers such as Teotihuacan and Tenochtitlán. Jane Jacobs (1969:143), discussing cities whose chief export is government, suggests they have much in common economically with company towns. Such urban centers can be characterized as administrative cities and are probably associated with larger, complex political systems. It is probable that, at the time of the conquest, Tzintzuntzan was adding economic functions to the political and religious functions it already had exported. The clustering of economic activities near and within the king's residence could easily have served as a stimulus to economic development, particularly in the export of highly processed and scarce resources such as feathers, capes, polychrome pottery, and copper, silver, and gold objects. Thus we can view Tzintzuntzan as an administrative city whose urban economic functions were a by-product of the centralizing power of its political functions. In addition, there remains the possibility that Tzintzuntzan was initially founded as a ceremonial center that later took on political functions as it developed into an urban entity.

Because Tzintzuntzan was the capital of a large empire, much of its structure can only be understood within the context of its region and state. It was the Lake Pátzcuaro Basin that provided the material basis for the growth of both the city of Tzintzuntzan and the kingdom as a whole, and that is the unit to which we now turn.

# CHAPTER 3

# THE POLITICAL CORE
## LAKE PÁTZCUARO BASIN

IN 1520 the Pátzcuaro Basin was the densely populated geopolitical core of the Tarascan kingdom (map 3.1). Known then as the region of "the lake of Tzintzuntzan," it functioned as the immediate hinterland of the capital. The relationships that existed among its various settlements affected the structure and development of the entire empire. Indeed, state religion defined the basin as the center of the Tarascan cosmos and a metaphor for the geography of the universe.

## HUMAN ECOLOGY OF THE BASIN

The population of the Pátzcuaro Basin was located in a variety of hamlets, villages, towns, and the capital city itself. The location and size of these communities and the interaction among them was to a great extent determined by the distribution of land and water resources found there. In this section I will detail what we know about the significant resources utilized by the Protohistoric population. In subsequent sections of this chapter, and in later chapters, it will then be possible to describe how the human ecology of the basin affected the political economy of the Tarascan core and the empire.

The Pátzcuaro Basin, encompassing an area of 929 sq km (92,890 ha), is located within the Tarascan central plateau (Gorenstein and Pollard 1983; Toledo and Barrera-Bassols 1984). This region has been classified as a humid temperate zone, with summer rains and dry winters. The average temperature varies between 12° and 18° C, with frost common from thirty-five to fifty days a year. Modern rainfall averages 900–1,250 mm (1,041 mm at Pátzcuaro), higher in the southern portion of the basin. This rainfall is markedly seasonal: 80 percent falls between June and September, primarily as thunderstorms.

## ENVIRONMENTAL ZONES

In 1520 the basin contained six environmental zones of significance to Protohistoric-period Tarascans (map 3.2). Paleocological reconstruction has established that three of these zones largely approximate their modern counterparts, but the three lowest zones differed in their extent (Pollard

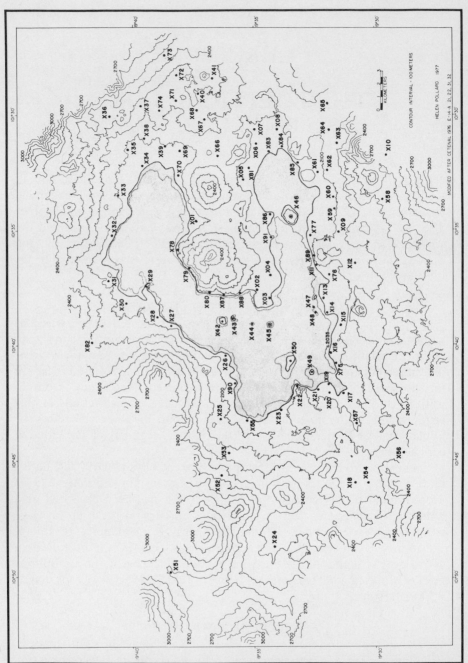

Map 3.1. Protohistoric Settlement in the Pátzcuaro Basin

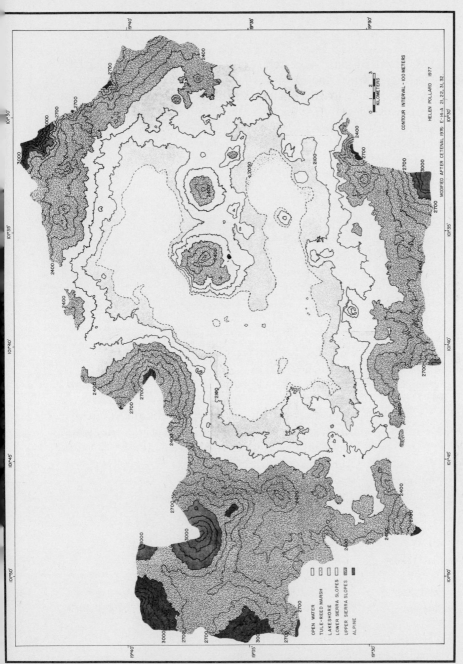

OPEN WATER
TULE-REED MARSH
LAKESHORE
LOWER SIERRA SLOPES
UPPER SIERRA SLOPES
ALPINE

CONTOUR INTERVAL – 100 METERS

HELEN POLLARD 1977

MODIFIED AFTER CETENAL 1976, E-14-A, 21, 22, 31, 32

0    1    2    3
KILOMETERS

Map 3.2. Environmental Zones of Protohistoric Pátzcuaro Basin

1979, 1983; Pollard and Gorenstein 1980; Gorenstein and Pollard 1983; Street-Perrott, Perrott, and Harkness 1987; Metcalfe and Harrison 1983; Metcalfe et al. 1987). During the sixteenth century the lakeshore was at 2,050 m above sea level, 15–19 m above its range in this century (fig. 3.1). Compared to now, this means that in 1520 there was a greater lake area, a different distribution of tule-reed marsh, and a smaller lakeshore zone. The six zones thus presented very different resources for the human population of the basin:

1. *Open Water*
   - area:           13,600 ha (14.6 percent of basin)
   - altitude:       lake level is estimated at 2,050 m
   - topography:     lake basin
   - rainfall:       average greater than 1,000 mm
   - frost season:   less than four months
   - soils:          none
   - biota:          open-water zone
2. *Tule-Reed Marsh*
   - area:           1,190 ha (1.3 percent of basin)
   - altitude:       ca. 2,050–2,070 m
   - extent:         Due to incomplete contour mapping this zone could only be estimated using aerial photographs and observing slope from vertical and oblique shots. The actual extent depends on the size of the lake, which could have been anywhere between the 2,045-m and 2,055-m contour lines.
   - topography:     shallows along the lakeshore
   - rainfall:       greater than 1,000 mm
   - frost season:   less than four months
   - soils:          lacustrine, alluvial
   - biota:          tule-reed marsh (hydrophilic vegetation)
3. *Lakeshore*
   - area:           11,340 ha (12.2 percent of basin)
   - altitude:       2,050–2,100 m
   - topography:     flattish floor of the basin, including lake islands, alluvial deltas, and plains
   - rainfall:       average greater than 1,000 mm
   - frost season:   less than four months
   - soils:          *charanda* predominant, also lacustrine, *uirás*
   - biota:          lakeshore vegetation with domestic plants and animals

4. *Lower Sierra Slopes*
   area:            29,600 ha (31.9 percent of basin)
   altitude:        2,100–2,300 m
   topography:      lower slopes of volcanic hills and mountains, some
                    lava flows
   rainfall:        entire range of the basin, 900–1,250 mm
   frost season:    about four months
   soils:           *charanda* predominant, (because of slope, the *char-
                    anda* is thinner than in the lakeshore zone), *t'upuri*
                    primary in southwest basin, some *uirás*
   biota:           probably more woodland and some pine/oak forest,
                    which would have had more oak and alder than now

5. *Upper Sierra Slopes*
   area:            33,500 ha (36.1 percent of basin)
   altitude:        2,300–2,800 m
   topography:      upper slopes of volcanic hills and mountains, also
                    includes small alluvial basins (West 1948:3)
   rainfall:        entire range of basin, but most land is in southern
                    portion, the average is probably closer to 1,100 m
   frost season:    four to six months
   soils:           *t'upuri* predominant, some yellow-brown
   biota:           pine and pine/oak forest; possible that the latter was
                    dominant

6. *Alpine*
   area:            3,660 ha (3.9 percent of basin)
   altitude:        2,800–3,200 m
   topography:      upper reaches of volcanic mountains
   rainfall:        varies, average 1,000–1,100 mm
   frost season:    six months
   soils:           yellow-brown, small amounts of *t'upuri*
   biota:           fir forest predominant, some pine forest

Human use of these zones was heavily determined by the soils, plants, and animals found within them. The basic soils and plant and animal communities found in the basin during the Protohistoric period are discussed below. Far more detail can be obtained from Gorenstein and Pollard (1983) and Toledo and Barrera-Bassols (1984).

## SOILS

Yellow-brown mountain soils, humic andosols, are located on the highest margins of the basin (map 3.3). West (1948) says this soil is the product of

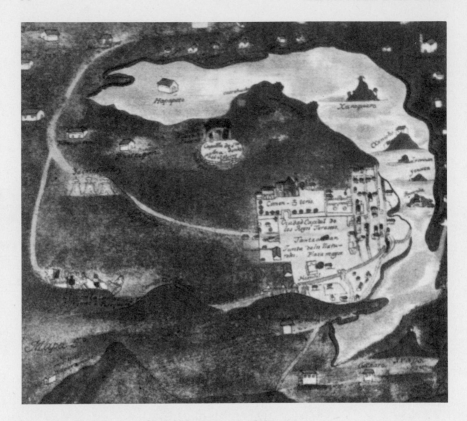

Fig. 3.1. Beaumont map of Lake Pátzcuaro, ca. 1540.

seasonally humid conditions under a fir-pine forest. It is the soil of the
upper slopes of the volcanic highlands. When stripped of vegetation the soil
becomes leached and infertile. After four to five years of agricultural
production the soil must be fallowed for several years. However, because it is
moisture retentive, crops can be planted before the spring rains, decreasing
the likelihood of frost damage before harvest. They are locally referred to as
"tierra de humedad."

The *t'upuri* soils (Tarascan, "yellow earth"), humic and vitric andosols,
are located on the slopes of volcanic hills surrounding the lake and are a
major soil of the basin. This is the most productive of the mountain soils,
with an extremely fine texture and moisture-retentive quality. "The surface
dries to a fine powder and acts as an insulator, preventing the evaporation of
moisture from the soil beneath" (West 1948:9). Thus, at the end of the dry
season (April–May) the soil will be moist below 7 cm from the surface.

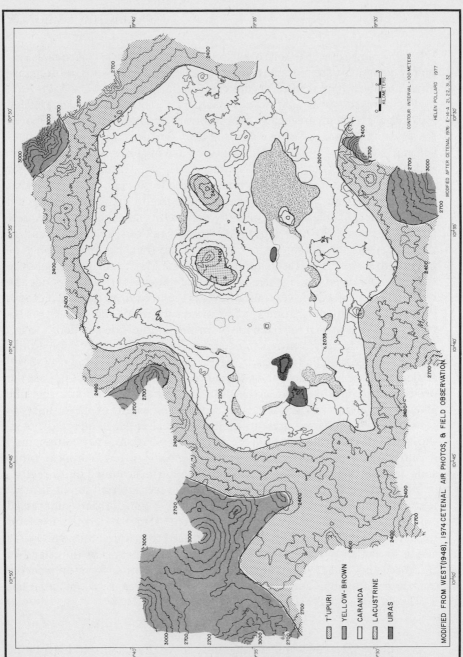

MODIFIED FROM WEST (1948), 1974 CETENAL AIR PHOTOS, & FIELD OBSERVATION

T'UPURI
YELLOW-BROWN
CARANDA
LACUSTRINE
UIRAS

CONTOUR INTERVAL - 100 METERS

KILOMETERS

HELEN POLLARD   1977

MODIFIED AFTER CETENAL 1976   E-14-A   21, 22, 31, 32

Map 3.3.  Soils of Protohistoric Pátzcuaro Basin

When the rains come, the soil soaks up the moisture, preventing serious erosion. *T'upuri* soils are more fertile than the yellow-brown soils, with higher humus content (6 percent), but deficient in lime, with a pH of 7.44–7.71.

The *charanda* soils (Tarascan, "red earth"), or luvisols, once called Mexican chernozem, are located over the lower mountain slopes and floor of the basin. This is a red-brown clay soil developed from the weathering of volcanic rock in a climate characterized by warm summers, mild winters, and broad-leaf vegetation. The texture varies (see Brand [1951:127] for results of four different samples) but averages 39 percent sand, 25 percent silt, and 35 percent clay. The clay content can rise to well above 40 percent (Brand 1951:127). This soil is generally deficient in nitrogen, but adequate in phosphorous (Gil Flores 1966). The soil does not retain moisture, and by the end of the dry season large cracks appear. Thus, crops can only be planted after the rainy season has begun (in late May to early June). As the rain hits this dried soil (generally in thunderstorms) it easily erodes the rather thin topsoil. Once vegetation cover is removed from this soil it erodes very easily, leaving deep gullies and exposed subsurface clay deposits. This clay is the raw material for red pottery for the region. The soil depth varies but generally decreases with distance from the lakeshore and slope uphill.

The lacustrine soils (*tamacua*, "tierra fertil y húmeda"; León 1888:94) are located in certain places along the shore of Lake Pátzcuaro. They are the product of deposition from arroyos draining the hillslopes and the lake when it was higher. In the sixteenth century the extent of these soils was considerably less than at present, their current abundance due to drops in the lake level and continuing soil erosion and deposition. They contain high organic content and sufficient essential chemicals, often lacking in other soils, to allow annual cropping, making them the most valued in the region.

The *uirás* soil (Tarascan, "white earth") is a very localized soil of "fibery-textured white clay" (West 1948:11) which is formed from compressed volcanic ash, and is extremely infertile. The Tarascan term is used for gypsum, and the subsoil of the *uirás* soil is used to manufacture white-gray adobe bricks and as a source of white clay for pottery. On the island of Jarácuaro this soil is overlain with lacustrine deposits, forming a fertile loam high in organics and calcium carbonate (7.7 percent). Alone, *uirás* has a pH value of 8.05–8.13.

## BIOTIC ZONES

Except for the open water and marsh zones of the lake itself, most biotic zones have been defined by prevailing vegetation, not fauna, because most animals move between land zones. By and large, modern vegetation zones are determined not by climatic features, but the impacts of human utilization of the basin for millenia. As West indicates (1948:8), the pine-oak forest localized on the upper slopes of the hills surrounding the lake once probably covered the entire basin.

## OPEN WATER

The dominant animals of the lake were fish and waterfowl. In the sixteenth century the fish would have included *Chirostoma* (Atherinidae), *C. estor* (pescado blanco, curucha urápiti), *C. bartoni* (charal, or c'arari), *C. grandocule* (c'uerepu), *C. patzcuaro* (c'uerepu), *Algansea lacustris* (acúmara, sardinia), *Allophorus robustus* (chehua), *Skiffia lermae* (t'irú), and *Neoophorus diazi* (choromu). The most common waterfowl were probably ducks of the genera *Aythya*, *Mareca*, and *Anas* (cuirísi) (Leopold 1959; Foster 1948). In the twentieth century the migratory ducks that wintered on the lake (late October to April) included *Aythya affinis* (lesser scaup, pato del tiempo), *Aythya valisineria* (canvasback, pato de los bosques), *Mareca americana* (baldpate, cotorro), *Oxyura jamaicensis* (ruddy duck, pato bola), *Anas acuta* (pintail, golondrino), *Anas discora* (blue-winged teal), *Anas cyanoptera* (cinnamon teal, pato zarceta), *Anas carolinensis* (green-winged teal, pato zarceta), *Anas strepera* (gadwall), *Spatula clypeata* (shoveller, pato cuchara), and *Nyroca collaris* (ringneck). The nonmigratory ducks included *Anas diazi* (Mexican duck, pato triguero) and *Dendrocygna bicolor* (fulvous tree duck, uacapu). Other waterfowl probably included *Fulica americana* (American coot, gallareta) and *Podilymbus podiceps* (grebe, iracu). Leopold (1959) believes the mallard (*Anas platyrhynchos*) once wintered in the lake.

## TULE-REED MARSH

The tule-reed marsh was found along shallow areas of lakeshore, probably no more than 4 to 5 m deep (fig. 3.2). This zone is extremely sensitive to lake extent fluctuations, and aerial photographs of the lakeshore taken in 1942 (USAF vertical and oblique coverage), 1952 (Companía Mexicana de Aerofoto), and 1974 (CETENAL) show marked changes in location and extent of the marsh. In addition, seasonal fluctuations create small marsh-grassland transition zones, which are seasonally flooded. The fauna would have probably included waterfowl, freshwater shrimp (sapitu), frogs (*Rana pipens*, cuanasa), water snakes, and herons (*Ardea herodias*, hapundarhu).

The zone is characterized by hydrophilic vegetation dominated by *tule* and reeds (Flores Mata 1971:30). The primary flora currently includes reed (*Arundo donax*, p'atamu, carrizo), tule comun (*Cyperus thyssiflorus*, p'acimu), tulillo (*Cyperus flaviconus*), chuspata (*Typha* spp., cattails), waterlilies (*Nymphaea*), water hyacinths (*Eichhornia speciosa*), and pond weeds (*Potamogeton luceus* and *foliosus*).

Fig. 3.2. Lake Pátzcuaro, tule-reed marsh.

## LAKESHORE VEGETATION

This zone occupies the lower slopes of the hills and the flattish floor of the lake basin. It is clearly the product of human use of the basin. The primary agricultural areas are within this zone, and all native forest and woodland has been removed. The predominant nonagricultural flora include grass, shrub, scrub oak, some pine, and cacti. The remaining fauna, apart from domestic animals, are small mammals and reptiles and birds.

The most common fauna found in this zone and the woodland zone currently include foxes (cúm iuátsi), squirrels (cuaráki), skunks (khuitsíci), chipmunks, gophers (cúmu), rats (hayác iuíri), hares (*Lepus callotis*, white-sided jackrabbit, chapási or cuambachu), mice (hayáci), lizards (ticuin), salamanders, leopard frogs and garter snakes. Also, there are many species of birds, especially hawks (tsapuki), owls (cocobi), ravens (cuaki), hummingbirds (tzintzúni), pigeons (hipúni), doves, towhees, and blackbirds (see Foster 1948:27).

## WOODLAND

This zone represents remnant stands of deciduous trees. The dominant tree species include oak (*Quercus* spp., tucúsi—more than twelve species known), scrub oak, colorín (*Erythrina americana*, purenchecua), madroño (*Arbutus xalapensis* and others), pine (*Pinus* spp.), and alder (*Alnus oblongifolia*, tepamu; *Alnus jorullensis*, aile; *Alnus cardifolia*, aile).

## PINE AND PINE/OAK FOREST

Pine forests are found on the upper slopes of most mountains encircling the lake basin (fig. 3.3). They were probably more extensive previously, although illustrations and descriptions in the RM (1956) refer to and show pine/oak vegetation only on upper slopes of mountains. Later accounts (Ponce 1968; *Inspección ocular en Michoacán*, 1799 [Bravo Ugarte 1960]) refer to the pine/oak forests encountered on the hills between settlements and place this zone very close to the modern distribution.

Stands of pine grade into mixed pine and oak stands at lower elevations. Minor amounts of other deciduous trees found in the woodland zone appear. The most common pine include *Pinus teocote*, *P. montezumae*, *P. michoacana*, *P. leiophylla*, *P. umbroides*, *P. harwegii*, and *P. pseudostrobus* (pucúri). At least twelve species of oak are known from the region (encino, roble) including *Q. crenatifelia* (encino blanco), *Q. incarnata trel* (encino rojo), *Q. microphylla* (encino capalincillo), *Q. punduriformes* (encino roble), and basswood (*Tilia* spp., cirimo).

The fauna includes small numbers of deer (axuni), rabbits (eastern cottontail, auani, *Sylvilagus floridanus*), squirrels, coyotes (ihuatsi), foxes (cum ihuatsi), lynx (misík pápu), raccoons, weasels, armadillo, opossum, tree quail, and skunks. Until the late nineteenth century the zone also contained larger mammals, with large numbers of deer (primarily white-tailed), peccaries (cuch shanu), wolves (úngurhiri, cui uíchu), jaguarundi (úngurhiri), mountain lions (mitspapu, púki), wild turkeys (*Meleagris gallopavo*, cúcuna), and chachalacas (*Ortalis vetula*).

## FIR FOREST

This zone is restricted to elevations above 2,800 m, where pine does poorly and fir well. This is spatially a very small zone of the lake basin, and judging by the small proportions of fir pollen in lake cores, this has always been the case (Hutchinson, Patrick, and Deevey 1956). The primary trees include fir (*Abies religiosa*, pinabete, t'cumbu, oyamel) and pine (especially *P. hartwegii*).

## PROTOHISTORIC LAND USE

When information about early sixteenth-century environmental zones, soil, and biotic zones are combined it is possible to determine the land-use classes and agricultural productivity of the Protohistoric basin. A fuller

Fig. 3.3. Lake Pátzcuaro, pine forest on upper slopes.


description of the modern land-use classes upon which the Protohistoric classes are based can be found in Gorenstein and Pollard (1980, 1983). A summary of the area of each zone and the agricultural productivity of each zone is found in table 3.1.

## AGRICULTURAL LAND

### Class I Land
Class Ia, permanently watered. This is land under permanent irrigation by either canal or pot/ditch techniques (map 3.4). It is generally found on either lacustrine or alluvial soils along the lakeshore or former lakebed. The soil is fertile and under continuous production. No fallowing is necessary, and two to three crops per year may have been grown.

Class Ib, seasonally watered. This is land under seasonal irrigation by floodwater techniques. A small amount of this land is terraced, and most is on naturally fertile stream alluvium and lacustrine soils. The literature is

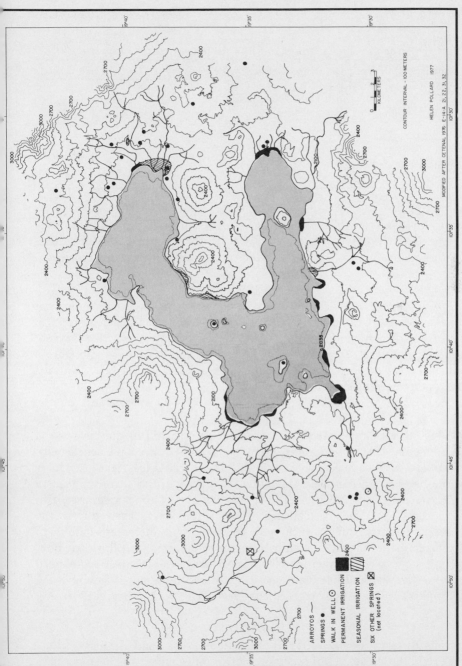

ARROYOS —
SPRINGS •
WALK IN WELL ☉
PERMANENT IRRIGATION ■
SEASONAL IRRIGATION ▨
SIX OTHER SPRINGS ⊠
(not located)

CONTOUR INTERVAL - 100 METERS

HELEN POLLARD 1977

MODIFIED AFTER CETENAL 1976 E-14-A 21, 22, 31, 32

Map 3.4. Water Resources of Protohistoric Pátzcuaro Basin

Table 3.1   Land-use Classes of Protohistoric Pátzcuaro

| Land Class | Hectares | Productivity (kg of maize/ha) | Fallow Cycle (years) |
|---|---|---|---|
| Class Ia | 321 | 2,200 | 1 |
| Ib | 212 | 2,000 | 1 |
| II | 11,922 | 1,000 | 1:2 |
| III | 29,600 | 450 | 1:4 |
| Forest | 36,045 | | |
| Marsh | 1,190 | | |
| Open Water | 13,600 | | |

mixed on the subject of fallowing this land. Belshaw (1967:8) indicates it is fallowed every other year, but West (1948:38) and Brand (1951:130) indicate continuous cropping. This land is often referred to as "tierra de humedad."

## Class II Land
This is land in the flattish floor of the basin (lakeshore environmental zone) and the alluvial basins of the upper slopes environmental zone. The land is farmed by rainfall agriculture (*tierra de temporal*) and is relatively more fertile, with deeper soils, than class III land. Generally the land is fallowed every other year, but various cycles have been described. The soils are generally *charanda* and *t'upuri*.

## Class III Land
This class includes the remaining agricultural land in the basin. It is found in the lower and (some) upper slopes environmental zones, with *charanda, t'upuri,* and yellow-brown soils. These are the least fertile hectares of the basin, with relatively thin soils. In addition, the altitude means a longer frost season and greater crop uncertainty. This is ameliorated in *t'upuri* soil zones, where planting begins a few weeks early due to the moisture-retentive quality of the soil. However, with increased slope there is greater chance of soil erosion in summer rainstorms, and this zone does include some of the most eroded land in Mexico. The soil must be fallowed every other year and in poorer sections rotated between maize and bean crops (first year fallow/maize, second year fallow/beans) (Brand 1951:130).

## FOREST
This category includes the woodland, pine/oak, and fir forest biotic zones and those portions of the lower sierra slopes, upper sierra slopes, and alpine environmental zones that contain these biotic zones. The forests provided a wide variety of resources, including lumber, firewood, pine oil,

medicinal plants, edible and wild plants, and animals (especially deer). For a detailed discussion of forest resources see West (1948) and Brand (1951).

## TULE-REED MARSH

Marshes provide the basic plant and animal resources of the basin. These include the reeds and tule for basketry and matting, marsh animals (frogs, salamanders, etc.), and shallow-water fish and wildfowl.

## OPEN WATER

The lake itself provides two basic resources, fish and waterfowl, in addition to acting as a primary means of transport.

## PROTOHISTORIC SETTLEMENT OF THE BASIN

The basic sources of information about Protohistoric settlement come from archaeological and ethnohistorical sources, including field identifications by Gorenstein and Pollard (1976–1977), partial survey by INAH (1981–1982), the RM, and several early Colonial maps. These have been analyzed by Gorenstein and Pollard (1983:13–96), and the following description is primarily drawn from that work.

## SETTLEMENT LOCATION

During the Protohistoric period the Pátzcuaro Basin is believed to have contained ninety-one settlements. Field observation by Gorenstein and Pollard located forty-seven of these settlements (the INAH partial survey recorded more than thirty), and nineteen others were confirmed by the RM or Colonial maps. Specific names could be attached to forty-eight of the archaeologically or ethnohistorically located sites, and sixteen other archaeologically located sites could not be assigned a name (table 3.2). Moreover, thirty-eight settlements were named in documents, but not assignable to a site. By utilizing settlement data from the decades soon after Spanish contact it was possible to project the likely location of twenty-five additional settlements, now buried under modern communities (see map 3.1). In this manner it was possible to assign a geographical location to settlements otherwise known to have existed only by name.

## SETTLEMENT SIZE AND FUNCTION

Of the ninety-one settlements in the Protohistoric basin, the areas and estimated populations of the four largest are known. These include Tzintzuntzan (674 ha), Ihuatzio (125 ha), Pátzcuaro (ca. 100 ha), and Eronguarícuaro (250–300 ha) (Pollard 1977, 1980). Based upon information from the mid-sixteenth century (see Gorenstein and Pollard 1983:chapter 2),

Table 3.2   Protohistoric Settlements

| | | |
|---|---|---|
| X01-Tzintzuntzan | X19-Haramútaro | X35-Cutzaro |
| X02-Cucuchuchu | X20-Nucutezepo | X36-Tirimicua |
| X03-Sipixo | X21-Tócuaro★ | X37-Caríngaro |
| X04-Ihuatzio | X22-Harocutín | X38-Cucupao |
| X05-Uemacuaro★ | X23-Urichu | X39-Serandangacho |
| X06-Hiripo | X24-Pechátaro | X40-Guanimao |
| X07-Sacapo | X25-Eronguarícuaro★ | X41-Itziparamucu |
| X08-Ichuen★ | X26-Puácuaro | X42-Pacandan |
| X10-Cuynaho | X27-Opongio | X43-Yenuán |
| X11-Ahterio | X28-Itzícuaro | X44-Ticuinun |
| X12-Pátzcuaro | X29-Házcuaro | X45-Xanecho |
| X13-Huecorio | X30-Tziróndaro | X46-Apupato |
| X14-Tzontzecuaro★ | X31-Purenchécuaro★ | X47-Utoyo |
| X15-Chapítaro | X32-Chupícuaro★ | X48-Urandén |
| X16-Pareo | X33-Uayameo | X49-Cuyameo |
| X18-Huiramángaro★ | X34-Irapo★ | X50-Xarácuaro★ |

X09, X17, X51–X91: names not assignable.

★Spelling differs from Gorenstein and Pollard (1983) to conform to the orthography used in this text.

these ninety-one settlements have been grouped into five size classes. Each class represents a range of settlement areas and population from the urban capital to dispersed hamlets. While many named or surveyed sites could be placed in a specific class, most of the smaller communities could not. Thus, while the overall number of places in each size class could be estimated, the exact location of all settlements in a class could not. The distribution of basic population is shown in table 3.3 (based on Gorenstein and Pollard 1983:63).

While the majority of class 3–5 settlements were generalized agrarian and/or fishing communities, a number of towns had additional specific functions within the basin structure. Eight communities were religious

Table 3.3   Settlement Classes

| Class | Number | Area Estimate | Population Range |
|---|---|---|---|
| 1 (capital) | 1 | Tzintzuntzan: 674 ha | 25,000–35,000 |
| 2 (center) | 3 | 100–300 ha | 3,000–5,000 |
| 3 (town) | 22 | 20–50  ha | 1,000–1,500 |
| 4 (village) | 40 | 10–20  ha | 100–500 |
| 5 (hamlet) | 25 | 1–10  ha | 30–80 |

centers, containing temples dedicated to a variety of Tarascan deities. These included Tzintzuntzan (X01), Ihuatzio (X04) and adjacent Sipixo (X03), Pátzcuaro (X12), the islands of Pacandan (X42) and Xarácuaro (X50), Ahterio (X11), and Itzícuaro (X28) (Gorenstein and Pollard 1983:64). Two settlements are known to have held marketplaces, Tzintzuntzan (X01) and Pareo (X16), with a third located at Asajo, immediately northwest of the basin. Tzintzuntzan functioned as the regional administrative center, in addition to being the imperial capital, while eight other communities functioned as local administrative centers. These included Eronguarícuaro (X25), Pechátaro (X24), Urichu (X23), Pareo (X16), Pacandan-Xarácuaro (X42–X50), Itziparamucu (X41), Uayameo (X33), and Pátzcuaro (X12). In terms of the basin social structure, the king and members of his lineage were resident at Tzintzuntzan and Ihuatzio. Other members of the nobility, the *achaecha*, also lived in nine other settlements; Uayameo, Pareo, Pechátaro, Eronguarícuaro, Urichu, Pacandan, Xarácuaro, Pátzcuaro, and Itziparamucu (Gorenstein and Pollard 1983:77).

## PROTOHISTORIC DEMOGRAPHY

Based upon the number and distribution of settlements during the Protohistoric period, the total population of the Pátzcuaro Basin is estimated to have been between 60,750 and 105,000 (mean: 80,000). By 1550 it had dropped to between 40,000 and 75,000 (Gorenstein and Pollard 1983:91), and by 1650 it was under 10,000. Not until the middle of the twentieth century did it return to the early Colonial levels (1940: 40,000), and only since 1980 did it reach Protohistoric numbers (greater than 80,000).

Nevertheless, throughout these five centuries, population has been distributed in a primate pattern, that is, one in which the largest settlement is more than twice the size of the next largest. During the Protohistoric period more than 36 percent of the population lived in the primate center, Tzintzuntzan, and more than 80 percent lived in communities with more than 1,000 people (table 3.4).

Table 3.4    Population and Settlements

| Settlement Class | Number | Population in Class | Mean | Percentage of Basin |
|---|---|---|---|---|
| 1 | 1 | 25,000–35,000 | 30,000 | 36.0 |
| 2 | 3 | 9,000–15,000 | 12,000 | 14.5 |
| 3 | 22 | 22,000–33,000 | 27,500 | 33.0 |
| 4 | 40 | 4,000–20,000 | 12,000 | 14.5 |
| 5 | 25 | 750–2,000 | 1,375 | 2.0 |

Thus, the Pátzcuaro Basin was characterized by a highly urbanized population distributed in a variety of functionally differentiated communities.

## ECONOMIC NETWORKS WITHIN THE BASIN

The primary mechanism for the exchange of goods and services within the basin was by means of barter at the three marketplaces that serviced the Pátzcuaro Basin (map 3.5). Given the high degree of urbanization and the variability of local resources, markets provided many of the basic commodities used in Tarascan households (see chapter 5). The three markets known to have been utilized by the basin population include those located in Tzintzuntzan, Pareo, and, just outside the basin proper, Asajo (Gorenstein and Pollard 1983:64–69).

We have no information about the frequency of occurrence of these markets, although the one at Tzintzuntzan was probably daily. Nor have we specific information about the relative variety of goods and services that each market offered. One way of evaluating the nature of the market network is by understanding the relative populations served by each market. Comparison to market behavior in the Pátzcuaro Basin during the twentieth century (Gorenstein and Pollard 1980; West 1948) suggests that populations will generally utilize marketplaces closest to them and that those populations midway between markets will attend both. If the settlement pattern, demographic, and marketing data are combined, they reveal the pattern shown in table 3.5.

Clearly Tzintzuntzan served the largest proportion of the basin population (67 percent) and largest number of elite, who were concentrated within the city. This probably means that a wider variety of goods and services were available there. However, the Pareo market would have still been quite large (the "gran mercado" of the RM [1956:61]). Both markets were accessible by lake transport, substantially increasing their value to Pátzcuaro residents, unlike the mountain valley location of Asajo. Finally, all settlements within the basin were located well in reach of local marketplaces.

Table 3.5    Protohistoric Market Structure

| Market | Number of Settlements | Population Served | Elite in Settlement |
|--------|----------------------|-------------------|---------------------|
| Tzintzuntzan | 51 | 55,230 | 6 |
| Pareo | 49 | 32,820 | 9 |
| Asajo | 13 | 13,655 | 1 |

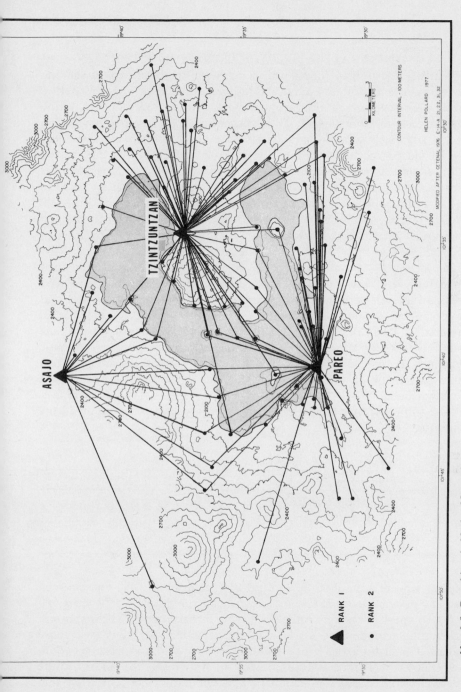

RANK 1 ▲

RANK 2 ●

CONTOUR INTERVAL - 100 METERS

KILOMETERS

HELEN POLLARD 1977

MODIFIED AFTER CETENAL 1976: E-14-A 21, 22, 31, 32

ASAIO

TZINTZUNTZAN

PAREO

Map 3.5. Protohistoric Market Networks

## ADMINISTRATIVE NETWORKS WITHIN THE BASIN

While Tzintzuntzan functioned as both the imperial capital and the regional center of administrative and judicial decisions, eight other settlements were governed by *achaecha*, or *señores*, who reported directly to the royal dynasty in Tzintzuntzan. These settlements included Eronguarícuaro, Pechátaro, Urichu, Pareo, Pacandan-Xarácuaro, Itziparamucu, Uayameo, and Pátzcuaro (map 3.6) (Gorenstein and Pollard 1983:69–72). Each would have had one of the *ocámbecha* to supervise tribute collection, maintain the census, and organize labor for public works. Larger communities may have had more than one, with a separate administrator for each ward.

Each of these administrative centers, including Tzintzuntzan, contained dependent villages and hamlets. Based upon the Caravajal Visitation of 1523–1524 (Warren 1977, 1985) and the first encomienda grants of 1523–1525 (Warren 1985), we know that the administrative hierarchy contained up to five levels (table 3.6). These documentary sources give information on these lower levels of the hierarchy for only a portion of the Pátzcuaro Basin. However, based upon these portions, Gorenstein and Pollard (1983:70) divided the basin into discrete and contiguous administrative units surrounding each of the higher-level centers (Thiessen polygons). These geographical units are believed to approximate the actual administrative units within the basin, although level 4 and 5 communities cannot be distinguished.

The administrative hierarchy of the Pátzcuaro Basin thus included the following:

Table 3.6   Protohistoric Administrative Hierarchy

| Administrative Level | Number of Settlements |
| --- | --- |
| 1 (capital: Tzintzuntzan) | 1 |
| 2 (basin center: Tzintzuntan) | 1 |
| 3 | 8 |
| 4 and 5 | 82 |

Each unit of administration within the basin would have had between one and sixteen dependent communities and represented between 2,500 and 9,800 persons (not counting the city of Tzintzuntzan). These approximated units contain fewer settlements, but higher populations, than those recorded in the Carajaval Visitation for other parts of the Tarascan kingdom (see chapter 6). Perhaps the administrative system was responding to the relatively high population numbers and population concentration that characterized the Protohistoric period.

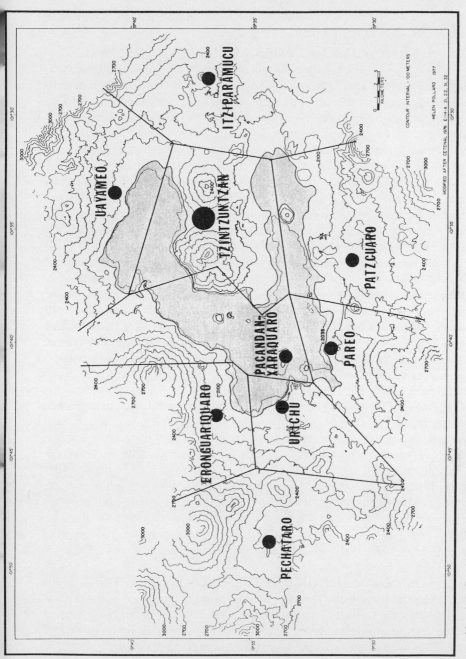

Map 3.6. Protohistoric Administrative Centers

## TRANSPORT NETWORKS WITHIN THE BASIN

During the Protohistoric period the movement of people and goods was limited to foot or canoe travel. On land, transport routes varied from well-defined roads up to 3 m wide to narrow paths (Gorenstein and Pollard 1982). Along them individuals traveled, information was transmitted, and, with tumpline carriers, goods were moved. Specialized porters could be hired in the markets and were also available through the royal palace. On the lake, travel was by canoe, *icháruta*, for both passengers and cargo. Smaller canoes, for two to six people with one or two paddles, and larger canoes, with four or more paddles, are illustrated in the RM. While the larger canoes have disappeared in the twentieth century, in 1980 there were still more than 700 canoes on Lake Pátzcuaro (Toledo and Barrera-Bassols 1984:193). Among the mayordomos in the central administration at Tzintzuntzan was a chief canoeman to whom paddlers were assigned (RM 1980:228).

Based upon the RM (text and illustrations), the early Colonial maps, aerial photographs, archaeological data, and field identification, the Protohistoric land and water routes have been mapped (Gorenstein and Pollard 1982, 1983). They reveal a high degree of interconnectedness between settlements and the focal significance of the lake and lakeshore in transport. The accessibility of each settlement from all other settlements was determined by counting the largest number of linkages, that is, other settlements through which one would need to pass, between any one place and all others. It was found that during the Protohistoric the highest number of such linkages was twelve (Gorenstein and Pollard 1983:75). The settlements that were more accessible needed fewer linkages to be reached. Seven settlements needed only seven or eight linkages to connect them with all other places in the basin and the routes leading out of the basin. None of these most accessible settlements was an important administrative, religious, or economic center, although Tzintzuntzan fell in the second rank of accessibility, needing nine linkages. All of the most accessible settlements were located on the lakeshore, clustered on the eastern shores of the lake.

## THE PROTOHISTORIC SETTLEMENT STRUCTURE

During the height of Tarascan political power in western Mexico more than ninety communities, containing 60,000–105,000 people, were located in the Pátzcuaro Basin. More than 90 percent of the settlements and population were found within two environmental zones, the lakeshore and lower sierra slopes. Indeed, 69 percent of the settlements and 74 percent of the population was found in the lakeshore zone alone, including the capital city, Tzintzuntzan (table 3.7) (Gorenstein and Pollard 1983:77).

Table 3.7    Settlements, Resources, and Population

| Environmental Zone | Percentage of Basin Land Area | Number of Settlements (%) |
|---|---|---|
| Lakeshore | 15 | 63 (69) |
| Lower sierra slopes | 37 | 20 (22) |
| Upper sierra slopes | 43 | 8  (9) |
| Alpine | 5 | 0  (0) |

| Environmental Zone | Population (%) |
|---|---|
| Lakeshore | 61,487 (74) |
| Lower sierra slopes | 16,875 (20) |
| Upper sierra slopes | 4,515  (6) |

| Soil Zone | Number of Settlements (%) |
|---|---|
| Charanda | 71 (78) |
| Uirás | 2  (2) |
| Lacustrine | 6  (7) |
| T'upuri | 11 (12) |
| Yellow-brown | 1  (1) |

A number of communities were functionally differentiated, and settlements varied considerably in their area and population. There was general congruence between the location of elite families and administrative centers, but as Table 3.8 indicates, this was not the case for other settlement functions. While the four largest settlements (Tzintzuntzan, Eronguarícuaro,

Table 3.8    Protohistoric Central-Place Functions

| Administrative Center | Resident Elite | Religious Center | Market |
|---|---|---|---|
| Tzintzuntzan | Tzintzuntzan | Tzintzuntzan | Tzintzuntzan |
| Eronguarícuaro | Eronguarícuaro | | |
| Pechátaro | Pechátaro | | |
| Urichu | Urichu | | |
| Pareo | Pareo | | Pareo |
| Pacandan-Xarácuaro | Pacandan-Xarácuaro | Pacandan-Xarácuaro | |
| Itziparamucu | Itziparamucu | | |
| Uayameo | Uayameo | | |
| Pátzcuaro | Pátzcuaro | Pátzcuaro | |
| | Ihuatzio | Ihuatzio | |
| | | Itzícuaro | |
| | | Ahterio | |
| | | | (Asajo) |

Pátzcuaro, and Ihuatzio) all contain some specialized functions, there was no direct relationship between number of functions and size of population. Indeed, only Tzintzuntzan was sufficiently differentiated to contain all community functions and was in addition highly accessible by the transport network (table 3.8).

This meant that Tzintzuntzan was a regional primate center on the basis not only of population size, but also its overwhelming control of all other functional hierarchies. No other settlement or elite group within the Tarascan geopolitical core could have challenged that control. On the other hand, it was the political and economic integration of this core that provided both the material *means* and the material *needs* for imperial conquest.

# CHAPTER 4

# THE EXPANSION OF THE TRIBUTARY STATE

THE expansion of the Tarascan state out of the Lake Pátzcuaro Basin and beyond central Michoacán involved the incorporation of varied populations, the control of large territories, and the defense of multiple hostile borders, including the long eastern frontier, along which Tarascan forces faced the westward movement of the Aztec Empire. The pattern of expansion and the effects of imperial conquest on the structure of Tarascan society reveal similarities to the political evolution of all Mesoamerican states and the historic and ecological differences that produced the distinctive Tarascan form.

## THE LEGENDARY AND HISTORIC EXPANSION
## OF THE KINGDOM

More than 75,000 sq km between the Lerma River in the north and the Balsas Basin in the south was dominated by the hereditary dynasty ruling from Tzintzuntzan. The historical sequence of conquest and consolidation of the kingdom over this vast region is primarily known to us from the RM. Supplementing and confirming the material are several documents written within the Tarascan region as part of the early Spanish colonial administration, including the RG of 1579–1580 (1985, 1987), the Caravajal Visitation of 1523–1524 (Warren 1977, 1985), the Ortega Visita of 1528 (Warren 1985), the *Suma de visitas de pueblos* of 1547–1550 (1905), and early encomienda grants of 1523–1525 (Simpson 1934; Warren 1985). Documentary sources recording Aztec conquests along the eastern Tarascan border provide an additional source of information (e.g., Contreras Ramírez 1987; Herrejón Peredo 1978; and Smith 1987). Finally, archaeological research within the Tarascan territory and along the frontiers amplifies the documentary record (Cabrera Castro 1986; Contreras Ramírez 1987; González Crespo 1979; Gorenstein 1985; Kelly 1949, 1985; Michelet 1986; Moedano 1946; Moguel Cos 1987; Noguera 1944; Weigand 1985).

The expansion of the Tarascan state has been the subject of research for several decades, and many detailed studies are available (Barrett 1973, 1974, 1975; Beltrán 1982; Brand 1943; Gorenstein and Pollard 1982, 1983; López Austin 1976; Paredes 1976; Pollard 1982b, 1987; Stanislawski 1947). In the present study I have utilized the available documentary and archaeological information to plot the actual sequence of conquests as reported in the RM. Using the Miranda edition of the RM (1980), I have numbered each set of conquests recorded. In general I have separated sets according to the sense of the passage or the separation of sentences. However, in several places the distinction has been arbitrary and cannot be interpreted as indicating separate military campaigns. The availability of accurate topographic maps at 1:50,000 and 1:25,000 (DETENAL 1977–1985) and increasing numbers of archaeological surveys have made such detail possible only recently.

In the legendary history of the Tarascans, the great culture hero Taríacuri established himself as lord of Pátzcuaro, and his two nephews, Hiripan and Tangáxoan, as lords of Ihuatzio and Tzintzuntzan, respectively. Between A.D. 1250 and 1350 this elite lineage under Taríacuri, the *uacúsecha*, effectively dominated political interaction within the Pátzcuaro Basin. By 1350, Taríacuri, with his lineage in control of the largest and richest parts of Pátzcuaro Basin (Pátzcuaro, Ihuatzio, and Tzintzuntzan), and his allies in Urichu, Eronguarícuaro, and Pechátaro, began to lead his followers on a series of military campaigns within and outside the Pátzcuaro Basin. The rationale for these conquests is presented in a mystical dream that Taríacuri had in which he forsaw the cosmic mission of creating a state. These conquests labeled 1 through 7, are represented on map 4.1, depicting Tarascan expansion from 1350 to 1440. Beginning with the southwest corner, the conquests moved to encircle it. At this point Taríacuri died, and under Hiripan, based in Ihuatzio, they moved out to the Lake Cuitzeo Basin. These territories were the most densely settled at contact and greatly enriched the *uacúsecha* elite who led these campaigns. However, it is quite clear that at this point the military expansion was little more than a series of raids for booty led by the war leaders Taríacuri and later Hiripan on behalf of a state that was little more than an amalgam of distinct polities with a series of "capitals," the residences of the highest-ranking members of the ruling lineage. The booty of military conquest was still being divided among the participating lords, and the conquests themselves were patchy. For example, the series of conquests in the Lake Cuitzeo Basin appear to have been accomplished by means of the lake, leaving large numbers of inland communities untouched, as well as many lakeshore communities (this we know from the list of towns conquered later).

Sometime around A.D. 1440, first under the leadership of Hiripan and later Tangáxoan, the first steps were made to institutionalize the military conquests and produce a tributary state. This involved the creation of an administrative bureaucracy and the allocation of conquered territories to members of the nobility. Rather than having individual lords lead raiding

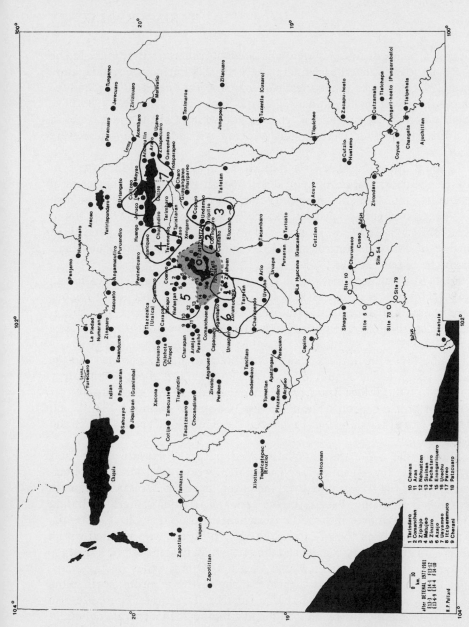

Map 4.1. Tarascan Expansion, 1350–1440

parties, a series of lineages were allocated bureaucratic positions. In the words of the *Relación*, the islanders (the lords of Xarácuaro, Pacandan, and possibly Urichu and Eronguarícuaro) took part of the *tierra caliente*, and the Chichimecs took the "right hand," or the Tarascan Sierra (RM 1980:198). Some communities previously "conquered" were retaken, and a series of administrative centers were established, from which future conquests were made.

In the following decades, the pattern of expansion forged for the conquest and incorporation of central Michoacán was used in the series of conquests that followed. These conquests are labeled 8 through 18 on map 4.2. The first target of expansion was the Tarascan Sierra (8 and 9), followed by the Balsas Basin (9, 10, 11, and 12). Subsequent conquests expanded the borders of Tarascan control in all directions and probably reached their maximum extent around 1470.

By 1470 those territories depicted on map 4.2, "Tarascan Expansion, 1440–1500" were part of the kingdom. In addition, a number of regions were conquered under the Tarascan king Tzitzipandáquare but subsequently lost through rebellion or Tarascan consolidation in the face of Aztec expansion.

By the 1460s the Tarascans had taken the province of Zacatula, on the Pacific coast at the mouth of the Balsas, advanced their northeastern frontier into the Toluca Basin, established centers north of the Lerma River (Cuecillo or Cerro Gordo, near Apaseo [Contreras Ramírez 1987]), and moved north of Lake Chapala in the west (see Herrejón Peredo 1978; Brand 1943, 1980).

During the 1470s the Tarascans faced military pressure along their eastern border from the Aztecs and along their western border with Colima. In 1476–1477 the Aztecs under Axayacatl retaliated for Tarascan conquests by a major campaign that captured a series of frontier centers, including Taximaroa, and moved into the Tarascan heartland as far as Charo. After the Tarascans took back their centers, the eastern border was fortified with a series of major military centers and the settlement of some ethnic Tarascans and several communities of Matlatzinca and Otomí exiles fleeing Aztec rule. The archaeological data suggest that the northern border, north of the Lerma River, was abandoned at this time by Tarascans. There are also indications that the Tarascans abandoned attempts to incorporate regions of Jalisco and Colima at this time, while consolidating their control in the Tamazula-Zapotlán and Coalcomán zones.

During the 1480s the Aztecs under Ahuitzotl either directly or indirectly, through their Matlatzinca, Chontal, or Cuitlatec subjects, launched a series of attacks along the southern Tarascan border in the Balsas Basin. These

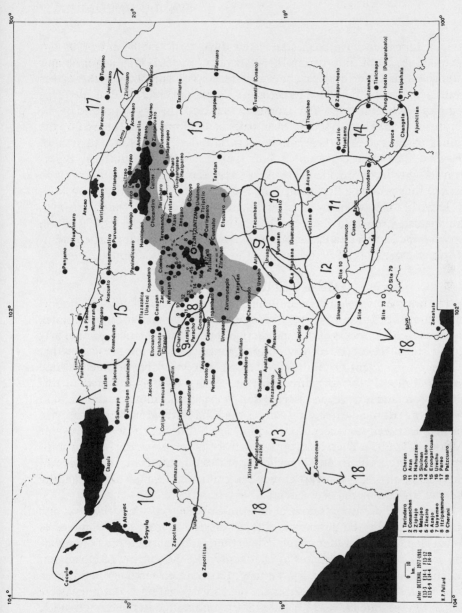

Map 4.2. Tarascan Expansion, 1440–1500

| | |
|---|---|
| 1 Tarindaro | 10 Cheran |
| 2 Comanchen | 11 Aran |
| 3 Zipiajo | 12 Nahuatzen |
| 4 Matujeo | 13 Sevinan |
| 5 Ziriciro | 14 Pechataro |
| 6 Azajo | 15 Erongaricuaro |
| 7 Uayameo | 16 Urachu |
| 8 Itziparamuco | 17 Pareo |
| 9 Cherani | 18 Patzcuaro |

10 Km.

after DETENAL 1977–1981
f13:3  f14:1  f13:12
f13:6–9  f14:4  f14:10

H. P. Pollard

attacks appear to have been stalemated during the 1480s and 1490s but occupied much of Tarascan military strategy. In 1517–1518 a final major offensive against the northern Tarascan border was launched by the Aztecs under Moctezuma II and led by the great Tlaxcallan chief, Tlahuicale. This campaign, which had reached Acámbaro in the north, was countered by the Tarascans in 1519 by two separate campaigns, one from Zinapécuaro into the Toluca Basin, and the other from the central Balsas to the Aztec fortress of Ostuma. The preoccupation of both powers with the southern Balsas frontier may have provided the leverage for the local chief of Zacatula to remove that province first from Tarascan and later from Aztec control.

Thus, in 1522, when the Tarascan king ceded Irechecua Tzintzuntzani to the Spanish Crown the Tarascans effectively controlled the 75,000 sq km between the Lerma and Balsas River systems from the modern Michoacán-Mexico border to the Sayula Basin in the west (tables 4.1 and 4.2).

## THE MULTIETHNIC STATE

The interrelationship between ethnic units and a central political authority is known historically to have been crucial to the operation of complex societies. In the process of this interaction, central authorities, particularly ruling elites, have created new ethnic groups, altered the attributes that define ethnic identity, and restructured relationships between ethnic groups (Enloe 1980:17ff.). Much of the society itself is revealed in this interaction, and it has been asserted that "perhaps the most crucial element in the dynamic of an expanding state is the kind of relationships it has with the people it seeks to incorporate and the way it initiates those relationships (Morris 1972:397). Therefore, the recognition of ethnicity, the relationships among ethnic units in plural societies, and the relationship between ethnicity and political control are subjects of central concern in understanding the pattern of imperial expansion.

The central defining feature of an ethnic group, self-identification, and categorization by the governing elite, is clearly beyond the resources of archaeologically derived research. Nevertheless, because ethnicity is generally associated with high rates of endogamy and the sharing of clusters of beliefs and values, marked by the use of a common language, and often territorially isolable, the discernment of ethnic variation is not impossible (Barth 1969; Enloe 1972, 1980) and is often highlighted in the ethnohistoric documents. Nevertheless, it is wise to remember that ethnic boundaries are fluid, contracting or expanding with major political and economic shifts in the society at large. Ethnic identifications coexist with other social identifications, meaning that occupational and class boundaries, for example, may cross-cut ethnic groups. Different artifact classes, or properties of

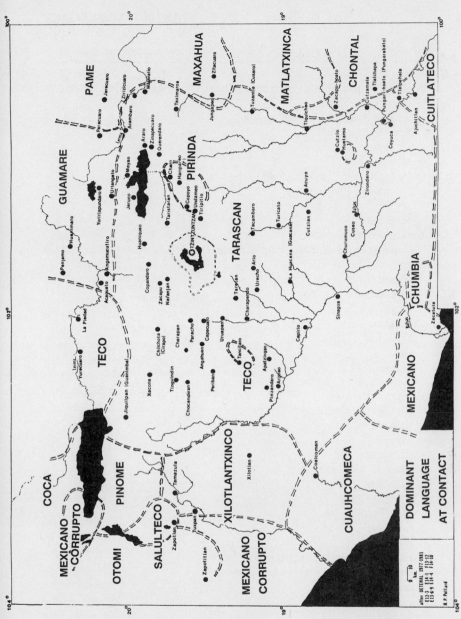

Map 4.3. Ethnic Groups within the Tarascan Domain

Table 4.1   Tarascan Conquests according to the RM (1980:191–99)

A. Early Conquests
  1. Within Pátzcuaro Basin: Hiuacha's villages (southwest portion)
        Zirapen (Zirahuén)
        Uiramu Angaru (Huiramángaro)
        Acuato (Jujucato)
        Chumengo
        Zizupan
  2. Outside the basin, immediately to the southeast
        Coyinguaro (Curínguaro)
        Tetepeo
        Turipítio
  3. Hetuquaro (Etúcuaro)
        Hoporo (Oporo in RG Tiritipio, Coapa?)
  4. Xaso
        Chucandiro
        Teremendo
        Huaniqueo
  5. Cumachen
        Naranjan
        Zacapu
        Cheran
        Siuinan
  6. Huruapa (Uruapan)
        villages of "nauatlatos"
        Hacauato
        Zizupan
        Chenengo
        Uacapu
        Tariyaran
        Yuriri
        Hopacutio
        Condebaro (Condembaro)
        Hurecho
     Taríacuari dies and is buried in Pátzcuaro
B. Conquests under Hiripan (based in Ihuatzio)
  7. Huriparao
        Charachutiro (Charo?)
        Tupataro
        Uarirosquaro
        Xeroco (Jeruco)
        Cuiseo (Cuitzeo)
        Peuendao (Apunda-lake)

Table 4.1    *Continued*

___

    Zinzimeo

    Araro

C.  End raiding and begin political incorporation of villages

    Appoint *caciques*

    Islanders took part of the *tierra caliente*

    Chichimecas took "the right hand"

      8.  Xénguaro (Capula)

          Cherani (Cheran/Cheranatzicuran)

          Cumachen

      9.  Tacanbaro (Tacambaro)

          Huruapan (Uruapan)

          Parachu (Paracho)

          Charu (Charapan)

          Hetocuaro (Etúcuaro)

          Curupu Hucazio

      These appear to be conquests and reconquests of previously raided communities.

      Division of towns among Chichimec and islander lords.

      Set up seats of government:

          In Curupu Hucazio: ten Chichimec lords

          In Hurapan: islander lords

          In La Guacanan (La Huacana): one lord

          In Paracho: one lord

          In Chupingo Parapeo: four lords

D.  Conquests in the name of the kingdom

    These lords then make *tierra caliente* conquests:

     10.  Casinda Angapeo

          Purechu Hoato

          Cauingan

          Tucumeo (Tocumeo)

          Marita Angapeo

          Hetuquaro Haparendan

          Zacango

          Cuseo

          Xanoato Angapeo

          Quayameo

          Apanoato

     11.  Continue these conquests, placing *caciques* in charge

          Uamuquaro

          Hacuizapeo

          Papazio Hoata (Papaseo)

          Tetengueo (Tetenxeo)

Table 4.1   *Continued*

        Puruaran
        Cuzian
        Mazani
        Patacio
        Camuqua Hoato
        Yurequaro
        Sirandaro (Zirondaro)
12. And continue:
        Copuan
        Cuxaran
     Under lord of La Huacana:
        Caxuruyo
        Sycuytaro (Zicuitaro)
        Tarinbo
        Hazaquaran
        Zicuytaran
        Pumuchacupeo
        Yacoho
        Ayaquinda
        Zinagua
        Churumucu
        Cuzaru (Cuzaro)
13. Under different lord:
        Paranzio
        Zinapan
        Zirapitio
        Taziran
        Turuquaran
        Urechu
        Ambaquetio
        Copuan (a nauatlato village)
        Euaqueran
        Charapichu
        Paraquaro
        Paques Hoato
        Euaquaran
        Tiristaran
        Puco Hoato
        Tanzitaro
        Eruzio
        Ziramaratiro
14. Continued conquering in *tierra caliente*:
        Uisindan

Table 4.1 *Continued*

    Hauiri Hoato
    Zinapan
    Zirapetio
    Hapano Hoato
    Cuyucan
    Hapazingan (Cutzamala [RG 1985:39])
    Pungari Hoato (Pungarabato)
15. Others conquered:
    Ambezio
    Tauengo Hoato (Tanhuato)
    Tiringueo
    Characharando
    Zacapu Hoato
    Peranchequaro
    Uasishoato
    Hucumu (Ocumo or Tuzantla [Warren 1985:281])
    Hacandiquao
    Haroyo
    Xungapeo
    Chapato Hoato
    Haziro Hauanio
    Taximaroa (Otomí village)
    Pucuri Equatacuyo
    Maroatio (Maravatio)
    Hucario (Ucareo?)
    Hirechu Hoato
    Acanbaro Hiramucuyo (Acámbaro)
    Teuendaho (Tarandaquao)
    Mayao (Maya)
    Emenguaro
    Cazaquaran
    Yurirapundaro (Yuríria)
    Cuypuhoato
    Uangaho (Huango)
    Tanequaro
    Puruandiro
    Zirapequaro (Zinapécuaro)
    Quaruno Ynchazo
    Hutaseo
    Hacauato (Aguanuato/Sta Fé del Río)
    Zanzani
    Uerecan (Yurécuaro)

Table 4.1   *Continued*

16. Son of Hiripan conquered:
    Carapan
    Father and grandfather of ruling king conquered:
    Tamazula
    Zapotlán
    pueblos de Avalos (Ortega 1528 in Warren 1977:411–25)
        Sayula
        Atoyac
        Teocuitatlan
        Techaluta
        Zacoalco
        Cocula
17. Tarascan king Tzizipandáquare (Tzintzuntzan) went toward Toluca and Xocotitlan. During time of Moctezuma's father (Hacangari) the Aztecs destroyed Taximaroa.
18. Then Tzizipandáquare went toward Colima and Zacatula and other towns (RM 1980:214).

Table 4.2   Military Service along the Tarascan Frontiers
(*Relaciones geográficas* 1579–1580)

|  | Eastern Frontier | Western Frontier |
|---|---|---|
| Acámbaro (1985:129) | Aztecs | Jalisco |
| Tuzantla (1985:206) | Aztecs | Jalisco |
|  | Matlatzinca |  |
| Ziróndaro (1985:140) | food to Cutzamala | Colima |
|  |  | Zacatula |
| Cuitzeo (1985:51) |  | Jalisco |
| Tiripitio (1985:180) | Aztecs |  |
|  | Matlatzinca |  |
| Chilchota (1985:64) |  | Colima |
|  |  | Jalisco (Amula, D'Avalos) |
| Tarecuato (1985:81) |  | Jalisco (D'Avalos) |
| Tinguindín (1985:78) |  | "Chichimecs" |
| Peribán (1985:85) |  | Jalisco (D'Avalos) |
| Jiquilpan (1985:74) |  | Jalisco (D'Avalos) |
| Tamazula (1985:153) |  | Colima |
|  |  | Jalisco (D'Avalos, west) |
| Tuxpan (1985:145) |  | Colima |
| Zapotlán (1985:149) |  | Colima |
|  |  | Jalisco (D'Avalos, west) |
| Coalcomán (1985:122) |  | Motines |

artifacts, may signal these different social boundaries. Moreover, within a single multiethnic, complex society the intensity of ethnic affiliation may differ, and along with this the number and kinds of markers used by a group to signal ethnicity may vary. Finally, the archaeologist deals with units of time that often compress ethnic "maps" and obscure the processes of ethnic emergence and change, and the ethnohistoric documents may give a false sense of permanence to affiliations that were in rapid flux.

The spatial parameters of the Tarascan state have been delineated according to available ethnohistoric and archaeological evidence. We can clearly distinguish the geopolitical core, the Lake Pátzcuaro Basin. In addition, the maximal and mean locations of the late fifteenth-century and early sixteenth-century military frontiers have just been described, marking the territorial extent of Tarascan tributaries and effective political control.

The Tarascan state appears to represent a simple, and historically common, pattern of a homogeneous ethnic unit, within which political power is centrally located, and surrounded by a ring of ethnically diverse populations incorporated by recent and/or continuous military expansion. Political systems like this are usually considered empires (Eisenstadt 1979) and are characterized by major political and economic segmentation into center and periphery (Ekholm and Friedman 1979; Larsen 1979). Centers are generally considered parasitic, drawing wealth as tribute from the periphery and controlling the primary means of production and exchange. Politically, centers are characterized by direct rule, while the periphery is characterized by indirect rule and local control of production. The relationship, in most general terms, is "imperialist."

However, in the Tarascan case the major political boundaries of core and periphery do *not* appear to have been congruent with the major ethnic boundaries of Tarascan and non-Tarascan. When the distribution of ethnic groups in the Protohistoric state is mapped (map 4.3) and then combined with the distributions of the tribute and market networks, it is possible to recognize two spatially nested units. The first, the tributary unit, covers the entire empire. It includes all communities outside the urban centers of the Pátzcuaro Basin. A second unit is limited to central Michoacán and is bounded by the marketing network that provided essential goods and services to basin populations (see chapter 5). This unit is co-terminous with the Tarascan central plateau and the northern rim, particularly the Lake Cuitzeo Basin, suggesting that it is an ecological or resource zone. An analysis of the relationship between the political/tributary unit, the ecological/market unit, and the actual distribution of ethnic groups in the Protohistoric period suggests the way in which ethnic variation was incorporated into the strategies of political expansion (map 4.4).

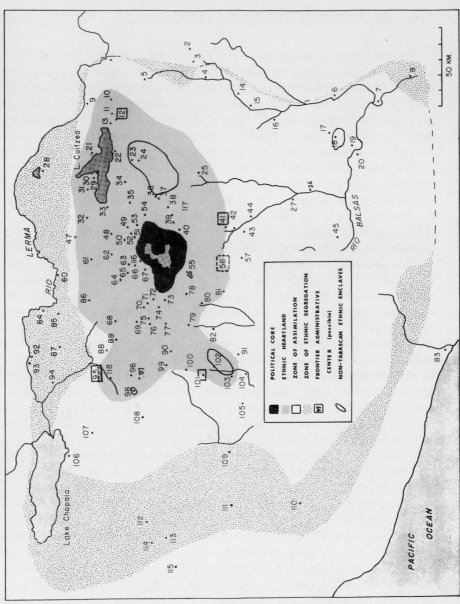

Map 4.4. A Model of Tarascan Ethnic Zones

Within the Tarascan sphere there appear to have been two distinct processes of ethnic boundary maintenance and change that dominated the Protohistoric period: ethnic assimilation and ethnic segregation. They are widely known from other times and societies and have been well defined in the literature (see Barth 1969; and Van Zantwijk 1973). To a great extent these distinct processes, assimilation and segregation, dominated community interaction in geographically separate zones of the Tarascan polity, and by 1520 they had resulted in the ethnic boundaries recorded in the early documents and mapped by Brand. By combining knowledge of the ecological, economic, political, and artifactual variation within this territory a series of ethnic zones can be proposed.

The first zone is that dominated by the process of assimilation. This is the territory within which Tarascan was the dominant language and cultural identity was ethnic Tarascan. It included at least two distinct regions. The first was the ethnic heartland, the zone within which the Tarascan political core existed, Tarascan values and norms were held by the bulk of the population, and there was a similar economic and settlement adaptation to the region (Stanislawski 1947). Thus, this zone defines the regional marketing network of the core, and the primary extent of Tarascan religion and ideology. The population within this zone, especially the elite, participated in a unitary social system dating to the political incorporation of central Michoacán (1350–1440) and the emergence of Tarascan identity (Gorenstein and Pollard 1983).

Within this heartland zone there are known to have been several cultural/linguistic groups in the period before the emergence of the Tarascan state (RM 1956, 1980). These groups were politically autonomous, and most were socially differentiated. Within the Lake Pátzcuaro Basin alone there were at least four such groups, including proto-Tarascan speakers, local Nahuatl speakers, and two separate groups of "Chichimecs" who had, at different times, migrated into the region during the Postclassic (A.D. 1000 and later) (RM 1956, 1980; RG 1985; Beltrán 1982; Brand 1943; Gorenstein and Pollard 1983). Each group was identified by the worship of specific deities, the performance of specific rituals, and the wearing of specific status markers (RM). The political unification of this zone was accompanied by the emergence of Tarascan ethnicity, marked by the universal use of the Tarascan language and the incorporation of all previously autonomous, culturally distinct groups. Political incorporation and the ideology of power that accompanied it are seen as primary in creating the homogeneous Tarascan zone that is documented in the sixteenth century. This rapid assimilation in the Pátzcuaro Basin from A.D. 1250 to 1400, and in the surrounding highlands from A.D. 1350 to 1440, was probably made possible by at least two factors: the bulk of the heartland was probably of "proto-Tarascan" culture, and the groups in question were not politically unified with a historical pattern of multiethnic complex society. Both possibilities can only be tested with (currently unavailable) archaeological data. I suspect a significant variable will prove to be the extent to which these legendary ethnic differences reflect truly different cultural traditions of entire populations or variations due to Postclassic migrations of small numbers of elites. Nevertheless, by the Protohistoric period, the ethnic unity of this zone would be archaeologically most noticeable in the common elite culture. Based upon the characteristics of elite culture at Tzintzuntzan, it would be expected that shared characteristics would have included ear and lip plugs, cotton garments (especially those embroidered, with feathers, and with copper bells), Tarascan polychrome ceramics, ceramic pipes, and state architecture associated with the patron deity Curicaueri.

The second region of assimilation can be referred to as the zone of active assimilation. This is the region within which local populations began assimilating to Tarascan identity during the Protohistoric, following their conquest by heartland Tarascans. Within this region Tarascan had become the dominant language at the time of Spanish contact (RG 1985; *Minas de cobre*, in Warren 1968; Ponce 1968; Brand 1943:51–52). The region represented an entrance of Tarascan identity into fundamentally different resource zones, dominated by subtropical and tropical ecosystems. Populations were relatively low in density and widely dispersed (Barrett 1975:16–24; González Crespo 1979; Warren 1968). The degree of assimilation by 1520 clearly varied, and as Brand found in the northern Tarascan zone, Tarascan ethnicity could vanish within decades of European control:

Combining the data from the Guzman *relaciones* and other sixteenth century sources, it would appear that the Tarascans had managed through conquest, colonization, and acculturation to impose their language over a presumptive Teco area from Jacona-Zamora down the valley of the Duero and into the Teco state of Coinan and the Coca state of Cuitzeo. During the first half of the sixteenth century Cuitzeo was predominantly Tarascan in speech, and Tarascan was spoken to a considerable extent in Coinan. However, in the next one hundred years Coca and Teco reasserted themselves only to be supplanted by Spanish and Mexicano. (Brand 1943:57)

The best evidence for the policy of cultural assimilation in this zone was the extension of the basic pattern of centralized political authority. Despite the possible existence of regional administrative centers, the RM indicates that local leaders in the zone of assimilation were directly appointed by the king, as in the heartland. Direct control of local decision-making is corroborated in several Colonial testimonies and will be treated in more detail in chapter 6.

Another policy fostering assimilation was the resettlement of Tarascans from the heartland into this zone. Such resettlements are known to have occurred from Jacona to Jiquilpan, to Turecuato, and to Periban (RG 1985; Stanislawski 1947). Smaller resettlements are known to have been made within the heartland and along the military borders, apparently to enlarge local populations in the face of active military threat (Stanislawski 1947).

Given the economic and political bases for the pressures of assimilation within this zone, there must have been great variability in the rate of cultural/linguistic assimilation. The existence of Tarascan elite polychrome ceramics has been documented at numerous settlements throughout this zone, sometimes associated with burials of individuals with ear and lip plugs adjacent to possible *yácatas* (González Crespo 1979; Maldonado 1980; Moedano 1946; Moguel Cos 1987; Muller 1979; Noguera 1944). Zones of particular economic or political interest to the core would have had the greatest interaction with Tarascans and may have been targeted for absorption. Thus, portions of the zone of assimilation near Jacona, in the west, and Zinapécuaro, in the east, two strategic military borders, had become heartland regions by 1520. At Huandacareo, a regional administrative center on the northern shore of Lake Cuitzeo, founded after the Tarascan conquest of this zone, there is variation in burial areas, from elite burials in formal tombs with ethnic Tarascan grave goods, mass burials of sacrificial victims with Tarascan ritual goods, and finally a zone of shallow pit graves with predominantly local undecorated wares. This suggested to the excavator, Angelina Macías Goytia, that local non-Tarascans were buried in this separate zone, while Tarascan state rituals and burial of local or core Tarascan elite took place in the rest of the center (Macías Goytia 1989). Within the zone of active assimilation, the retention of Tarascan as the primary native language in the southeastern portion of Michoacán in 1750 attests to the relatively high degree of assimilation reached in this important metal-producing region, due in part to the groups of ethnic Tarascans who were moved south to work in the mines of the Balsas, and smelters sent to the major smelting centers during the Protohistoric period (Pollard 1987).

The final geographical unit is the zone of ethnic segregation. This zone includes ethnic enclaves located within the zone of assimilation and those large territories along the military frontiers within which were a variety of ethnic groups. It is possible that there may have been ethnically distinct populations within the heartland that held specialized occupational roles.

This kind of segregation was known in other parts of Mesoamerica, although the documentary sources do not specify this for the Tarascan domain.

Rather, ethnic enclaves within the zone of assimilation occupied distinct communities, primarily as political refugees. One group of such communities was occupied by Matlatzincas escaping Aztec domination of the Toluca Basin. They were settled in the Charo-Undámeo zone and were referred to as *pirindas* (RM 1956, 1980; RG Necotlán 1985). This Tarascan term, meaning "those in the middle," referred to the physical placing of these settlements within the Tarascan heartland. These communities may have been established on patrimonial land belonging to the king or on land that was previously unsettled (as per Archivo General de la Nación Hospital de Jesus, 1635, leg. 29, vol. 51, exp. 34, f. 55). According to Matlatzinca sources, the fleeing groups included members of the Matlatzinca nobility (settled at Charo), others of the lower nobility (settled at Undámeo), and commoners (Quezada Ramírez 1972:51). In a description of the expansion of Corínguaro into this zone during the period of first consolidation of a unified Pátzcuaro Basin, Corínguaro is said to have captured land from the Otomí living there (RM 1980:140–141). It is not clear whether the Otomí referred to were the later *pirinda* or whether Otomí-speakers were already established in this zone by the early Postclassic. Matlatzinca communities were also established in the tropical zone at Huetamo (RG Cuseo 1985), and other Otomí groups fleeing Aztec rule were settled in the Balsas zone, perhaps near Huetamo (RG Necotlán and Taimeo 1985).

Along the military frontiers ethnic enclaves often provided their tribute in the form of specialized military service (Carrasco 1969:219; RM 1956:14, 248; RG 1985; Brand 1943:54). Many of the frontier centers and fortified towns were multiethnic and non-Tarascan in origin, including as many as four different ethnic groups, in addition to small Tarascan communities sent to colonize the center. Taximaroa is first referred to as an Otomí village (RM 1980:191–99), and Tuzantla is known to have been Ocumo in Tarascan (Ucumu), which means Otomí (Warren, personal communication, 1989, based upon the Tulane dictionary, pt. 2, f. 126v). These communities were administered separately by ethnic group. Thus the Tarascan governor sent out to Acámbaro was in charge of the Tarascan community only (RG Celaya 1985). Local lords of each ethnic group were selected, with the approval of the Tarascan king, to administer their own communities. When they fought in Tarascan military campaigns they remained within their own military units, although serving under Tarascan leaders. These non-Tarascan ethnic groups spanned the political borders of the state and can only be detected archaeologically by the continuity in ceramic forms and architecture that are interrupted by military fortifications (Gorenstein 1985; Contreras Ramírez 1987). Such groups were able to serve as buffers along active military lines and as cultural brokers between Tarascan and non-Tarascan communities.

The reality of these ethnic distinctions, and the ability of archaeology to discern them, has been demonstrated at the Tarascan capital, Tzintzuntzan. Here one locality of the city contained relatively large quantities of a clearly nonlocal ceramic ware. Research along the northeast border indicated this ware was the dominant form there during the Protohistoric, probably of an Otomí-speaking group (Gorenstein 1985; Pollard 1977). The presence of this border population in the Tarascan capital suggests that future archaeological research will reveal a more complex pattern of ethnic relations than that suggested in this chapter, and at the same time supports the political role such border populations served within the state. The existence of Los Alzati, a Late Postclassic center near Zitácuaro with cultural affiliation to the Matlatzinca of the Toluca Valley (Macías Goytia 1988), indicates the variability inherent in a border zone and the ability of archaeology to discern ethnic variation.

With the demise of the autonomous Tarascan kingdom in the early sixteenth century, these poorly articulated zones separated. The rather "thin veneer" of Tarascan identity in the zone of active assimilation was easily eroded as historical and ecological differences took precedence. The cohesive unit remained the fundamental cultural and economic unit, the ethnic heartland.

## TARASCAN WARFARE

Taríacuri may have believed that the domination of a great territory by himself and his heirs was divinely ordained, but the empire itself was created and maintained by military action. The primary weapons were bows and arrows, lances, clubs, and poisoned darts, while shields and cotton armor were used for protection (RM 1980; Gorenstein 1985:112f.). Non-Tarascan soldiers fought with their traditional weapons, and their skills were well known and strategically used. Thus, the "Chichimecs" (Tecos) at Acámbaro were used as specialized archery troops (Gorenstein 1985:112). The Otomí used the macana and slings and excelled at hand-to-hand combat.

The Tarascans advanced through a combination of military conquest and intimidation (RM 1980:248–49). They placed a premium on intelligence, asserting, "To be warned is to have three-quarters of the battle won" (Craine and Reindorp 1970:135). Accordingly, they maintained spies, often using Otomí along the eastern border, who gathered information on enemy military activity and terrain (Gorenstein 1985:112). Once the battle strategy was decided, the army marched forward. Each unit included men following their village or ward leaders, accompanied by standard bearers and priests. The RM (1980:241–47) describes the taking of a village with twelve squadrons of soldiers, each squadron containing 400 men (fig. 4.1). The army marched with the warriors from Tzintzuntzan in front, accompanied by 200 feather banners (or standards) and the priests of the major Tarascan deities. They were followed by double columns of six squadrons. While the unit of recruitment for the army was a subward or village of about twenty-five households administered by the *ocámbecha* (see chapter 2), these were clearly combined to form larger fighting forces.

The army as a whole included ethnic Tarascans from the heartland ("those of Michoacán"), others from the ethnic enclaves within the heartland ("Chichimecs and Otomí who are subjects" and Matlatzincas), those from the ethnic enclaves in the zone of assimilation (for example, the Uetamaecha, from near Huetamo), and those from the ethnic enclaves along the frontiers (including Chontales and those of "Tuxpa, Tamazula, and Zapotlan"). Non-Tarascans remained with their own leaders in separate squadrons, under the general direction of the "captain general" (RM 1980:241ff.).

Once a village was captured the population was removed, unless they had negotiated a surrender to the Tarascan forces. The aged, infants, and wounded would be immediately sacrificed on the battleground; the adults would be brought to major temples, often in Tzintzuntzan, for sacrifice; and the children would be brought back to the Pátzcuaro Basin and put to work in the agricultural fields of the king (RM 1980:248). The Tarascans were quite vehement that slaves were *not* acquired by warfare, but were purchased with blankets (RM 1980:185).

During the consolidation of the Pátzcuaro Basin, the culture-hero Taríacuri set up a battle between the communities of Pátzcuaro and Pacandan (RM 1980:163) to provide sacrificial victims for the temples in the newly built ceremonial complex of Querétaro, located at Ihuatzio. Similar negotiations between ruling elite were apparently undertaken to provide sacrificial victims for the funerals of great leaders. What is described is clearly a flower war, as it has been defined for late Postclassic central Mexico (Hassig 1988:10). Therefore, the Tarascans knew of, and in earlier centuries had utilized, this form of warfare. There are, however, no indications that they had engaged in flower wars after the emergence of the unified state. The supply of sacrificial victims from the tribute of conquered territories may have made this unnecessary.

By the early sixteenth century much of the military activity along the frontiers was defensive in nature. The RM is quite explicit about the need

Fig. 4.1. "How they destroyed a village." (From *The Chronicles of Michoacan*, translated and edited by Eugene R. Craine and Reginald C. Reindorp, Copyright © 1970 by the University of Oklahoma Press, plate 6.) "Como destruían o combatían los pueblos" (RM 1956:190).

for this defensive activity. In discussing the assignment of troops within the state, some men were sent to the Mexican front "to fight the Otomís who are brave men" ("which was why Moctezuma put them on his frontiers"), while others were sent to fight with those of Cuynaho. Corona Núñez has interpreted *Cuynaho* as *Cuinao*, a community on the Santiago River northwest of Lake Chapala, and believes this refers to defensive attacks made in the early sixteenth century to protect the northwest frontier by Lake Chapala (RM 1956:191, note). In response to repeated Aztec aggression along the eastern frontier, the Tarascans established a series of fortified, strategically placed settlements. These fortifications were located at the major passes from the Lerma River in the north to the Balsas River in the south, and while they were generally staffed by non-Tarascans, they often included Tarascan colonists, and all were controlled directly by Tarascan administrators from Tzintzuntzan.

Hassig (1988:209) sees in this the emergence of a new imperial form in Mesoamerica, that of the territorial empire. Since he sees this type of perimeter defense only on the Tarascan/Aztec border, he views the Tarascan system as quasiterritorial. Considering that it was only along this border that the Tarascans faced a far greater centralized expanding empire, which had strategic interest in access to the Lerma and the gold, silver, and copper mines of the Balsas, it is not surprising that they maintained their autonomy only by innovation (see Gorenstein 1985). Had they not innovated in organization and structure, it is quite likely that large portions of the Tarascan domain would have become part of the Aztec Empire, or at least become part of the economic periphery of Protohistoric Mesoamerica. Instead, the Tarascan heartland, and particularly the Lake Pátzcuaro Basin, became a core region itself, reorganizing economic networks in the name of the state.

# CHAPTER 5

# ECONOMIC INTEGRATION WITHIN THE TARASCAN FRONTIER

WHILE Tzintzuntzan's increasing control of the Pátzcuaro Basin may have made military expansion *possible* during the Late Postclassic period, by the beginning of the Protohistoric both the centralized control of the basin and the expansion of the state were *necessary* to maintain the large, dense population in the core. During the florescent Tarascan state in the early sixteenth century, the population of the Lake Pátzcuaro Basin was located in more than ninety settlements and totaled between 60,000 and 105,000 people (see chapter 3). Between 25,000 and 35,000 persons lived in the capital city, Tzintzuntzan (see chapter 2). Recent research in the Zacapu region, just northwest of the Pátzcuaro Basin, indicates a marked drop in population following the Late Postclassic. Michelet (1988) has suggested that this may reflect migration into the Pátzcuaro Basin. Certainly the rapid growth of Tzintzuntzan associated with the large number of settlements indicates population increases within the basin that cannot be understood by internal growth alone.

## THE ROLE OF ECONOMIC EXCHANGE

Given the increasingly dense basin occupation during the Protohistoric, new economic mechanisms were required to support local populations. By calculating the annual dietary needs of the population, it is possible to determine indirectly the ability of the basin to support its population. To that end, I have proposed a hypothetical Protohistoric Tarascan diet based on foods that were consumed in the basin in the early sixteenth century and weighted in significance according to ethnohistoric evidence and ethnographic diets (Pollard 1982; Pollard and Gorenstein 1980; Gorenstein and Pollard 1983). The range of foods utilized by the Tarascans included more than fourteen genera of domesticated plants, four genera of local fish, various local waterfowl, small mammals, deer, domestic turkey, several wild plants, condiments (cacao, honey), lime (in maize preparation), and, of course, salt (fig. 5.1) (Gorenstein and Pollard 1983:appendix III). The following daily diet has been proposed: maize/amaranth (600 g, 90-percent digestible, 1,950 usable calories); fish (100 g, more than 90-percent digestible, 67 usable calories); other fruits and vegetables (200 usable calories).

Fig. 5.1. Janitzio, Lake Pátzcuaro, fisherman with nets.

This diet would provide 2,400 calories and utilize the most abundant resources of the lake basin. Maize and/or amaranth would provide 80 percent of the calories, well within the range of ethnographic diets from the basin (Brand 1951:180—408–1,400 g daily, rural average 700 g, urban lower-class average 560 g; Smith 1965:33—560 g; PLAT 1968—700 g, average for basin) and close to the ethnohistorically derived diet for protohistoric Tetzcoco (Ivanhoe 1978—680 g for commoners and 400 g for the elite). It is impossible to determine the relative proportion of amaranth in the diet, which varied by age, sex, and class. In addition, fruits and vegetables were particularly abundant in the summer and early fall, making the 200 calories allotted to them clearly an annual average. Certain foods may have been socially restricted to the elite (e.g., cacao) or limited by their relative scarcity and cost. Those believed to have been utilized primarily by the elite include amaranth, maguey (as a drink), cacao, waterfowl, deer, and tropical fruits (fig. 5.2).

To evaluate the accuracy of the diet, I tabulated the nutritional value of the basic foods in their suggested portions. Only those elements often deficient in maize diets were tabulated, including protein, amino acids, niacin, iron, calcium, and zinc. Vitamins derived primarily from fruits and vegetables were omitted from analysis. The analysis included recommended daily intakes and the value of maize/amaranth, beans, and fish, which would have constituted at least 90 percent of the proposed diet. The results revealed that a 100-g portion of fish (based on *C. estor* [white fish] of Lake Pátzcuaro) adequately completes the protein and amino acid requirements and fulfills calcium requirements when the fish are consumed whole but

Fig. 5.2. "How the masters of the Chichimecs took the daughter of a fisherman and married her." (From *The Chronicles of Michoacan*, translated and edited by Eugene R. Craine and Reginald C. Reindorp, Copyright © 1970 by the University of Oklahoma Press, plate 20.) "Como los señores de la laguna supieron de la mujer que llevaron los chichimecas, y como les dieron sus hijas por mujeres" (RM 1956:31).

leaves a diet highly deficient in niacin, iron, and (possibly) zinc, elements that often pose health problems in maize-dominated diets. For the Proto-historic Tarascan population to maintain adequate diets, particularly in times of nutritional stress (pregnancy, lactation, illness), they needed some nonfish-derived meat. A 100-g portion of deer or rabbit provides 7–8 g of niacin, while similar amounts of wild duck and domestic turkey provide 5–6 g. Similar portions of these meats provide 3.0–3.5 g of iron and allow the absorption of iron contained in maize. While it is clear from ethnohistoric and ethnographic data that fish were, and are, the primary meat source in the diet, I proposed that two nonfish meat portions per week were substituted for fish. This is close to ethnographic diets in the basin (e.g., Foster 1948), but I am unable to tell if twice a week is sufficiently frequent to prevent iron and niacin deficiencies. Thus I may have slightly overrated the use of fish in the basin and underrated the use of other meat.

Given the population of the basin in 1520, and given the modified diet as just presented, it is now possible to determine the quantity of basic food resources needed to sustain the core Tarascans. For a population between 60,000 and 100,000 persons, the following foodstuffs would be consumed annually: 13,140,000–21,900,000 kg of maize/amaranth; 1,920,000–3,200,000 kg of beans; 1,560,000–2,600,000 kg of fish; and 624,000–1,040,000 kg of meat (primarily deer, rabbit, duck, and turkey).

By determining the Protohistoric land-use zones (see chapter 3), it has also been possible to estimate the maximum productivity of the basin in these products. The methods and assumptions used in calculating the productivity of the basin in maize/amaranth, beans, fish, and meat are detailed in Gorenstein and Pollard (1983:appendix IV). The figures listed in table 5.1 must be understood as estimates, particularly that in the meat category, which is based on limited data and does not include several species of small mammals and birds that were consumed. Dogs, an important meat source in other parts of central Mexico, are known to have been common in Tarascan communities but are never referred to as food. While this may reflect class differences in diet and/or the ethnohistoric bias of native elite and Spanish interests, without such positive documentation I have omitted them from the quantifications. However, for every reason one might increase the figures (such as the lower proportion of maize in an elite diet), there are other reasons to decrease them (such as loss due to spoilage and food preparation). Therefore, with the exception of the meat category (certainly underestimated), the figures can be taken as reasonable approximates.

When these productivity figures—expressed either as kilograms produced per year or as numbers of people who could be supported—are compared to the needs of the basin, certain relationships become clear. The basin was clearly unable to produce sufficient maize/amaranth for its population. The deficit was large, and between 25 and 55 percent of the

Table 5.1    Productivity and Population

| Food | Estimated Productivity* | Population Supportable** |
|------|-------------------------|--------------------------|
| maize/amaranth | 9,821,200 kg/year | 45,000 |
| beans | 2,331,050 kg/year | 73,000 |
| fish | 4,732,800 kg/year | 182,000 |
| meat (deer, rabbit, duck, domestic turkey) | 330,000–490,000 kg/year | 32,000–47,000 |

*See Gorenstein and Pollard (1983:appendix IV).

**Based on hypothetical diet. If elite ate more meat and less maize and constituted 5–10 percent of the population, then the 45,000 figure could rise to 48,000. Crop losses due to spoilage, vermin, and waste would have lowered the figures by 5–10 percent.

maize consumed in the basin must have been imported. Beans were consumed in smaller quantities; either the basin was able to produce a slight surplus of this item or, if the population was above 70,000, it was importing up to 27 percent of its needs. The figures for meat are notably equivocal but suggest a deficit relationship of some unknown size. Of the basic resources consumed in the basin, only fish clearly produced a surplus, with up to 62 percent of the harvestable crop available for export. The fish-productivity figures used in this analysis were particularly conservative, and I would guess that the actual available crop was far larger than projected, although the harvest was probably considerably below maximization of the yield.

Other basic materials were produced in the basin, including wood products (especially firewood and lumber), basketry, mats, ceramic clays, and basalt. However, the basin naturally lacks salt, obsidian, chert, and lime, all products used by most households in the Protohistoric period; it also lacked a wide range of goods utilized by the elite.

It is clear that economic interchange within the state was not simply a matter of acquiring colored feathers for the elite and that the flow of goods in the expanding tribute system was not simply a political expression of obedience. The core of the Tarascan state in 1520 was not a viable economic unit. It existed, even thrived, only by the exchange of goods and services in regional and supraregional patterns.

## THE NATURE OF EXCHANGE WITHIN THE TARASCAN STATE

Goods and services flowed through several institutional channels, which fell into two basic classes: local and regional markets, and state-controlled agencies. The state-controlled agencies are believed to have included the tribute network, official long-distance merchants, state agricultural lands, state forest lands, state mines, and official gift exchange.

## MARKET EXCHANGE

The primary ethnohistoric sources for information about protohistoric Tarascan economic networks, the RM and the RG, say relatively little about markets and marketplaces. Nevertheless, we do know they existed and can locate specific centers at Tzintzuntzan, Pareo, Asajo, and Uruapan (RM 1956:223, 61, 92, 114, respectively). Gilberti recorded Tarascan terms for marketing (*mayapeni*), trade (*mayapecua*), merchant (*mayapeti*), and marketplace (*mayepeto*) (1975:67, 403). The RM even includes a drawing of the Asajo market, similar in many respects to modern regional markets (fig. 5.3). Women are depicted as the sellers, produce is sold from baskets placed on the ground and spatially grouped by product, and there is eating of prepared food (fig. 5.4). From the RM text we know that market activity

Fig. 5.3. "Taríacuri finds his lost mother and nephews." (From *The Chronicles of Michoacan*, translated and edited by Eugene R. Craine and Reginald C. Reindorp, Copyright © 1970 by the University of Oklahoma Press, plate 29.) "Como Taríacuri buscaba sus sobrinos Hiripan y Tangaxoan" (RM 1956:91).

included the renting of services, such as water carrying (RM 1956:114) and maize grinding (RM 1956:114); begging food; and the selling of slaves (RM 1956:92, 178). Gilberti (1558) gave specific terms for one who sells prepared medicines (herbs), *sipiati uri*, and the place from which they are sold, *sipiati hatacuaro* (Sepúlveda y H. 1988:102, 104). The most specific indication of the barter actually taking place is revealed in the insistence that slaves are not acquired by war, but purchased with blankets (RM 1980:185). There is no indication of the size of these markets and only hints about the relationship between market activity and the state. There is no indication that the markets were state-controlled or regulated, despite an extensive description of the judicial system in the RM. On only two occasions, the death of a Tarascan king and the appearance of Spaniards in the Tarascan capital (RM 1956:246, 223), does the king forbid market activity. Both of these occasions are extraordinary, although they do indicate the ultimate subordination of marketing to centralized political control. Perhaps more revealing of the market/state relation is the basic Lake Pátzcuaro Basin settlement pattern. During the Protohistoric period there were three major markets serving the basin, at Tzintzuntzan, Pareo, and Asajo. Only two of these, Tzintzuntzan and Pareo, were also administrative centers. The noncongruence of market and administrative centers int he Tarascan core, and, I believe, in Protohistoric central Michoacán generally (Pollard 1980) suggests minimal politi-

Fig. 5.4. Pátzcuaro market, 1970.

cization of the markets. The markets themselves appear to have been more heterarchical than hierarchical in the goods and services they offered and the populations they served. The exception to this appears to have been Tzintzuntzan, where manufactured and elite-utilized goods were associated with the large concentration of artisans and craftsmen in the capital.

Within the Lake Pátzcuaro Basin, many goods and services flowed through the markets. Those for which there is specific documentation include maize, beans, chile peppers, amaranth, local fruit, ducks, local bird feathers, fish, cotton cloth and clothing, slaves, prepared food, medicinal plants, and household services. Other goods were utilized by the general population and widely distributed in the basin but are not mentioned, or rarely mentioned, in any market or state agency exchange. Some of these are believed to have flowed through market networks, including squash, gourd or gourd plates, nopal cactus, quail, doves, parrots, *cuinique* (squirrel), dogs, maguey fiber, wild plants (in addition to those used for medicinal purposes), wood products (especially firewood and lumber), rabbits, turkeys, and honey bees. There are other goods that were limited in their availability because of their natural occurrence (basalt outcrops, fine clays, marsh environments), the restriction of their natural habitats (deer), or their concentration in the immediate hinterlands of a limited number of basin settlements. These goods are not documented as being under any state agency, and their general use by the basin population suggests they too flowed through market networks. They include reeds and their products (mats, baskets, nets), clays and ceramic vessels, basalt and basalt tools, and possibly deer. Finally, several goods utilized by the general population and not available locally are projected as having been imported into the basin through the market networks. These include obsidian (gray, black, and black with red), chert, jasper, agate, opal, copal, lime, and salt. Current analyses of gray-black obsidians from Tzintzuntzan indicate they came from Zinapécuaro, Ucareo, and Zináparo. They have been designated as market imports because they do not appear on tribute lists or even lists from settlements at or near the resource (and in the case of obsidian, places from which they are specifically known to have come).

## THE TRIBUTE SYSTEM

The most significant state agency involved in economic interchange was the vast, centralized, and hierarchically organized tribute network of the Tarascan state (map 5.1) (see especially RM 1956; RG 1958, 1987; Paredes 1976, 1979; Gorenstein and Pollard 1983). This network was fundamentally a political institution, the bulk of goods passing through various levels, from various regions of the state, ultimately finding their way to the capital, Tzintzuntzan, where they were placed in central storehouses. To the extent that they were consumed within the basin by the royal family, the political bureaucracy, the religious functionaries of the state temples, as gifts to foreign emissaries, and as emergency stores for the local population, they represent a significant portion of the local economy. In addition, these items were used to maintain the army, which during periods of war would have supported large numbers of men from the basin.

The tribute system was under total control of the Tzintzuntzan-based royal family. Tribute was collected from regional tribute centers, each with its own known tributaries, on a fairly regular basis (e.g., every eighty days; see Warren 1968). Specialized bureaucrats in charge of the collection, storage, and distribution of the tribue are well described in the RM. Tribute itself took the form of both goods and services. On the local level, tribute was used to support local state representatives, both administrative and religious, and only a portion was passed on to the regional collection center. From regional centers the amassed tribute was sent to Tzintzuntzan or the military borders. The most common items appearing on tribute lists of goods that actually went to the capital include maize and cotton cloth and clothing. Other goods that regularly appear include slaves, sacrificial

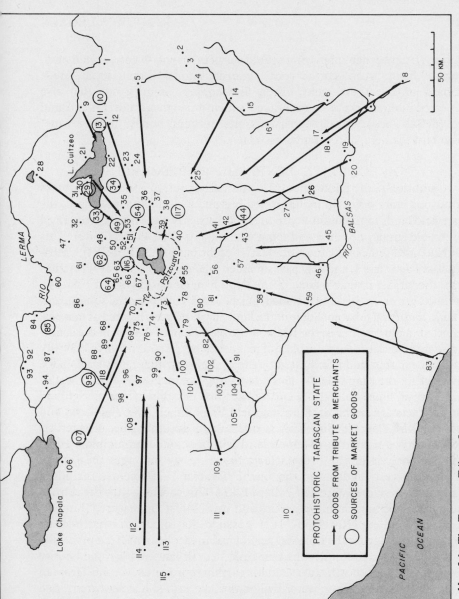

Map 5.1. The Tarascan Tribute System

victims (from border zones), household services, metal objects, armaments, tropical fruit, cacao, cotton (raw), gourds, animal skins (jaguar, etc.), tropical bird feathers, gold, silver, and copper. Some goods that also appeared in the markets are occasionally mentioned in tribute contexts and include salt, beans, chile peppers, rabbits, turkeys, honey, maguey wine, local bird feathers, and ceramic vessels.

## DIRECT STATE OWNERSHIP OF RESOURCES

In addition to the tribute network, the state acquired goods and services in various other ways. In the most obvious and well-documented case, the state held lands in the basin to produce food directly consumed by the royal household, upper nobility, and temple attendants (RM 1956:173–80). This land included some of the most productive of the basin (RM 1956:184), probably class 1 and class 2, and may have included much of the Llanos de Tzintzuntzan, the largest irrigable zone in the Protohistoric basin (Brand 1951:24). Products grown on this land included maize, beans, chile peppers, squash, amaranth, fruit, and tobacco. Some of the land may have been planted as maguey, reflected in illustrations in the RM and the settlement of Aterio on the southern shore of the lake (Atero = place of maguey honey; Romero Flores 1939:18). The value of this land is indicated by the capital punishment proscribed for "neglecting the king's fields" and "damaging the maguey" (RM 1956:12).

The royal household also seems to have had possibly exclusive rights to the products of certain local forests, including lumber, firewood, deer, and rabbits (RM 1956:173–80). This is difficult to document because forest/woodland was treated as common land within colonial municipios. However, an analysis of the Protohistoric basin clearly indicates the lack of extensive forest lands near the major Tarascan settlements, including Tzintzuntzan (Gorenstein and Pollard 1983). This conflicts with the continual mention of royal hunting parties and royal forest "managers," lumbermen, and hunters (RM 1956). It is possible that much of what became common land during the Colonial period had in fact been utilized primarily by the Tarascan elite under the principle that all lands within the empire belonged to the god Curicaueri and his earthly representative, the Tarascan king. In a similar manner, waterfowl on the lake and, to a lesser extent, fish from the lake, are referred to as being provided to the royal household by royal duck hunters and royal fishermen (RM 1956:173–80). These may have been tribute items from lakeshore settlements—tribute made in the form of hunting service—or they may have reflected elite rights to certain portions of the basin's general resources.

Unclear though the possible state "usufructs" within the basin are, indications exist that some of the copper mines were under the direct exploitation of the resident elite of Tzintzuntzan. In a document from 1533, workers from the copper region of Turicato-La Huacana-Sinagua along the central Balsas River drainage indicated that delivery to Tzintzuntzan of copper occurred every eighty days or whenever the king asked for more (Warren 1968:47, 50). Paredes (1979:10) suggests that the king sent workers to these mines to meet his needs. This seems to indicate a relationship greater than one defined by tribute alone (see Pollard 1987 for detailed discussion of the state's relationship to the mines). State gifts, from both foreign visitors and Tarascan leaders, are known to have brought into Tzintzuntzan such items as tropical fruit, cotton and cotton cloth, and manufactured metal objects (RM 1956:228, 238).

Artisans attached to the palace in Tzintzuntzan produced a wide range of goods for the royal household, including basketry, mats, pottery, feather-work, and metal objects of gold, silver, and copper (RM 1956:173–80; Pollard 1972), and three thousand construction workers produced public buildings in the capital (or basin?) (RM 1956:174–75). It is unclear whether these people were retained by the royal household or were paying their tribute in specialized activities and goods.

The last institutionalized mechanism by which goods flowed into the basin was through the state long-distance merchants. These merchants were apparently retained by the royal household to provide specialized, rare goods obtainable only from the far reaches of the state borders or from outside the state itself. At the king's behest they acquired cacao, animal skins, marine shell and bone from the Pacific, tropical bird feathers, turquoise, rock crystal, serpentine, jadeite, gold, silver, and slaves (RM 1956:178, 171–72). Copal, used by the palace household and in state ceremonies, may have been acquired by the merchants, along with other lowland products. Red, green, and possibly some clear obsidian, used in limited quantities by the elite (Pollard 1972, 1977) and obtained from outside the state borders, may have been among the "precious stones" obtained by the merchants. Preliminary analyses of obsidian from Tzintzuntzan, being conducted under my supervision, indicate the green specimens were probably from the Llano Grande of Jalisco (just west of modern Guadalajara). Some green obsidian came from Pizarrín and Pachuca, under Aztec control; red and clear from Zináparo, near the Tarascans' northern border on the Lerma; and small amounts of gray-black from Zaragoza and Tozongo in the eastern central plateau. There is no indication whether these merchants sold any of their goods in the regional or Tzintzuntzan markets. One reference to merchants who sold slaves (RM 1956:184) may refer to these specialists or to local individuals who dealt strictly with local products.

## PRODUCTION OF GOODS AND SERVICES

Of the goods and services produced within the basin, there is a sharp dichotomy between those goods utilized by the commoners and those utilized by the elite. Commoners obtained goods through local markets or subsistence activities, while the elite obtained goods primarily through state-controlled agencies, especially state lands and usufructs.

Local tribute, though poorly documented, was probably a main source of household services and some manufactured goods. This means that within the basin, those settlements having immediate access to valued resources, such as prime agricultural land, marsh lands, and fishing zones, could exchange local surpluses for nonlocal items in the marketplace. Not surprisingly, more than 65–70 percent of all settlements were located with immediate access to these resources. However, the local elite, possibly including merchants, artisans, and other specialists, only minimally participated in such market exchange, obtaining similar products by outright ownership of production or by tribute.

In return for the large quantities of goods flowing into the basin, Tarascans exported some goods and many services. Fish, dried to aid preservation and reduce bulk weight while maintaining full nutritional value, was exported through regional markets, primarily in those zones from which bulk foodstuffs were imported. Thus, fish provided the primary exchange for maize/amaranth, beans, and chile peppers and was therefore the most significant export product. Undoubtedly, this simplifies a complex pattern including full-time fishermen on the lake islands and in some lakeshore settlements who exchanged fish for a variety of needed goods, both locally produced and imported. Fishermen may have also traveled outside the basin to directly exchange their fish for other foodstuffs (see Smith 1965 for ethnographic parallels). Bird feathers from lake waterfowl and heron were also exported, although in comparatively small quantities (RM 1956:44).

Besides fish and some feathers, only manufactured goods appear to have been traded outside the basin. These probably included basketry, mats, ceramic vessels, and metal objects. Given the resources available to the bulk of the population, and the large and varied assortment of imports they needed, these manufactured goods played a significant role in balancing the economic flows of the commoners. By specializing in manufactured goods, particularly basketry, matting, and ceramics, whose raw materials were available locally and not under the control of the elite, the basin occupants in a sense created new resources that sustained the import of other goods. This is remarkably similar to the ethnographic and historic patterns of the basin in times of population growth or resource depletion (see Gorenstein and Pollard 1980).

Goods that were imported into the basin consisted of two types: resources not available locally and foodstuffs supplementing those produced in the basin. Commoners obtained their goods primarily through markets, and the scale of these imports must have been considerable. Thus, for example, 90 percent of the lithic artifacts collected in my survey of Tzintzuntzan were obsidian (see appendix 3), all imported from at least 80 km away. The resource analysis of the basin suggested that approximately 44 percent of the maize and 9 percent of the beans consumed were imported. While some of these imported goods came into the basin through the tribute system, food obtained this way appears to have solely maintained the elite. Meanwhile, much of the best land in the basin was also used for the support of the elite and for state functions, leading to the conclusion that large quantities of foodstuffs representing significant proportions of commoners' diets must have been imported through market networks. These networks were regional and local, and two adjacent zones are documented as suppliers of foodstuffs for the basin: the Asajo zone to the northwest, covering the rich agricultural land of Comanja and Naranja; and the Curinguaro zone to the southeast, covering the lands of Tiripitio and Huiramba (Caravajal 1523 in Warren 1977:386; RM 1956:13, 24, 33, 121, 211; RG Tiripitio 1985). These zones functioned as supplementary "bread baskets" for the Tarascan core. Other goods used by the commoners were imported from sources throughout central Michoacán, especially the sierra to the west, the north, and the Lake Cuitzeo zone (see map 5.1).

The elite obtained goods primarily through state-controlled institutions. These included basic resources not available in sufficient quantities in the basin, such as maize, and also a wide variety of goods not available in the basin at all, such as turquoise. The first category of goods was circulated primarily through the tribute network, while the second group was also obtained by state merchants, through state mines, and, in the case of war captives, by the exploits of the army. Several observations about this importation can be made. Unlike the imports used by the commoners, these goods (even maize, a bulky item needed in large quantities) were not geographically restricted to central Michoacán. Rather, imports for the elite came from all corners of the Tarascan state and beyond (see map 5.1; all settlements listed were Tarascan tributaries except number 83; only those for which specific tribute items are documented have been marked with arrows). From outside the state came turquoise from the northwest; marine shell from the Pacific; cacao from the Balsas delta; rare obsidian and other stone from eastern central Mexico (Hidalgo, Puebla) and to the west in Jalisco; and serpentine, jade, and pyrites from Oaxaca and farther south (highland Guatemala?). The farther the source of the item, the fewer the channels of acquisition, and the rarer the use. The function of these imports was largely (but not exclusively) to maintain status differences between members of the elite and the rest of society (i.e., they are "luxury" goods). Finally, of the foods imported for the elite, a notable proportion included sources of meat protein, such as deer and rabbit, which are not documented in market contexts. This may have produced substantial nutritional differences between the social classes.

The elite, however, primarily exported state services that included administrative control, religious functionaries, and military security. In return for tribute and state control of lands, forests, and minerals, the elite exported "elite culture," a state religion, and the organization necessary to maintain and defend the borders of the kingdom. To the extent that these exchanges were coerced, ideological, and clearly unequal in either the relative living standards they produced or the power they concentrated, the economic flows within the Tarascan state maintained and intensified an asymmetrical relationship between the basin and the rest of the state. Finally, to the extent that the production of state services was concentrated in the capital, Tzintzuntzan, the economic networks maintained an asymmetrical relationship between the capital and its immediate hinterland, the Lake Pátzcuaro Basin.

# CHAPTER 6

# ADMINISTRATION OF THE STATE

AS the territorial extent of Tarascan control increased, the central dynasty ruling from Tzintzuntzan faced those problems common to conquest states: how to politically incorporate populations of varying ethnic status, in widely differing ecological zones, and still achieve the two fundamental goals of conquest—the economic exploitation of populations and resources, and the protection of the integrity of the state frontiers. The Tarascan solution involved a high degree of centralization of administrative functions, the creation of a common Tarascan ethnicity within the primary zones of economic exploitation, and the ethnic segregation of populations along the major military frontiers.

## THE STRUCTURE OF AUTHORITY

The structure of the Tarascan administrative system has been the focus of study by numerous authors, most recently including Beltrán (1982, 1986), Carrasco (1986), Castro-Leal (1986), García Alcaraz (1976), Gorenstein and Pollard (1983), López Austin (1976), Paredes (1976), Pollard (1972, 1977, 1980, 1982b, 1987), and Pollard and Gorenstein (1980). They all are based primarily on the documentary sources, especially the RM, and what follows is a summary based on their work.

The central administration of the state was located in the capital. There the Tarascan king, *irecha*, held his court, administered justice, and received emissaries from within and outside his territory. The court included members of the Tarascan nobility in a series of hierarchically organized offices, including the following:

*Irecha*. Head of *uacúsecha* lineage; king or *cazonci*.
*Angatacuri*. Governor or prime minster.
Captain. Military leader in warfare.
*Petámuti*. Chief priest.
Tribute minister. Steward in charge of tribute collectors.
*Caracha-capacha*. Governors of four quarters of state.
*Achaecha*. Other members of nobility acting as advisors.

Below the court was a large bureaucracy composed of members of the nobility and commoners. This included:

*Quangariecha*. Captains of military units in wartime.
*Ocámbecha*. Tribute collectors.
Mayordomos. Heads of units that stored and distributed tribute, produced crafts and service within the palace (at least thirty-four different units known).
Priests. Hierarchy of ten levels below chief priest serving in temples dedicated to state religion.
*Angámecha*. Leaders of towns and villages, referred to as caciques or señores (fig. 6.1).

All positions appear to have been hereditary from father to son, with preference given to sons of senior wives. However, in most positions the Tarascan king had final approval of the office holder. Local leaders were chosen by the king from among a number of possibilities, and could be replaced, and their decisions could be overruled by the king. In some instances the ties between the central dynasty and local leaders were reinforced by marriage to one of the king's daughters. In the Lagunas dictionary of 1574 (1983:221) these people are called *angámecha*, "los que tenian bezotes entre la barba y el labio" (those who had lip plugs between the beard and the lip). In the RM the removal of lip plugs is the symbolic act marking punishment by the king and removal from office (RM 1956:201–2). This group included members of the hereditary nobility, *achaecha*, and apparently also included some commoners rewarded for military service. Lagunas (1983:22) defined the verb *angámeni* as "poner los tales bezotes que el Rey ponia a los señores y valientes en la guerra, señalando los con esta hydalguia, quasi por sustento, pilar, favor y amparo de la otra gente plebeya, y assi los tales podian tambien interceder, induzir, importunar y bolver por ellos como," (to put in those lip plugs, which the king put in for the lords and men who were valiant in war, marking them with this nobility, as though for the support, pillar, favor, and protection of the other commoners, and thus such men could also intercede, persuade, importune, and stand up for them). Gilberti in 1559 (1975) had used *angámucuni* to indicate "standing at the door" or "the shore of a lake." The definition emphasizes the role of village leader as the link between the Tarascan dynasty and the commoners, stressing the flow of authority from the central government and not from the local nobility.

This flow of authority from the center to the village was supported by the fundamental system of land and resource ownership. All land titles within

Fig. 6.1. "Concerning the general administration of justice." (From *The Chronicles of Michoacan*, translated and edited by Eugene R. Craine and Reginald C. Reindorp, Copyright © 1970 by the University of Oklahoma Press, plate 19.) "De la justicia general que se hacia" (RM 1956:11).

the Tarascan domain were justified by having come from the king. This even included agricultural lands, fishing rights, mineral resources, and hunting territories within the Pátzcuaro Basin itself. Thus, for example, the people of Tiripitio had fishing rights in Lake Pátzcuaro, despite their not being a basin community (RG Tiripitio 1985), by a grant from the king. Similar grants from the king are credited with laying out the lands and fishing rights of Xarácuaro, Zurumútaro, and Carapán (García Alcaraz 1976:228–29). The mechanisms for ensuring this distribution of resources is clear. In Carapán we are told that if someone used fields not belonging to them, local judges would issue a death sentence, and the individual would be sent to Tzintzuntzan to be "offered to the gods."

Beltrán (1982) and Carrasco (1986) have studied the land tenure and isolated a series of categories including patrimonial lands of the royal dynasty (*uacúsecha*), fiscal lands of the state on which tributary goods were produced, lands allotted to local lords, and the lands of the commoners. To these categories I would add usufruct rights for hunting, fishing, and lumber, the control of state mines, and the control of long-distance merchants (Pollard 1982, 1987).

Labor to work the state lands was recruited from among the general commoners (*purépecha*), with additional lands worked by slaves. The slaves (*teruparacua-euaecha*) included war captives, criminals, those who sold themselves into slavery, and others bought in the market. In addition there were *acípecha*, who appear to have been servants of the nobility (Carrasco 1986:80–81). Finally, each son of the ruling king was granted lands that were maintained by his mother's family, although how labor was actually recruited is unclear.

## TERRITORIAL DIVISIONS WITHIN THE STATE

Administrative control was accomplished by the creation of a series of centers, each with a number of dependent communities. Map 6.1 shows the location and extent of the administrative and tribute centers about which there is sufficient data. The data come primarily from the available fragments of the Caravajal Visitation of 1523–1524 (Warren 1977, 1985) and the first encomienda grants of 1523–1525 (Warren 1985), before depopulation and Spanish colonial administration had altered the Protohistoric pattern.

The administrative centers of these units reported directly to the palace in Tzintzuntzan. They in turn contained dependent villages and dispersed hamlets, and in several instances were divided into subcenters. Beltrán (1982:118) suggests that these sub-*cabeceras* were the result of the splitting off of the noble lineages that ruled in the centers. Thus the administrative hierarchy contained up to five levels. Of the five units known in detail from the Caravajal Visitation, the number of subject communities varied from 12 to 44, and the number of "casas" reported varied from 244 to 863. At an average of six persons per household, the units reported varied from 1,464 to 5,178 persons. Despite the low density of population in regions further from the Tarascan core, the units remained fairly similar in size, allowing one day's travel time between any community and its administrative center.

There are many parts of the political geography of the state that are currently unclear. Foremost, it is not clear whether there were any units above the level of these mapped centers and below the level of the capital. Documentary sources suggest, for example, that Tancítaro was a center for tribute collection for much of the southwestern territory. Furthermore, Xacona is described as one of the four centers for the administration of the Tarascan territory, under the supervision of one of the four *caracha-capacha* (administrators). Analysis of the documentary sources suggests that the four-quarters division was solely symbolic, as part of the cosmic design of the imperial enterprise, or that these centers served as military massing centers in conjunction with their possible role as tribute collection points. Thus, for example, we know that major military campaigns were organized from Xacona, Tacámbaro, and Zinapécuaro.

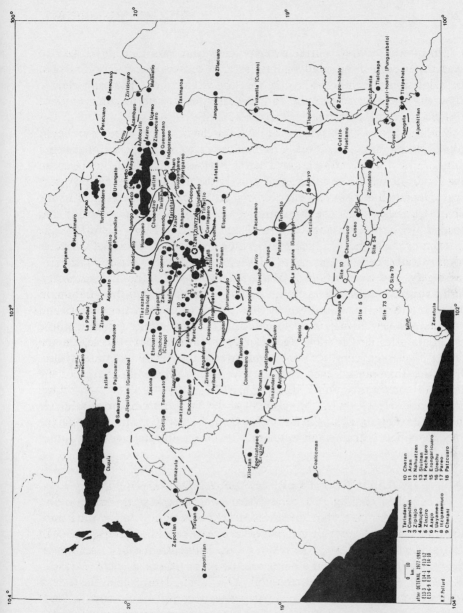

Map 6.1. Tarascan Administrative Centers

The power of the central dynasty, however, was directly linked to headmen in each of the smaller administrative centers, and direct control of local decision-making could reach even the village level. For example, we know that the king sent a judge to settle disputes within the community of Tetlamán, near Tepelcatepec (Carrasco 1969:219).

Within and along the frontiers of the Tarascan kingdom were a number of non-Tarascan ethnic enclaves. These enclaves were composed of distinct communities, which were granted lands by the king within the Tarascan heartland, or were communities of non-Tarascans along the military borders. Documentary sources suggest that in the case of Matlatzinca in the Charo-Undámeo zone, the communities were administered as a group and headed by Charo (Quezada Ramírez 1972:43; Warren 1977:247–50). As the location of the highest-ranked Matlatzinca nobility, the choice of Charo as administrative center implies little Tarascan "meddling" within Matlatzinca society, and a retention of Matlatzinca-defined status and authority. Along the military frontiers ethnic enclaves often provided their tribute in the form of specialized military service. Many of the frontier centers and fortified towns were multiethnic, including as many as four different ethnic groups in addition to small Tarascan communities sent to colonize the center. These communities were administered separately by ethnic group. Thus the Tarascan governor sent out to Acámbaro was in charge of the Tarascan community only (RG Celaya 1985). Local lords of each ethnic group were selected, with the approval of the Tarascan king, to administer their own communities. When they fought in Tarascan military campaigns they remained within their own military units, although serving under Tarascan leaders.

## POLITICAL POWER, CLASS, AND ETHNICITY

As stated in chapter 4, I believe that two processes, assimilation and segregation, were part of deliberate administrative policy during the Protohistoric period. Despite clear indications of earlier ethnic heterogeneity in central Michoacán (RM 1956, 1980), by the sixteenth century the population was self-identifying and being identified by others as solely Tarascan (RM 1956, 1980; RG 1985; Warren 1968, 1977, 1985). However, at the time of Spanish contact there was not congruence between ethnic and political borders. The political core of the state was located approximately in the center of the ethnic heartland, as defined by shared ideology and economy.

As the territory of the state enlarged, the economic and political success of the Protohistoric Tarascans required that the increasingly distinct communities be integrated to ensure the economic exploitation of populations and resources and to protect the integrity of the state's frontiers. This integration was designed to serve the best interests of the political core, the Lake Pátzcuaro Basin. Particularly, it had to serve the interests of the sociopolitical elite residing in Tzintzuntzan.

Within the heartland local leaders dealt directly with the central administration (RM 1956, 1980; Gilberti 1975; Lagunas 1983; Caravajal Visitation, in Warren 1977). This region appears to have been under the direct control of the political capital. All local leaders were approved by the Tzintzuntzan elite. Their loyalty was assumed, and intervention in local affairs was considered unusual (RM 1956:201–2). Such loyalty to the Tarascan royal dynasty was repeatedly demonstrated during the early Colonial period (Warren 1977, 1985).

The second zone, that of active assimilation, presented quite different problems. Many resources basic to elite identification came from this zone, including tropical fruit, cacao, cotton, copal, jaguar skins, tropical feathers, gold, silver, copper, and tin (Pollard 1982a; Gorenstein and Pollard 1983; Pollard 1987). This zone, absorbed into the expanding state only after 1440, was increasingly basic to the maintenance of Tarascan elite society. If the kingdom was to successfully expand beyond this zone, the political loyalty of these tributaries had to be ensured. Revolts or insurrections, while unlikely in this region of low population density, nevertheless would have strained core Tarascan resources. To the core elite, the loyalty of these peoples would have been best assured by a policy of gradual assimilation into the mainstream of the Tarascan social system and by the adoption of Tarascan ethnic identity.

Assimilation as a process can only take place when individuals are motivated to change their individual and collective behavior. It was not enough that Tarascan elite saw political/military advantages to assimilation; local populations had to perceive parallel benefits. The benefits perceived were the prestige and power gained by identification with the Tarascan social structure. Local village leaders, *angámecha* in Tarascan (*caciques* or *señores* in Colonial documents), were people who wore lip plugs given them by the king (Lagunas 1983:22, 221) and who were thus elevated to noble status. By controlling access to local political offices the core elite also controlled the local elite's access to power and prestige, now definable on Tarascan terms. There is no indication that local elites within this zone derived land claims from prior historical myths of legitimacy, which would have bound them to a particular place and people (see Brumfiel 1988). By extending the Tarascan political ideology throughout this zone, non-Tarascan-based access to resources and social status became illegitimate and over time would have become irrelevant.

Within the zone of ethnic segregation, along the military borders, loyalty to the Tarascan elite was assured in exchange for the security provided by the state military structure. Administrators were sent from the political core to articulate with the local population and ensure this loyalty. Nevertheless the populations were regarded as subject allies, rather than subjects, and tribute included war captives and slaves (RG 1985). The inclusion of zones of segregation within the state was highly desirable; the risk to the state of losing their ultimate loyalty was balanced by the benefits of using these populations for military support, sacrificial victims, and economic brokers with neighboring societies. Carlos Herrejón Peredo (1978) has detailed the valuable role played by Matlatzinca and Otomí communities, both along the eastern border and at enclaves at Charo-Undámeo, in the Tarascan repulsion of the 1476–1477 Aztec military campaign. Such support brought harsh Aztec reprisals in the Toluca Valley itself and resulted in additional refugees' fleeing to Tarascan territory.

This ethnic strategy differed from that of the Tarascans' contemporary neighbors, the Aztecs, among whom ethnic diversity was woven into the basic economic and political fabric of society (Carrasco 1971; Van Zantwijk 1973). There is no Aztec ethnic heartland, but a zone of culturally similar populations sharing the Basin of Mexico, often sharing individual communities, for their mutual (if not equal) benefit. Traditional ethnic markers included language, dress and adornment, marriage patterns, deities and ritual, and even occupational specializations. Here ethnic boundaries were maintained, even cultivated, by the Aztec elite, although the markers and significance of the boundaries surely changed as Aztec power increased. Beyond the political core of the state, Aztec policy was largely one of indifference to ethnic distinction, with the result that conquered communities, regions, and states retained previous ethnic boundaries unaffected by Aztec administrative units or economic networks. Contact between Nahuatl-speaking, ethnic Mexica, related Nahuatl speakers of the Basin of Mexico, and groups in conquered territories was extremely limited and hierarchical, consisting primarily of interactions between tribute collectors and conquering armies, on the one hand, and local ethnic leaders and defeated peoples, on the other. Robert McC. Adams has suggested that an important reason for the absence of "measures that were intended to lead toward the cultural, linguistic and political incorporation, or even long-term pacification, of the conquered peoples" may have been the overwhelming demographic dominance of the core population over its peripheries (Adams 1979:64).

While Tarascan ethnic strategy may have been distinctive in sixteenth-century Mesoamerica, it exhibits many characteristics common in the structure of ethnicity of complex societies. The policy of assimilation, and its implementation by control over positions of power and prestige, is a fundamental component of the military strategies of many expanding states, including the Inca (Morris 1982; Rowe 1982; Wachtel 1982), the Roman (Salmon 1982), and the Assyrian (Larsen 1979). One of the best documented cases is that of the romanization of central Italy (Salmon 1982). The spread of Roman ethnicity took more than three hundred years to be achieved in central Italy and was a product of specific policies of the expanding Roman state. These policies included the granting of specific privileges to some members of conquered communities, the use of the Roman language in all economic and legal affairs, the establishment of Roman colonies in conquered zones and the locating of markets within them, and the granting of land to migrants who had been uprooted in the various wars. Assimilation during these centuries was aided by the linguistic diversity existing in the region, which made the use of a lingua franca desirable, and the fluidity of Roman religion in its acceptance of regional variation. A consistent feature of this process was the direct administration of peoples by Roman law and the severing of communities from their ethnic homelands. While Salmon found no evidence of a deliberate Roman policy of cultural assimilation, he noted that the methods that stimulated such changes were patterned early in Roman history (by 338 B.C.; Salmon 1982:56) and, given their success, were incorporated in all later territorial expansion. Indeed, the high degree of political centralization found in such polities may be directly related to an elite perception of the role of ethnicity as an integrating mechanism, and to the larger goals of expansion. By promoting assimilation in the larger Tarascan territory, the elite of the geopolitical core could better ensure the economic exploitation of this zone, uninterrupted by rebellions and retaliatory campaigns. This exploitation was increasingly necessary to feed the growing population of the Pátzcuaro Basin and maintain the conspicuous consumption of the state (Pollard 1982, 1987). From this perspective, the ethnic strategy was an adaptive mechanism, increasing the stability of the Lake Pátzcuaro Basin ecosystem.

Ethnic segregation along military borders is also common, particularly the use of such populations in a military capacity. Enloe (1980:25–29) has termed this the "Ghurka Syndrome," characterized by the maintenance of ethnic boundaries in regions that are usually mountainous, along historic invasion routes, and geographically distinct. In the Tarascan case, such groups served not only military functions, but also economic ones.

The high degree of political centralization that characterized the Tarascan state was an extension of a pattern historically successful in the political core and adopted during the formative phase of Tarascan political unification (Gorenstein and Pollard 1983). It consisted of the adoption of a unitary elite social system, manifest in Tarascan ethnicity and state religion. The process by which this unitary system was established involved the appropriation of the material bases of power by the *uacúsecha* elite and the appropriation of the ideological bases of power (López Austin 1976) by the central dynasty. Along military frontiers this structure was altered to encompass other ethnic groups, who would provide security. Rather than imposing the direct rule that characterized the state, these communities retained their local leaders and were ruled only indirectly by Tarascans.

Rapidly expanding complex societies often exhibit a characteristic pattern of rapid territorial increase followed by periods of consolidation and absorption of the conquered territory. The political unit soon after conquest is multiethnic and heterogeneous and is often termed an empire. The assimilation that follows expands the center, absorbing increasing portions of the periphery, until the resultant polity is best viewed as a territorial state. In A.D. 1521 the Tarascan polity was actively in the process of this internal incorporation, reflecting the strong political motivations of expansion and the high degree of centralization of administrative functions. The type of state that resulted appears to have been the product of the economic needs of the expanding Tarascan nobility centered in the Lake Pátzcuaro Basin (chapter 5; Pollard 1982a; 1987; Gorenstein and Pollard 1983; Pollard and Gorenstein 1980) and the absence of competing state societies in Late Postclassic Michoacán. Clearly the Tarascan elite were aware of other types of imperial control, and central Michoacán had been culturally part of Mesoamerica for more than two millennia. Nevertheless, the case of the Tarascan state demonstrates one variant of Mesoamerican states and the emergence of an expanding state in a region where none had existed before.

# CHAPTER 7

# THE IDEOLOGY OF POWER
## THE STATE RELIGION AND THE TARASCAN INTELLECTUAL TRADITION

THE creation of the Tarascan state and the emergence of the *uacúsecha* elite was accompanied by the establishment of a new ideology. Indeed, as Eric Wolf has stated, "The construction, deconstruction, and reconstruction of cultural units implies also the construction and destruction of ideologies" (1987:590, my translation). This ideology, or system of ideas, values, and attitudes served to unite the elite into a legitimately bounded social class and culturally unify the larger population. However, an elite is by definition an interest group, and elite culture serves to "enhance and maintain its power" (Cohen 1981:126). For this reason Tarascan ideology represented beliefs imposed by the dominant social class on the rest of society to justify its political and economic power (López Austin 1976:197). The primary means by which this was accomplished was to "universalize" symbols of benefit to the elite centered in Tzintzuntzan to the status of cosmic truth.

The process of producing a state religion is not direct or simple. Ideas, rituals, sacred places are all developed and acted upon over long periods of time. The populations of Postclassic Michoacán came from different cultural traditions and related to the emerging elite in varying ways. "There are thus no well-thought-out design, no clear intentions, no consistent logic, and no coherent body of ideas" (Cohen 1981:229–30). The new ideology emerges out of existing beliefs and newly performed ritual. Thus there are at least two sources of difficulty in understanding protohistoric religion: the limited sources of information and the changing nature of the belief system.

With that said, we can isolate the core beliefs that empowered the royal dynasty to obtain the loyalty of an empire. The royal lineage, and to a lesser extent the nobility as a whole, were believed to have obtained "power" or "force" from their personal relationship to the universal power of the god Curicaueri. The "force" was maintained by leading a virtuous life, and the elite at birth had more of it than commoners (López Austin 1976:236–37). The elite would therefore use this force on behalf of the commoners for their general good. The means of explaining how this came about, and how it could continue, fell to a series of state cults and an official history or creation myth. This history included a migration legend with a heroic struggle against adversity, and a hero in human form. This hero, Taríacuri, a charismatic leader with a special relation to sacred power, was the tool for the creation of secular power.

Among the many deities known, Cuerauáperi, Curicaueri, and Xarátanga are mentioned most often. The greatest number of temples seem to have been constructed to them, and they were linked most directly to the Tarascan state. The earth was conceived of as the body of the great creator goddess Cuerauáperi. This goddess represented the forces that controlled fertility, including rain, birth, and death. She was the mother of all the gods and was actively venerated throughout the Tarascan territory (RM 1980:15–17). The sky forces were associated with major celestial bodies, including the sun, the moon, and stars. The sun was embodied in Curicaueri (or Curita Caheri), the great burning god and the god of fire. He was both the messenger of the sun (the sun's rays), connecting the earth and sky, and the warmth of the hearth. As a sky force he was referred to in different terms for the rising, noon, and setting sun; as an earth force, these phases of the sun were related to directions. As the original patron god of the Tarascan royal dynasty, he was a warrior and the god of the hunt. The moon goddess, Xarátanga, the daughter of the earth creator and wife of the sun, was associated with childbirth and fertility.

The worship of Cuerauáperi and Xarátanga share many features of Mesoamerican societies that were widespread by the Classic period. These include autosacrifice (especially bloodletting from the ears), human sacrifice, flaying and wearing of sacrificial skins, female figurines, snake and butterfly associations, the rubber ball game, and conch shell trumpets. The worship of Curicaueri is explicitly linked to the "Chichimec" heritage of the royal dynasty and is associated with bow and arrow hunting of deer, eagles, wood fires (especially on mountain peaks), stone projectile points, animal skin garments, the aggressive hummingbird, and warfare. The forging of the centralized state after A.D. 1300 required the creation of a common language of cosmic forces. The patron gods of the dominant ethnic elite were elevated to celestial power, while the various regional deities and worldviews, which were themselves products of generations of change, were elevated, incorporated, or marginalized.

The clearest evidence of this process involves the joining of the ethnic Chichimec deity, Curicaueri, with the ethnic "islander" or *purépecha* goddess, Xarátanga. In the prophetic language of a great epic, it was written, "Curicaueri will conquer this land, and you for your part will stand with one foot on the land and one on the water. . . . and we shall become one people"

(RM 1980:40). Their joint worship at Ihuatzio and Tzintzuntzan was a direct product of this unification, reinventing them as husband and wife.

But elevating their rival's goddess to the stature of their god was not sufficient to produce a coherent state religion. Patron deities of various communities were reinterpreted within the dual system of the four quarters (Curicaueri's four brothers) and the five directions, uniting all the solar deities in a manner that made the Lake Pátzcuaro Basin the cosmic center. One of the final conqeusts in the political unification of the Pátzcuaro Basin was the defeat of the island of Pacandan. The island's patron deity became the god of sacrifice, exile, and the center direction. In the ritual of Ecuata Conscuaro, before the recounting of the official Tarascan history, the chief priest would turn to the east and invoke the goddess Cuerauáperi, turn to the west and invoke the goddess Xarátanga, turn to the north and invoke the solar god of Zacapu (Querenda-Angapeti), turn to the south and invoke the gods of the hot lands, and finally look up to the sky and invoke the spirit of Curicaueri, the great sun (Hurtado Mendoza 1986:139–40). But a number of practices associated with other deities were given little role in the state religion, such as the rubber ball game. The use of the calendrical system to divine good or bad days, as in selecting a day for battle, was known to exist at earlier Xarátanga cult centers, but it was considered unnecessary by Curicaueri warriors (RM 1980:184).

Thus, the particular combination of beliefs that formed Tarascan state religion, described in this chapter, reflect those belief systems in existence by about A.D. 1300. The dominant themes of the Curicaueri sun-warrior cult can be documented along the Lerma River by the Early Postclassic, while the Cuerauáperi rain-fertility deity was probably a widespread complex by the Late Preclassic Chupícuaro culture. Kirchhoff saw Cuerauáperi added to the Tarascan pantheon after the conquest of the Cuitzeo Basin (RM 1956:xxiv), although more recent archaeological documentation of the spread of Chupícuaro in the Late Preclassic makes this unlikely. It is in the Xarátanga cult that specific Classic/Epiclassic beliefs and rituals appear to cluster, and they may represent historical continuity between the elite of, for example, Epiclassic Tingambato and the ethnic "islander" elite of the Early Postclassic Pátzcuaro Basin. But whatever the origins of the components of Tarascan state belief, by the early sixteenth century it had become a new variant of Mesoamerican religion.

## STATE CULTS AND DEITIES

The Tarascan deities did not constitute a neatly defined unit or "family." Most of the information about the gods is indirect and focused on individual beings. Rarely do we get a glimpse of the way in which they were viewed together, and even then, the information is often contradictory. However, on at least two state occasions major deity cults were brought together. First, in the official order of mention at state ceremonies (RM 1980:280, 282), the cults were listed in the following order: Cuerauáperi, celestial origin gods, gods of the Four Quarters, gods of the Right and Left Hand, god of the underworld, Curicaueri and his brothers, Xarátanga, and Uiránbanecha (not always listed). Second, in the account of the official procession from Tzintzuntzan at the commencement of war (RM 1980:242), there appeared first five priests of Curicaueri and then four priests of Xarátanga.

The main dieties and their primary characteristics are listed below. This information summarizes analyses based on the RM, the RG, León (1903), Corona Nuñez (1957), and Hurtado Mendoza (1986).

## CUERAUÁPERI

Cuerauáperi was the Tarascan creator goddess controlling birth and death. She was associated with the vapor from hot springs, which rises to form clouds that bring rain. Specifically, she sent rain from the east and could withhold rain and send famine. As the mother of all the gods of the land, her name means "that which creates" and "our grandmother."

### ASSOCIATIONS

Cuerauáperi's cult included thermal springs with idols at Araró and Zinapécuaro, although there were temples dedicated to her in most communities. She was depicted in female figurines, especially those dressed with corn, with her face painted yellow. At the feast of *sicuíndiro* (the flaying), dedicated to Cuerauáperi, sacrificial victims were flayed and the hearts of the victims placed in the hot springs of Araró to encourage rain. Her priest-imitators wore an artificial snake and paper butterfly around their waist at *sicuíndiro* (RM 1980:11–15). The dance at this feast included two nobles representing four clouds—white (frost), yellow (dew), red (soft wind), and black (running water); four priests representing other deities associated with Cuerauáperi; one priestess representing the goddess (dressed in a snake and paper butterfly); and two sacrificial victims (slaves).

### RELATED DEITIES

Turec-Upan was the goddess of Naranjan and other sierra centers. She was also known as Tarecupane, "she who brings food," and appears to be depicted in a figurine from Naranjan of a deity dressed with corn (in the Lumholtz collection, American Museum of Natural History, New York).

Camauaperi was a goddess of Pacandan and possibly a sister of Cuer-auáperi.

Auicanime was a goddess of hunger, an aunt (sister?) of the sky gods, represented by a reddish mouse. Hurtado Mendoza (1986:95) says *auicanime* refers to the sisters of the moon deity, who are referred to as the grandaunts, once women who died in childbirth. When they came to earth they were believed to presage hunger, calamity, and death.

Guach-Hozcua were "the girl stars," the Pleiades, or seven stars.

Tam-Hozcua were "the four stars," or the Southern Cross.

## XARÁTANGA

Xarátanga was the daughter of Cuerauáperi, the goddess of the moon, wife of the sun deity, and patronness of childbirth and fertility (fig. 7.1). Her name means "she who appears in diverse parts," "that which appears" (the moon), and "our mother." She is known to have had the power of concealing fish in the lakes to hide them from fishermen.

### ASSOCIATIONS

The Xarátanga cult was associated with ball courts and thermal springs. On the southern side of Xarátanga's temples were said to be baths called *pucue huringuecua* (*puque huringuequa*) (jaguar baths) (RM 1980:174). She could take the form of an old woman, a coyote, or an owl and was represented by yellow. There were major temples dedicated to her at Xarácuaro and Tzintzuntzan, but a portable idol was moved with the center of her cult, which apparently shifted during the Postclassic. Her temples are referred to as "house of the parrot feathers" ("casa de las plumas de papagayos") and "house of the turkey feathers" ("casa de las plumas de gallina") (RM 1980:174). In addition to standard priestly dress, her priests also wore black and red varieties of chile, beans, and maize strung on necklaces, bracelets, or wreaths. Her temples received offerings of ducks and quail. In her ball courts the gods were fed at midday, and she was often depicted as a half moon, snake, coyote, or vulture.

### RELATED DEITIES

Peaume was a goddess of Zacapu and appears to have been a local equivalent of Xarátanga. She was the wife of Querenda Angapeti.

Acuizecatapeme was the "serpent locked up in water," a water goddess associated with death (snakes). She had a temple on Xarácuaro and was related to Xarátanga.

Purupe Cuxareti was a sister of Hacuizecatapeme.

Fig. 7.1. Tzintzuntzan, figurines, possibly Xarátanga (Museo Michoacano, Morelia).

Mauina was a goddess of love and the daughter of Xarátanga.

Manouapa was the son of Xarátanga. Offerings to him were included in the treasury. His name means "sun of movement," and he may have been associated with a star or planet.

## CURICAUERI

Curicaueri was the patron deity of the Tarascan state, represented on earth in the form of the Tarascan king. As Curita Caheri, the great burning or the great fire, he was a sun god. In addition he was associated with obsidian, black, and a large white eagle. Curicaueri was represented by a face painted yellow and black. He received offerings of deer, especially skins, wood (for fires to keep him warm on his mountaintop), and blood. The blackening of his face represented the soot from the smoke of these fires. He was also referred to as Tiripeme Curicaueri (RM 1980:20). At least four different aspects of the Curicaueri cult can be isolated. They acknowledged Curicaueri as fire god (hearth, warmth, burning wood offerings); sun god (nourishing, fertility, grandfather, rays of the sun, messenger of the sun, human sacrifice, autosacrifice); warrior god (Thiume, the black squirrel; white eagle); and tribal god of the *uacúsecha* (with the Tarascan king as his earthly form; a hunting god; and an obsidian knife kept by the *uacúsecha* leader).

## RELATED SKY DEITIES

As the sun god, Curicaueri was also linked to various deities representing the phases of the sun, and to other regional sun deities. Of greatest prominence were the following.

Cupanzueri (also Apantzieri) was the old sun, who played the ball game and was associated with the west.

Achuri Hirepe, whose name refers to "the night that hurries" and who at Xacona was called the "house of the night," probably refers to the waning sun or moon deity.

Sirata Taperi was the young or morning sun. Cuerenda-Taperi was a solar god of Zacapu, "god of the rock that is worshipped." He was believed to have houses in all four quarters and the underworld.

## CELESTIAL FIRST-BORN GODS: THE SKY GODS

The sky gods include several male deities, each of whom was once the patron celestial being of a distinct community or region. Within Tarascan state religion they appear to have occupied a minor role, except as they were reinterpreted as brothers of Curicaueri.

Urendecuaecara was the god of light and once the patron deity of Corínguaro. In the Tarascan state religion he was also known as Tiripeme-Cuarencha, and was a brother of Curicaueri.

## TIRIPEMENCHA

The tiripemencha (tiriuapeme) refers to a group of five deities called "golden or beautiful water." They once may have been separate patron deities of different communities, but in the state religion they were placed within a unified system of directions, colors, and geographical centers encircling the Pátzcuaro Basin.

Tiripeme Xugapeti was the yellow god of the north, who breaks bare soil. His home was Pechátaro.

Tiripeme Turupten was the white god of the west or setting sun, whose name is also written as Tupuren. His home was Iramuco (possibly Urichu).

Tiripeme Caheri was the black god of the south or the noon sun. He was the patron of Pareo.

Tiripeme Cuarencha was the red god of the east or the rising sun, or the morning star, Venus. He was associated with red and white and was the patron of Corínguaro. As Huren de Cuavecara (Urendecuavecara) he was specifically associated with red and white clays.

Chupi Tiripeme was the blue god of the center, or the god of capture, exile, or sacrifice. He was also the patron deity of Chupícuaro and Pacandan.

## GODS OF THE FOUR QUARTERS

These deities are mentioned in the RM only in the context of official chants where all the great supernatural powers are enumerated. It is not clear whether they refer to the Tiripemencha or another set of deities.

## GODS OF THE RIGHT AND LEFT HANDS

These deities are named only in official chants. The Uiránbanecha are referred to as the Gods of the Left Hand. As a group of deities associated with the south, their identification suggests that these two categories included those deities associated with the south (left) and north (right) directions.

## UCUMU (UHCUMO)

Ucumu was the lord of the underworld and death, and the patron of Cumiechucuaro, the place of death. He was associated with gophers, moles, mice, and snakes, and could be reached through caves.

## SOME MINOR DEITIES

Several deities about whom we know nothing are listed in the RM. Others who occupied minor roles in the state religion do reveal the diverse cultural roots of the Tarascan pantheon.

Pungarencha, the war god, was the messenger of death in battle. He was a plumed or feathered god, based on the translation of his name.

Sirunda Aran, "the black twin," was also a messenger of a sun god (the sun god of Zacapu), who used the Milky Way as his road.

The Uiránbanecha, the gods of the hot lands, were associated with the caiman, perhaps some stars, and the gods of the left hand (RM 1980:174).

Inpiechay (Inpiencha) was a sea god associated with the conch shell and the west.

Taresupeme was the lame god of pulque (fermented maguey juice), who lived in the south. This deity was a patron of Cumanchen.

Uazoricuare, a local god, was "the rays of the sun." He was generous and a giver of food.

## TARASCAN WORLD VIEW, COSMOLOGY, AND RITUAL

The Tarascans' basic conception of the world shared fundamental principles with those of all Mesoamerican societies. Nevertheless there were differences in emphasis and particular practices that serve to distinguish Protohistoric Tarascan ideology and that are still reflected in the structure of the modern Tarascan language (Friedrich 1984). The bulk of our understanding of these principles comes from the RM, supplemented by other ethnohistorical documents, including the sixteenth-century Tarascan grammars and dictionaries.

The universe was believed to have been made up of three parts: the sky (*arandaro*), represented by eagles, hawks, and falcons; the earth (*echerendo*), believed to be a goddess with four quarters; and the underworld (*cumiechucuaro*), which was the place of death associated with the mouse, gophers, moles, snakes, and caves.

The four quarters of the earth were associated with cardinal directions, to which was added the center, and each direction was associated with a particular color. These included black (*turis*): south; white (*urauas*): west; red (*charapecua*): east; yellow (*tsipambecua*): north; and blue (*chupicua*): the center (color names from Gilberti 1987). North south were also referred to as the right and left, respectively, based upon their direction seen from the vantage of the rising sun. Not surprisingly, given the geography of Michoacán, the west was also associated with the god of the sea, and the east with the earth goddess, Cuerauáperi, the direction from which she brought the rains.

Deities were seen as active in the affairs of humans and capable of moving from their divine spheres to communicate with people on a personal and group level. The sky gods, and particularly the sun god, Curicaueri, were believed to descend from the heavens when invoked from high places and spiritually called by smoke (especially bonfires and incense). Thus they were propiated on mountains, although in addition there was a wooden pole placed in the center of the plaza of the temples, "down which the gods descended from the heavens" (RM 1980:144). In a similar manner, dreams, through which the gods often communicated, were believed to occur when a person was sitting at the base of a tree. Individuals were seen to have a relationship to a patron diety that was established at birth. Thus even after marriage a woman retained a special tie to the patron deity of her home community (RM 1980:25–26).

Friedrich (1984) has noted that in modern Tarascan there is a sharp line drawn between humans and animals, and further between humans/animals and all else in nature. Reflecting the latter division of animate forms, the Protohistoric deities were believed to be able to appear in both human and animal form. In addition, humans were believed to be able to be possessed by deities.

In an agrarian civilization, it is perhaps expected that much of life would be dominated by the agricultural cycle. In the Tarascan case this took the form not only of the ordering of time and ritual, but also in the pervasive role of maize in the language, from the enormous focus on the parts of the plant, phases of growth, season of harvest, and types of food preparation, to a metaphor for birth, strength, and renewal in the society as a whole.

There are a number of central Mexican traits, associated with basic belief systems, that have no counterpart in the Tarascan intellectual tradition. Perhaps most significant is the relatively small number of major religious cults in the Tarascan state religion and the (unsuccessful) attempt on the part of the Tarascans to relate the major deities to a divine "family." There is no clear indication of dualism as a fundamental principle of Tarascan ordering, and few of the deities have clear male/female counterparts. The major deities, whether male or female, control multiple forces of nature. Major central Mexican deities are not worshiped at all, or may have a Tarascan counterpart in a minor (usually regional) deity. Thus, there is no Tarascan Tlaloc, and rain is the province of the earth goddess Cuerauáperi. There is no Quetzalcoatl, although Hurendecuavecara (Tiripeme Cuarencha) may have aspects of a Quetzalcoatl-like deity.

Finally, there is little indication that the Tarascans saw a need to record their beliefs in books. That they were aware of the Aztec books is clear from the RM. From the sixteenth-century dictionaries we have the following terms: *carani*, to write or paint (Lagunas 1983:164); and *siranda*, paper or book (from the word for the amate tree, used to make paper in prehispanic times (Gilberti 1987:98). Despite these words, there are no known preconquest pictorials or any writing system associated with this civilization.

At least two contradictory origin myths are known from the Tarascan area, although both were based on late-sixteenth-century sources. The portion of the RM that was lost would have included the official state version. A single line in the RM suggests this official view would have included a series of creations, in which the Tarascans lived in the fifth cycle or sun ("oh dioses del quinto cielo"; RM 1980:238). This would have reflected a common Mesoamerican theme that included the belief in cycles of creation and destruction, each dominated by a new sun or sky.

A rather distinct cosmogeny emerges from a 1585 document published in the Miranda edition of the RM (1980). In it eight balls of ashes mixed with blood from the ears of the messenger of the sky gods, Curita Caheri (the sun), are turned into four men and four women. They are not perfect and were subsequently destroyed. This is repeated again, and on the third try all the gods are destroyed by a great flood. The first god created after this is Cuerauáperi, mother of all the gods, who on the fourth try succeeds in creating the first people, the earth, and the underworld. The earth is then made from a goddess lying down with her head to the west (represented by the god of the sea), her feet to the east (represented by Cuerauáperi herself), and each arm extending to the north and south. (RM 1980: Appendix, *Relación sobre la residencia de Michoacán (Pátzcuaro) hecha por el Padre Francisco Ramírez, 4 abril 1585*).

Seventeenth-century priests recorded an alternative origin myth in which Curicaueri, the sun god, is the original being, who creates a companion, Achuri-Hirepe (a moon deity). She becomes pregnant, and as Curicaueri is aging, speeds his death, and buries him in the east. That night she gives birth to a son, Siratataperi ("of the father's lineage"). This son in turn fathers Tuitze, who is sent to earth in the form of a deer to live among people. These are the various aspects of the sun deity, Curicaueri. All living things are the creation of the offspring of the sun deity and his consort, Achuri-Hirepe. This offspring is the mother goddess, Cuerauáperi, who then creates the living world (table 7.1) (Hurtado Mendoza 1986:49–55).

It is unclear whether there were several origin myths recounted during the Protohistoric period, reflecting the partial incorporation of various local cults during the Postclassic, or whether the second version, in which Curicaueri is the creator deity, reflects the influence of Christian, male-dominated origin myths.

There were, broadly speaking, two types of major rituals represented by the monthly feasts. The first acknowledges the yearly cycle of birth and death in an agrarian society, including the rebirth in spring, the fall harvest, and the return of migratory animals. These festivals were primarily devoted to Cuerauáperi, Xarátanga, or one of the related fertility deities. The second type had as its main focus the glorification of the state and the legitimation of the king. Thus "the great gathering" was the scene for the retelling of official state history (as in the RM), the "imprisoning of rebels" allowed communities to publically renew their loyalty to the state, and the "initiation of warriors" gave social and moral prestige to the military power of the empire. Not surprisingly these festivals were devoted to the Tarascan patron deity, Curicaueri, and other sky gods associated with warfare. The ceremonies about which there is information are listed in table 7.2.

Most celebrations included giving "food" to the gods in various forms. In addition to traditional human foods these gifts included:

| | |
|---|---|
| Wood, fires | Curicaueri |
| Bloodletting | Curicaueri |
| Human sacrifice | Cuerauáperi, Curicaueri, all major gods; two to four victims except when associated with warfare. |
| Flaying of sacrificial victims | Cuerauáperi |
| Eating of sacrificial victims | Not clear; probably most. Flesh divided among priests. |
| Ducks, quails | Xarátanga |

Dogs (?)                          Two dog burials in ceramic vessels
                                  excavated at Zinapáecuaro (Moedano
                                  1946).


Table 7.1    Prehispanic Tarascan Religion

1.  The universe
    sky (*arandaro*): eagle, hawk, falcon
    earth (*echerendo*): goddess with four quarters
    underworld (*cumiechucuaro*): place of death; mouse, gopher, mole

2.  Major cults
    *Cuerauáperi*: earth goddess, bringer of rain, fertility
    *Xarátanga*: moon goddess, Venus, childbirth, ball game
    *Curicaueri*: sun god, fire god, warrior god, patron god

3.  The quarters

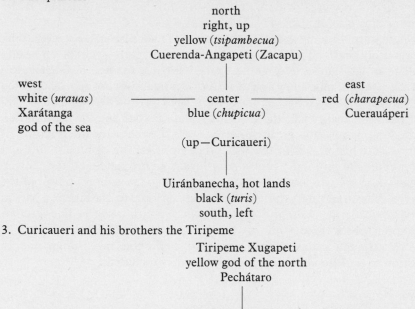

north
right, up
yellow (*tsipambecua*)
Cuerenda-Angapeti (Zacapu)

west
white (*urauas*) ——————— center ——————— red (*charapecua*)
Xarátanga                blue (*chupicua*)                Cuerauáperi
god of the sea

(up—Curicaueri)

Uiránbanecha, hot lands
black (*turis*)
south, left

3.  Curicaueri and his brothers the Tiripeme

Tiripeme Xugapeti
yellow god of the north
Pechátaro

Tiripeme turupten (tupuren)    Chupi Tiripeme       Tiripeme cuarencha
white god of west           — blue god of center —  red god of east
Iramuco (Urichu?)             Chupícuaro/Pacandan    Corínguaro

Tiripeme caheri
black god of the south
Pareo

Table 7.2    Major Celebrations*

| Name | Possible Translation | Major Deity | Center |
| --- | --- | --- | --- |
| Ecuata Conscuaro | "the great gathering"; "render justice"/recounting of state history | Curicaueri | Tzintzuntzan |
| Hanciuanscuaro | "the imprisoning of rebels"/ military campaigns at borders | Curicaueri | Ihuatzio |
| Hicuandiro | "feast of purification" | Cuerauáperi | Zinapécuaro |
| Sicuindiro | "feast of flaying skin"/ temple repaired | Cuerauáperi | Zinapécuaro, Araró |
| Charapu Zapi | "feast of small moss" | Cuerauáperi | Tzintzuntzan |
| Caheri Uapanscuaro | "great joining of barrios"/ Maize harvest | Cuerauáperi | All centers |
| Curindaro | "feast of the bread offering" | Cuerauáperi | Tzintzuntzan |
| Purecatacuaro | "initiation of warriors" | Curicaueri | Tzintzuntzan, Zacapu |
| Cuingo | "white heron" | Curicaueri Cuerauáperi | Tzintzuntzan |
| Caheri Conscuaro | | Curicaueri | |

*Includes only those about which there is any information in addition to the name.

## PRACTITIONERS

The state religion was administered by an elaborate hierarchy of priests and supported by the village leaders and elite bureaucrats. At the top of the hierarchy was the king, who as the earthly representative of Curicaueri participated in all major rituals. Below the king was the chief priest or *petámuti*. He was in charge of all other priests and presided over the most important ceremonies in Tzintzuntzan, both civil and religious. He wore a black shirt, gold tweezers at his neck, and a woven wreath on his head, and his hair braided with a feather. On his back he carried a large turquoise-encrusted gourd filled with tobacco, and he carried a flint-tipped lance on his shoulder (RM 1956:181–82). As the moral leader of the empire, he acted as chief judge for all but the most serious crimes. It was he who presided over the month-long court held at Tzintzuntzan (Ecuata Conscuaro) and passed sentences (RM 1956:11–14). During the rest of the year complaints were first submitted to him, and if action was warranted, sent on for consideration by the king (RM 1956:201).

Below the *petámuti* were the *curitiecha*, who acted as traveling priests, officiating at ceremonies and ordering firewood to be collected for the temples (fig. 7.2). They also wore gourds on their shoulders, and in this manner "they had all the people on their shoulders" (RM 1956:181).

Each temple had a head priest and a number of lower priests called *cura*, or grandfather. These priests were married and inherited their positions "por linaje." It is unclear whether that refers to a patrilineal inheritance, as existed for the position of king. However, all of these generalized positions were probably limited to the nobility. The *cura* were charged with knowing the histories of the gods and their feasts (RM 1956: 181).

In addition to these priests, there were a series of special-function priests. It is possible that not all served full-time, especially those drawn from the nobility. The full hierarchy thus included (RM 1956:181–82):

*Generalized Priests*
  *petámuti*
  *curitiecha*
  temple head priest
  *cura*

*Specialized Priests*

| | |
|---|---|
| *curizitacha* | Burned copal (incense) and brought branches for particular ceremonies. Gilberti (1975:40) recorded *curihtsitari*, "fogonero de los ydolos," or "stoker of the hearth." |
| *thiuimencha* | Carried the images of the gods on their backs and thus accompanied the army. They were named for the deity they carried. |
| *áxamencha* | Sacrificers, "who took out hearts" (Lagunas 1983:164). The king and upper nobility held these positions. |
| *hopitiecha* | "Those who held the hands and feet" of victims on the sacrificial stones. One priest was in charge of them. |
| *patzariecha (pazariecha)* | Keepers or guardians of the images of the deities. |
| *atápacha* | Drum-beaters. |
| *pungacucha* | Trumpet or horn blowers. |
| *hatepatiecha* | Heralds who chanted while walking in front of war captives. They had a steward in charge of them. |

Fig. 7.2 "The priests of the temple." (From *The Chronicles of Michoacan*, translated and edited by Eugene R. Craine and Reginald C. Reindorp, Copyright © 1970 by the University of Oklahoma Press, plate 4.) "Estos son los sacerdotes y officiales de los cúes" (RM 1956:179).

| | |
|---|---|
| *cuicuiecha* | Carried the sacrificed victims to where their heads were raised on poles. |
| *hirípacha* | Chanted prayers and incantations, burning tobacco, in the priest's houses before going to war. |
| *cuirípecha* | Performed the rituals associated with war. |

The power held by the priesthood appears to have been limited to that
power held by priests as members of the nobility or in their other roles as
political leaders. The bulk of the religious practitioners appear to have been
subordinate to the state bureaucracy. Thus, while much of the tribute
collected in the empire was destined for use as offerings in the temples,
there is no indication that the priesthood had any control over the tribute
system, save the collecting of firewood. In a similar manner, while the
largest public works were the temple complexes, there is no indication that
any religious authority controlled the corvée labor necessary for their
construction or maintenance.

## THE CALENDAR

The Protohistoric Tarascans divided time into parts of the day, days of
the months, and months of the solar year. The basic calendar was the
*huriyata miucua* or sun count (Gilbert 1975). This solar year (*uexurini*) was
divided into eighteen months of twenty days. The month was the *cutsi
miucua*, or moon count (Gilberti 1987:292), with five extra days. Within the
month, units of five or ten days were recognized, and often delimited the
length of festivals. The day itself was a solar unit, *huriatecua* (Gilberti
1987:188). The day was divided into four parts, based upon the movement of
the sun, and the night into four corresponding parts (Gilberti 1987:331–38).

The solar year was also divided into seasons: spring, *tzitzicuicurarenscua*
(time of flowers); summer, *hozta (cua)* (for heat or star, *hozcua*); autumn,
*haniscua* (or *hanicua*, rain); and winter, *iauanscua* (ice) (León 1888:39,
Gilberti 1987:94, 98). There is no evidence of the naming of days or the
ritual 260-day calendar known from other parts of Mesoamerica. In the
RM, reference is made to the counting of named days (cane day, water day,
monkey day, knife day, etc.) and the use of day signs in fortune telling, but
only as a practice used by "others," including a group of communities just
southwest of the Pátzcuaro Basin (1980:184). This suggests that the ritual
calendar was part of the cultural heritage of some Postclassic groups in
Michoacán. The RM does *not* document its use by the Protohistoric
Tarascans, as has been assumed most recently by Edmonson (1988:238).

Attempts to reconstruct the Protohistoric Tarascan calendar began before the turn of the century by Paso y Troncoso in 1888 and were continued
by Seler (1908) and León (1903). The most detailed effort was by Caso (1943,
1967), who also compared the Tarascan calendar with other Mesoamerican
systems he was studying. All of these studies are primarily based upon the
fragmentary information given in the RM, especially the dates for a few
months, which were correlated with the year in which the RM was recorded
(1541).

Table 7.3, a comparison of the Tarascan, Matlatzinca, and Aztec calendars is based upon Caso (1967), Berdan (1982), and Hurtado Mendoza (1986). The Tarascan dates given in the RM are underlined, the first dates of the Aztec months are given in the last column, and the five extra days, marking the end of the solar year, are also underlined.

It should be noted that Hurtado Mendoza (1986:126) believes that some of the festivals, and therefore the months listed above, occurred at different times. He bases his disagreements with Caso on statements by early friars or on the seasonal context of the rituals themselves. His differences include: Ecuata Conscuaro (July, not June); Hanciuascuaro (December 21, not July); Curindaro (October, not December); and Cuingo (late October, not February). He also believes that the celebration of Sicuindiro was held every four years (leap year), at the end of the year, during the last five days plus the extra day (the 366th).

Apart from the more fragmentary nature of the Matlatzinca and Tarascan calendars, the purpose of the comparison is to demonstrate the general similarity of the solar calendars found in sixteenth-century Mesoamerica. Within the general similarity, however, the closer correspondence of the Tarascan calendar to that of the Matlatzinca suggests that they all share a common ancestry, with geographic proximity and cultural interaction determining the degree of specific congruence through time. There is no need to see the Tarascan calendar as a trait acquired from the "Puebla-Mixteca culture" or copied from the Aztecs, both suggestions common in the literature, but which contradict Michoacán prehistory, Tarascan linguistics, and the cultural dynamics of the Late Postclassic and Protohistoric periods. Edmonson has suggested that the specific form the Tarascan calendar took in the Protohistoric period had emerged by the Early Postclassic (A.D. 1000) and was based upon an earlier Teotihuacan calendar that underwent multiple shifts during the Classic/Epiclassic (1988:104).

## SACRED PLACES

### NATURE: MOUNTAINS, SPRINGS, AND CAVES

The Protohistoric Tarascans viewed mountain peaks as the natural domain of the sky gods, especially Curicaueri. Mountains were seen as the logical mediators between the earth and the sky and were the location of rituals, individual spiritual guests, and refuge in time of chaos. Bonfires located on mountain peaks kept Curicaueri warm (a reference common in the RM) and served to communicate with distant communities. Specific mountains, including Cerro Tzirate, Cerro Tariácuri (Tariacaherio in the RM) in the Pátzcuaro Basin, and Cerro Tancítaro in the sierra, were

Table 7.3   The Prehispanic Tarascan Calendar

| Tarascan Months 1541 | Matlatzinca Months | Aztec Months (1521) |
|---|---|---|
| Apr 9–28 (?) | In Thacari (great time) | Hueytozoztli Apr 14 (long watch) |
| Apr 29–May 18 (?) | In Dehuni (to roast maize) | Toxcatl May 4 (dry thing) |
| May 19–Jun 7 Mazcuto | In Thecamoni (?) | Etzalcualiztli May 24 (maize/beans meal) |
| Jun 8–27 Ecuata Conscuaro (great gathering) | In Thirimehui (small change) | Tecuilhuitontli June 13 (small feast of lords) |
| Jun 28–Jul 17 Caheri Conscuaro | In Tamehui (great change) | Hueytecuilhuitl Jul 3 (great feast of lords) |
| Jul 18–Aug 6 Hanciuascuaro (catch rebels) | In Iscatholohui (small death) | Tlaxochimaco Jul 23 (small feast of dead) |
| Aug 7–Aug 26 Hicuandiro (purification) | Ima Thitohui (great death) | Xocotlhuetzi Aug 12 (great feast of dead) |
| Aug 27–Sep 15 Sicuindiro (flaying) | Itzbacha (broom) | Ochpaniztli Sep 1 (sweeping) |
| Sep 16–Oct 5 Charapu Zapi (small moss) | In Toxiqui (small moss) | Teotleco Sep 21 (gods arrive) |
| Oct 6–Oct 25 Uapanscuaro (barrios join) | In Thaxiqui (great moss) | Tepeilhuitl Oct 11 (mountains) |
| Oct 26–Nov 14 Caheri Uapanscuaro (great barrios) | In Thechaqui (night heron) | Quecholli Oct 31 (flamingo) |
| Nov 15–Dec 4 (?) | In Thechotahui (the twins) | Panquetzaliztli Nov 20 (raising flags) |
| Dec 5–Dec 24 Peuanscuaro | In Teyabihitzen (fall from above) | Atemoztli Dec 10 (water falls) |
| Dec 25–Jan 13 Curindaro (bread offer) | In Thaxitohui (grandfather) | Tititl Dec 30 (shrunk) |

Table 7.3   *Continued*

| Tarascan Months 1541 | Matlatzinca Months | Aztec Months (1521) |
|---|---|---|
| Jan 14–Feb 2 Tzitacuarenscuaro | ? | Nemontemi Jan 19 Izcalli Jan 24 (resurrection) |
| Feb 3–Feb 22 Purecatacuaro (warriors) | ? | Nemontemi Feb 8 Atlcahualco Feb 13 (leave water) |
| Feb 23–Mar 14 Cuingo (white heron) | ? | Tlacaxipehualiztli Mar 5 (flaying of men) |
| Mar 15–Apr 3 Hunisperacuaro | ? | Tozoztontli Mar 25 (short watch) |
| Apr 4–Apr 8 extra days | In Thacari | |

particularly sacred and were the location of major rituals and the scenes of many sacred myths.

Springs, especially warm mineral springs, were the home of the earth goddess, Cuerauáperi. The clouds of vapor rising from the pools of hot water were a metaphor for the life-giving rain the deity provided. As the patron of fertility and childbirth, the deity Xarátanga was also worshipped at these springs, although she was at times identified with lakes and marshes.

Natural caves were believed to be spiritual entrances to the underworld, and as such, they were centers for the worship of the deity Ucumu. A large cave on Cerro Tzirate in the Pátzcuaro Basin has been found to contain figurines of gophers and other animals associated with the underworld (Brand 1951). Caves were also used as places of repentance during mountain spiritual renewals, and they are occasionally referred to in the RM as shelter.

## SACRED CONSTRUCTIONS

Tarascan ceremonial architecture is found within urban settlements functioning only partly as religious centers and at ceremonial complexes whose primary function was ritual activity (Pollard 1980). Both types of construction were generally adjusted to the conformation of the land (often sloping) and were added to in a rather unplanned manner over time.

There were, however, exceptions to this lack of planning, although at the present time I can document only one ceremonial complex that appears to have been ritually oriented. This is the ceremonial center of Ihuatzio, located near the center of the Pátzcuaro Basin, and constructed probably in the early fourteenth century. Of the 125 ha of the settlement, more than 40 percent (50 ha) was allocated to the religious functions of the center, which were concentrated in a large zone enclosed within thick rubble walls. The stone walls and major structures are generally aligned to the cardinal directions, with the principal axis running north-south. The north section of this zone consists of two rectangular pyramid platforms facing east over a large enclosed plaza referred to in the RM as the ball court, *querétaro*. Directly east of this complex are three small hills (Cerritos los Coyotes, or *iuatzi*). A line projected east from the corridor between the two temples falls midway between the two northern hills, and when viewed from this corridor the peaks of the two hills bracket one lunar phase cycle either side of the equinox (Anthony Aveni, personal communication, 1989). The north-south axis of the site seems to align with a hill immediately to the north (a southwest extension of Cerro Tariácuri). Hurtado Mendoza (1986:144–46) reports that for the festival of Hanciuanscuaro, taking place in Ihuatzio as the celebration of war initiating a major ritual military campaign, the timing of rituals was related to the appearance of the sun (or possibly Venus) on the crest of one of these hills. ("Two days before the celebration, the king ordered firewood brought to the patios of the Ihuatzio *yácata*, and when the morning after appeared bright in the sky, on the crest of a mountain which served as a clock, they lighted an enormous bonfire atop the sacred precinct."). Later in the festival, at midnight, a procession would lead from Ihuatzio to the crest of Cerro Tariácuri (located 30° east of north), where an altar was prepared and songs were chanted. When the fire was lighted, simultaneous fires appeared on mountain tops throughout the Pátzcuaro Basin, conch shell trumpets were sounded, and, with the sunrise, the procession returned to the temples at Ihuatzio.

## TEMPLES

Tarascan religious structures were generally located on the sides of mountains, increasing their visibility, not occupying prime agricultural land, and remaining close to the sacred spaces of the deities. Of the temples for which we have ethnohistoric identifications, most appear to have been devoted to the worship of a particular deity. These include the *yácatas* at Tzintzuntzan devoted to Curicaueri "and his five brothers" and the pyramids at Zinapécuaro devoted to Cuerauáperi. At Ihuatzio there are three *yácatas* and two rectangular pyramid platforms (figs. 7.3, 7.4). It is not clear whether the rectangular platforms, adjacent to the ball court, were associated with the worship of Xarátanga while the *yácatas* were associated with

Fig. 7.3. Ihuatzio, ball court and rectangular pyramid platforms.

Fig. 7.4. Ihuatzio, close-up of pyramid platforms.

Curicaueri, or whether they were all used interchangeably. Temples were generally arranged along one or more large platforms, with secondary temples located throughout settlements (see chapter 2). At Zacapu there is evidence of temple-altar-plaza compounds (Michelet 1986; Michelet, Ichon, and Migeon n.d.), and at Huandacareo there is evidence of a central cluster of at least three plazas, one of which was sunken, and two temples, one stepped rectangular and the other semicircular (Macías Goytia 1989). Here the major festivals to the deities were celebrated, judgments of the priests were issued, and members of the nobility were buried within or adjacent to the temples.

## BALL COURTS

There is little attention to ball courts in the RM, possibly because there was none at Tzintzuntzan. But there were ball courts in other Tarascan centers, continuing a tradition known in Michoacán from at least the Late Classic period and, if the figures from El Opeño are ball players, known from the Preclassic. The sixteenth-century dictionaries provide Tarascan words for the ball game (*querehta*), the ball court (querétaro), and the ball (*taranducua*) (Gilberti 1975). Within the Pátzcuaro Basin a ball court was located at Ihuatzio. According to the RM it was built on the orders of the goddess Xarátanga, and it was here that the gods were to be fed at midday ("Allí tengo de dar de comer a los dioses a medio día.") (1980:174). The ball court was located on the northern end of the ceremonial precinct ("la mano derecha") and appears to be the large walled rectangular plaza (ca. 200 m by 140 m) whose main axis runs east-west, and which is still referred to as *querétaro* by the modern inhabitants. No special ball court architecture can be discerned at present, unlike both earlier and contemporary courts in Michoacán.

At Zacapu at least two ball courts are known. They include an I-shaped court in the zone of Las Milpillas, and another I-shaped court in the zone of El Palacio (Michelet 1986; Michelet, Ichon, and Migeon n.d.). The first is oriented east-west on the long axis and measures 34 m by 14.2 m. The second is oriented north-south and is similar in size (no dimensions are given). At least twenty-two other ball courts are reported from other sites in the Zacapu Basin (Taladoire 1989:91).

The ethnographically recorded ball games in the Sierra Tarasca (Beals and Carrasco 1944) and the Lake Cuitzeo Basin (Corona Nuñez 1957) employ some of the same Tarascan terminology found in the sixteenth-century dictionaries but are referred to as *uárucuni*, or some variant. This word, meaning horizontal obstacles to movement through a narrow opening, reflects the nature of the game, which is to prevent an opposing team from moving a ball along a street or corridor using wooden sticks (somewhat like modern street hockey). Only the use of a flaming maguey root as the ball in Cuitzeo (Corona Nuñez 1957:22) suggests the relation of the game to the prehispanic solar deities. There is no evidence to indicate whether the Protohistoric game used such sticks, or whether the modern survivals are part of more widespread rituals, which would have been performed in villages, wards, and towns parallel to the large state ceremonies.

## BURIALS AND DEATH

The primary treatment of the dead appears to have been cremation, giving us no indication of cemeteries. However, the nobility, war captives, and sacrificial victims were buried in a variety of contexts that are often complemented by ethnohistoric descriptions of funeral celebrations. The goal of the burial rite and the goods deposited with the deceased was to speed the individual to the underworld, land of the dead. Based upon the excavations at Tzintzuntzan, Urichu, Zinapécuaro, Huandacareo, and Zacapu, and the many reports of looted burials, I believe the range of burial types included primary extended burials in tombs adjacent to major temples, primary group extended and flexed burials of more than thirty-five individuals, primary flexed burials adjacent to temples in minor centers, secondary burials in ollas, ossuaries of disarticulated bones, and isolated skulls or skulls added to primary burials. In addition, there was probably separate treatment for infants, but this is undocumented archeologically.

In the RM there is a lengthy description of the burial of a dead king, which seems to reflect the two primary tomb burials. It is stated that at the death of male and female nobles, others were killed to help them along the road to the underworld. Their bodies formed a bed on which the noble person would be buried, and others would cover the person, "thus preventing the earth from touching him" (RM 1980:163).

Secondary olla burials are also described in the RM (1980:58). At the death of the two lords Uapeani and Pauacume, a funeral took place at the temples in Pátzcuaro. The bodies were burned as conch shell trumpets were blown. Then the ashes were placed in ollas, each containing a gold mask, necklaces of turquoise, and green feathers. The trumpets were sounded again as the ollas were buried.

The many "extra" and disarticulated bones found within ceremonial precincts were the burials of sacrificial victims after they had been killed and dismembered, or skulls of sacrifices after they were removed from the skull rack adjacent to the main temples. Along with such burials have been found intentionally striated long bones (Lumholtz and Hrdlicka 1898; Macías Goytia 1989; Rubín de la Borbolla 1939, 1941).

## STOREHOUSES

Sacred objects and other ritual paraphenalia were stored in the palace storehouses in Tzintzuntzan and adjacent to major temples throughout the empire. Cabrera Castro (1987:549) excavated a series of rooms that may have been used for storage of such goods adjacent to the *yácatas* at Tzintzuntzan (see appendix 1). Among the many goods in the king's treasury in the royal palace (RM 1956:152, 257) was the "idol" of Curicaueri. It was believed that injury to this "idol" would cause illness. It is not clear whether "idol" refers to a statue of the deity or to the obsidian block referred to as the heart of the deity, taken from Zacapu in the legendary history of the *uacúsecha*. Also included in the ritual objects were mirrors and flint knives made by *pinguiri*, who were artisans of "espejos y pedernales" listed by Gilberti (1987:99).

## ILLNESS, TREATMENT, AND THE SOCIAL GOOD

The health of individuals, and indeed the general health of the community and state, was believed to be related to the actions of the deities, supernatural beings, and the breaking of the moral code. Illness, both physical and emotional, was dealt with through two approaches. One was to redress the breaking of the moral code through the judicial system, by designating punishment or by locating witches. Highly punished breaches of the moral code, especially among the nobility, included drunkenness and adultery, and were often used to explain natural disasters or military defeats in the RM. The second approach was to treat the illness itself. In a recent study of Protohistoric Tarascan medicine, Sepúlveda y H. (1988) has used the information provided by the RM, the RG, and the Gilberti dictionary (1975) to understand the Tarascan medical system. The following discussion is drawn primarily from this analysis.

The primary causes of illnesses listed in the sixteenth-century dictionaries are accidents or traumas (more than twenty terms in Gilberti 1975); infectious or contagious diseases (more than forty-five terms); emotional upset (four terms); and other specific agents, such as pain, blindness, and clouded eyes (cataracts) (more than forty terms). Certainly some of the terms for infectious diseases are compounds used to describe the symptoms of European-imported diseases. The illnesses themselves were believed to be the product of witchcraft, including possession, the evil eye, injury from falls, animal bites, burns, and the product of deliberate abortions.

There were a series of medical specialists, some probably full-time and others part-time. They included *xurimecha*, general doctors or curers, who made diagnoses, sometimes resolved domestic disputes, applied herbal cures, and did some dental work. A group of curers served the royal palace and had an official (chief curer?) to supervise them. The Gilberti dictionary distinguishes among *xurimecha*, who are inexperienced and try experimental cures, and those who teach. *Peuatahpe* were the midwives, older women or widows serving the goddess Xarátanga and her mother, Cuerauáperi. There are names for a group of medical specialists, including a doctor for the eyes (*tzinanganicuhperi*), a doctor for the ears (*cheexahcuhpeti*), and a blood letter (*chucuhpe*). Finally there were the herbalists, *sipiati miteti*, who prepared and sold herbal remedies in the markets.

Diagnosis was a complex activity and involved divination by means of seeing the reflection of the sky in a bowl of water (*itsi eramanstani*), by luck or omens (*sicuamechan micurini*), by the reading of dreams (*uintsiyandacuareni*), by an astrologer (*auanda ambongasri*), by interpreting hallucinogenic trances brought on from eating "intoxicating" mushrooms (*cuaicua tarecua*), by seeing into a burning flame (*exehrapeni* and *erantzcani*), and by reading the patterns of dry maize on a plate or maize floating in water. While many of these sources of diagnosis were common throughout Protohistoric Mesoamerica, the use of the burning flame was limited to the Tarascans and Huastecs (Sepúlveda y H. 1988).

Treatment included a wide range of options, from surgery to inducing vomiting, bleeding, puncturing, applying plasters or *ungüentes*, setting bones, using gargles, and taking medicinal plants. In addition, they practiced circumcision of boys (*tzihuecua sicuiri*), another practice shared with the Huaxteca. There are terms for abortion (*huuan*) and a drink to induce childbirth. Finally, taking baths in thermal springs was seen as beneficial, especially as a means to increase fertility in women. For these baths women went to the thermal springs of Zinapécuaro, Araró, and Chucándiro, all associated with the mother goddess Cuerauáperi, bringer of fertility. There are at least fifteen locations in the Cuitzeo Basin with thermal springs, several more in the Lerma River Basin, and a few in the Balsas Basin. Except for the mention of baths associated with the temples to Xarátanga at Ihuatzio, there are no indications of steam baths (*temascales*) within structures before the late sixteenth century.

Based upon the botanical inventories of Hernández and Ximénez, in addition to the Gilberti dictionary, more than 100 medicinal plants are mentioned in Tarascan, 10 more in Náhuatl that were also used by Tarascans, and many other plants whose names are given in Latin or Spanish, but whose use by Tarascans is indicated. The plants included tobacco (*Nicotina tabacum*) and certain mushrooms used in diagnosis, treatment, and religious ceremonies. A recent ethnobotanical study of the Tarascan zone indicates that the mushrooms probably included *Psylocybe mexicana* and *P. cubensis*, the only hallucinogenic mushrooms currently found in Michoacán

(Mapes, Guzmán, and Caballero 1981:61–62). They would have been widely available in the Tarascan central plateau, including the Pátzcuaro Basin. A stone sculpture in a mushroom shape, found in 1963 in the Pátzcuaro region, appears to depict a young phase of the mushroom *Amanita muscaria*. This mushroom was easily identified by Mapes's informants, who used the same name as the sixteenth-century sources. It is now considered poisonous and avoided. Other varieties of mushrooms were used in healing (and still are), as well as mesquite, maguey, achiote, and many other wild and domestic plants.

Based upon all the information studied, Sepúlveda y H. suggests that the most frequently recognized illnesses were due to infections, both intestinal and bronchial, skin problems, and injuries. The Protohistoric Tarascans took diagnosis and treatment seriously, and failure to cure a patient could result in death to the doctor. In this and the general approach to illness and treatment, the Tarascans share the basic intellectual tradition of Mesoamerica. A small number of specific traits were shared solely with the Huaxteca and may reflect early and continuing ties along the Lerma Basin and the northeastern Mesoamerican frontier.

## THE MATERIAL EXPRESSION OF BELIEF: TARASCAN ART

Tarascan art represented the unified ethnicity of central Michoacán and the political power of the Tarascan state. In both roles, the art communicated information about religious beliefs, social status, and political power. It served as the primary bearer of Tarascan elite culture and political domination. As such it reflected the common Mesoamerican heritage of Postclassic Mexico, while revealing features that were limited to western Mexico or unique to Tarascan civilization.

The media of known Tarascan art primarily included architecture; public stone sculpture and petroglyphs; lapidary arts and metalwork; wood sculpture; featherwork; clay figurines, tobacco pipes, and pottery; and textiles. The finest works were produced by master craftspersons, some of whom were resident specialists housed within the royal compound at Tzintzuntzan. Other artisans lived in distinct communities or wards, and at least some had inherited their occupational specialties.

## ARCHITECTURE

Tarascan architecture was characterized by large artificial platforms on which were built one or more stepped pyramids. The platforms and pyramids were constructed of rubble-core volcanic stone and faced with dressed stone. Whenever possible, the natural slope of a hill was terraced to produce platforms with minimal building effort, but of a size (up to more than 300 m wide) that when faced with dressed stone and viewed from below were monumental in impact (for example, Tzintzuntzan, Pátzcuaro, Acámbaro, Zinapécuaro, and Huandacareo). A specialized pyramid form, the *yácata*, consisting of a keyhold shape, was constructed at major religious centers associated with the Tarascan sun god, Curicaueri (see chapter 2 and appendix 1). Temples of wood were constructed on top of these platforms. Other buildings illustrated in the RM (1948) included specialized residences for priests, royal compounds, elite and commoner houses, granaries, and treasuries. These were of wood, often with stone foundations, and roofs of wood or straw. Temples and elite residences included carved wooden lintels and portals with painted posts and walls. Ball courts are known from Ihuatzio, Zacapu, and Huandacareo.

## STONE SCULPTURE

A number of stone sculptures have been found adjacent to major temples. These include three *chacmool* forms (fig. 7.5) and an animal sculpture (53 cm high), generally interpreted as a coyote, from the site of Ihuatzio. These basalt sculptures are stiff and formal, with little detail. Sculptures similar to these were destroyed by the Spaniards in the first years of contact because of their association with native ritual, including human sacrifice. Like the temple architecture, they are simple but powerful expressions of the patron gods, especially the earthly representative of Curicaueri, the Tarascan king.

Petroglyphs, pecked designs on basalt outcrops and pyramid facing stones, are known from Tzintzuntzan, Acámbaro, and many other Tarascan centers. At least forty-seven have been found on the facing stones (*xanamu*) at Tzintzuntzan and the sixteenth-century chapels nearby (primarily from *xanamu* taken from the pyramids) (fig. 7.6). The most common motifs were spirals, double spirals, bulls-eyes, and curving meandering lines. At Acámbaro more than seventy petroglyphs are recorded from basalt outcrops on the sides of the frontier fortress on Cerro del Chivo (fig. 7.7) (Gorenstein 1985). The most common designs are spirals, ladders with a hole at the top, stairways of temple models, and wandering lines. The spirals are most common on the north side and the ladders on the east and west. The occurrence of similar designs on Tarascan facing stones confirms a Protohistoric date for many, although similar petroglyph designs were made as early as the Late Classic period in portions of the Lerma River system. Mountjoy (1987) has documented identical petroglyphs in the Lerma-Santiago drainage basin and at San Blas, Nayarit, he has confirmed Classic and Postclassic associations of spirals, ladders, and pits. In the Tomatlán area he has found 747 boulders covered with bull's-eyes, pits, circles, and some spirals, primarily Postclassic. Mountjoy has suggested that these

Fig. 7.5. Ihuatzio, *chacmool* (Museo Michoacano, Morelia).

designs may be associated with a sun/fire god and seasonal ritual sacrifice, with the spiral and bull's-eye symbolizing the eye or face of the sun god— an interpretation that fits well with the mountain/hillside rituals that were performed to the Tarascan god Curicaueri, so frequently described in the RM.

## LAPIDARY AND METALWORK

Small objects of carved and polished obsidian (red, green, gray, and striated), turquoise, quartz crystal, bone, marine shell, opal, serpentine, jadeite, and pyrite—especially ear and lip plugs, beads, and pendants— were used for personal adornment by Tarascans of high social status. They were also used as offerings and ritual paraphernalia in public celebrations of the state religion. The common designs, which include nonrepresentational lines, spirals, and dots, were similar to those found on decorated pottery. In addition a number of animal effigies and human masks were made. Rare and precious stones were also used as inlay and mosaics in combination with metal and wooden objects.

Metalwork of gold, silver, copper, copper alloys of gold or silver, and bronze alloys (copper-tin and copper-arsenic) were made into bells, beads, pendants, pins, disks, animal effigies, masks, figurines, and a variety of

Fig. 7.6. Tzintzuntzan, petroglyph.

tools (such as needles, awls, tweezers, axes, punches, and fishhooks) (fig. 7.8) (Pollard 1987; Hosler 1985, 1988a; Castro-Leal 1986). Ores were obtained by shaft mining or, in the case of gold, by panning nuggets from rivers (Barrett 1981; León-Portilla 1978; Warren 1968). Ores were then smelted down in clay braziers or in pits in the ground and cold hammered and cast, using the lost-wax process. Decoration was produced by guilding, embossing, soldering, and (probably false) filigreeing (Bray 1984; RM 1956; Rubín de la Borbolla 1944; Warren 1968). In style and form the Tarascan metalwork was different from that of contemporary central and southern Mexico, reflecting both the long West Mexican metallurgical tradition and specific Tarascan design canons. Only in gold design does the Tarascan

Fig. 7.7. Cerro Chivo, Acámbaro, petroglyph.

metalwork reveal ties to central and southern Mexico (Chadwick 1971:690–91; Kelly 1985:153–79); Mountjoy 1969:28; Pendergast 1962:536).

## WOODWORK, FEATHERWORK, AND TEXTILES

Much of Tarascan art was made from perishable materials that have rarely survived. Our knowledge of them is largely limited to descriptions and illustrations in early historic documents. Thus relatively little can be said about techniques of manufacture, design elements, or, sometimes, their social meaning. While our greatest information pertains to woodwork, featherwork, and textiles, tribute lists included carved gourds, basketry, leatherwork, and rare animal skins. Large carved and painted gourds were carried on the back of high priests during major rituals. Gilberti (1987:103) distinguished *cueres*, unpainted gourds, from *urani*, painted gourds, indicating their significance in Tarascan life.

Tarascans utilized wood as the primary building material, unlike the peoples to the east and south, who relied upon wattle and daub, adobe bricks, and stone. Wood was also used for furniture, house posts, canoes, weapons, ceremonial drums, and figurines. Illustrations in the RM indicate

Fig. 7.8. Tarascan metalwork, including necklace of copper and alloy bells, hoe, tweezers (Museo del Estado, Morelia).

that furniture, especially stools and storage chests, and house posts were painted and carved. House posts are shown painted in geometric patterns of alternating bands of red, white, yellow, and blue. The Tarascan king, chief minister, and major priests carried carved and painted staffs adorned with feathers and stone spear points. From Spanish tribute lists and occasional archaeological preservation, it is known that objects of wood were inlaid with precious stones, and that lacquer decoration was also used.

Featherwork was a highly specialized and prestigious occupation. Feathers of local and rare tropical birds were used to decorate costumes, shields, standards, and spears of noble-ranked warriors. Feathered capes and headdresses were worn by the royal rulers for major public rituals. As illustrated in the RM, standards carried into battle by units of Tarascan warriors representing different wards or villages were uniform in design, bearing alternating red and white bands. Shields were decorated with bull's-eye designs in alternating circles of white and red. Elite warriors may have carried shields with specific symbols, but the sixteenth-century illustrations are not clear enough to discern them.

Tarascan textiles were made of woven maguey fiber and cotton. As with all Mesoamerican textiles, Tarascan cloth was woven on the backstrap loom in varying widths depending on the nature of the garment or blanket being produced. Pottery spindle whorls are common artifacts at Tarascan sites and in elite female burials, suggesting that women, both commoner and elite, produced most of the cloth. One of the basic obligations of the king's women was to weave cloth for Curicaueri (RM 1980:134). Anawalt's (1978) study of Tarascan garments found that male clothing included the hip cloth, open-sewn tunic, cotton quilted armor, and specialized robes for warriors, priests, and ministers. Women wore wraparound skirts, small versions of the triangular shirt or *quechquemitl*, and draped capes. Most fabric shown in the RM illustrations was colored in alternating bands of red, blue, yellow, or white. Some of the ceremonial robes were woven in a stepped fret or checkerboard pattern. In two illustrations of robes worn by a Tarascan leader, a large red circle is shown on the upper back. Each has a central red dot and red lines or triangles radiating from the red circle, probably representing the sun god, Curicaueri. Small remnants of cotton cloth, which were preserved because of their contact with copper bells sewn to the cloth, indicate that additions to elite and ritual garments with metalwork, stone beads and pendants, and featherwork was probably common.

## CLAY OBJECTS

The most abundant media for the expression of Tarascan beliefs and styles were in fired clay. Among such objects were pottery vessels, tobacco pipes, spindle whorls, beads and pendants, figurines, and musical instruments. Pottery vessels included a range of bowls, plates, and jars common in Postclassic Mesoamerica (see appendix 2). Certain forms were limited to the elite, used for ritual offerings, or part of major religious and political ceremonies. These were highly decorated, finely finished, and particularly characteristic of Protohistoric Tarascan art (fig. 7.9). Of note were miniature bowls with tripod supports (3–6 cm in diameter), miniature jars, modeled jars in animal and plant forms, spouted vessels with solid or hollow handles (with or without supports), and spouted vessels in animal forms, often birds.

The range of form for body shape, handles, and supports is extremely large in the category of decorated pottery. This fineware was usually slipped in red, cream, pink, white, or gray. Red, white, and black paint was used in varying combinations to produce color zones and design motifs. Decoration was also achieved by adding appliqué pellets, excision, incision, and negative or resist painting. The most common design elements included red and white vertical dashes, lines of white dots, thin parallel lines, hatching

Fig. 7.9. Tzintzuntzan, polychrome tripod bowl (Museo del Estado, Morelia).

and checkerboard, S-shaped and Z-shaped elements in bands, spirals with small ticks or lines, double spirals, and X-shaped elements. Complete vessels indicate that these elements were generally combined to form decorative panels, especially on rims, handles, and interiors of bowls, many of which divide the vessel into halves or quarters. Others include animal shapes similar in form to stone and clay figurines. Still others have animal forms appliquéd to rims and bodies.

The variety of form and decorative treatment characteristic of polychrome pottery was also found among clay pipes, used by priests and other members of the nobility in association with religious ceremonies. They were commonly slipped in white, red, or cream and could be polished, incised, or appliquéd. Most pipe stems were twisted, and many also were grooved, producing a composite cross-section. Others were in animal or plant shapes. Some of the pipes may have been used for metal smelting, as illustrated in the RM (1956:172, lamina xxix).

Some clay spindle whorls were painted, incised, or modeled in shapes of bells; others were undecorated. Small figurines, pendants, beads, and musical instruments of clay were treated in similar ways, generally slipped or painted in red, white, cream, or black, with limited design elements.

In general, Tarascan ceramics can be characterized by curvilinear and plastic shapes, limited and relatively simple combinations of decorative elements, and a high degree of variability. The absence of mass production of plainware and fine ceramics accounts for far less standardization than that which characterizes many other Mesoamerican civilizations.

## IDEOLOGY THROUGH ART

The limited archaeological research in this region, the reliance on unprovenienced artifacts, and the use of the term *Tarascan* to cover earlier time periods and other regions of West Mexico has led to the characterization of the art as "eclectic" (Kubler 1984:198). Compared to other Proto-historic elite art, such as Mixtec or Aztec, the Tarascan material seems without clear roots and is difficult to interpret. Our need to rely on the RM for almost all of our information about Tarascan ideology has fostered the use of non-Tarascan sources for iconography, and with them the belief that Tarascan religion was a patchwork of recently adopted beliefs from elite migrants. However, research in western Mexico suggests that many traits once considered late imports, such as circular ceremonial structures, complex metallurgy, and spiral motifs on ceramics and petroglyphs have long cultural traditions in the regions between the Lerma and Balsas River systems. The Tarascan art style was a product of these regional traditions transformed into state art on behalf of an aggressively expanding dynasty.

# CHAPTER 8

# THE TARASCAN KINGDOM WITHIN MESOAMERICAN PREHISTORY

IN the preceding chapters the Tarascan polity has been analyzed in a number of different dimensions, defined geographically and structurally. The present chapter is designed to integrate these various threads within the context of Mesoamerica and the study of early states. Such an integration will begin with the world in which the Tarascan state existed, Protohistoric Mexico, particularly as it was influenced by the powerful neighbors to the east, the Aztecs, or Mexica (map 8.1).

## THE SHADOW OF THE AZTEC EMPIRE: TARASCAN-AZTEC RELATIONS

It is often assumed that if two societies are contemporary and geographically relatively close, communication between them is high and unrestricted. But the degree and nature of communication and exchange between populations of independent states is a function of both the military/political relations between them and the ability of central authorities to control interactions across their borders. The interaction between the Aztec and Tarascan states was dominated by military hostility that restricted the flow of individuals, including members of the elite, and allowed the creation of ethnic stereotypes that persist to the present.

### MILITARY AND POLITICAL ENGAGEMENT

The Tarascans are generally considered to have been the foremost enemy of the Aztecs (Davies 1987:291). From the 1450s until the Spanish conquest these two powers were continually engaged in offensive or defensive military actions. The sequence of interaction is summarized on table 8.1, based upon material reported in Hassig 1988, Herrejón Peredo 1978, Brand 1943, Contreras Ramírez 1987, Warren 1985, the RM (1541), and the RG (1579–1581).

It is clear that both the Tarascans and the Aztecs had economic interests in portions of the disputed territory. The middle Balsas is a zone of metamorphic rock with copper, silver, and gold deposits; greenstone; and localized salt production. Smith (1987:27) points out the role of Alahuistlán (Ajuchitlán) in salt production, seeing the Aztec effort to protect that

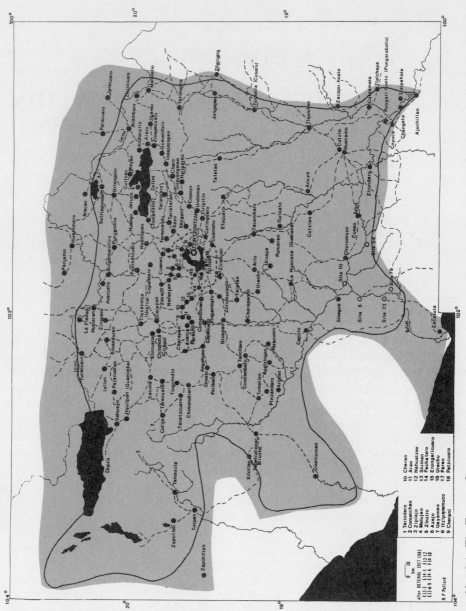

Map 8.1. The Tarascan State

| | |
|---|---|
| 1 Tarindaro | 10 Cheran |
| 2 Comanchen | 11 Aran |
| 3 Zipiajo | 12 Nahuatzen |
| 4 Matujeo | 13 Siunan |
| 5 Zicuiro | 14 Pichataro |
| 6 Aiatajo | 15 Erongaricuaro |
| 7 Uayameo | 16 Urechu |
| 8 Itzipanamuco | 17 Pareo |
| 9 Charani | 18 Patcuaro |

after OETEMAL 1977/1981
EI3:3  EI4:1  FI3:12
EI3:4,9 EI6:4  FI4:10

N.P. Pollard

Table 8.1    Tarascan-Aztec Military Engagements

| | |
|---|---|
| 1430s | Aztecs under Itzcoatl began conquests in the Toluca Basin. |
| 1440s | Aztecs under Moctezuma I (Motecuczomah Ilhuicamina) conquered south and west of the Toluca Basin, including Oztoman. |
| 1455–1462 | Tarascan conquests, under Tzitzipandaquare, into Toluca Basin as far east as Xiquipilco, previously conquered by Itzcoatl. |
| 1472 | Aztecs under Axayacatl retook areas of Toluca Basin and defended area from Tarascan attempts to take region. Hassig (1988:185) places this as part of the 1477–1478 campaign. |
| 1475–1477 | Aztecs under Axayacatl conquered central and western portion of Toluca Basin and move south to Oztoman and its neighbors. |
| 1479–1480 | Aztecs' third major western campaign under Axayacatl moved against Tarascan territory after Toluca Basin was placed under military rule. The army, including Tezcuanos, Tepanecas, Chalcas, Xochimilcas, Chinampanecas, and Otomies, massed at Toluca (Tollocan). It took Taximaroa and marched towards Queréndaro up to Charo-Undámeo. Aztecs were defeated here by combined Tarascan-Matlatzinca force, and all communities were retaken to frontier at Taximaroa. A small force harassed the Aztec force back to the Toluca Basin. This was a major battle involving up to 50,000 Tarascan and 32,000 Aztec soldiers; up to 30,000 Aztecs are said to have died. |
| 1486 | Ahuitzotl crowned *tlatoani* in Tenochtitlán. The Tarascans refused to attend. There was an Aztec military campaign to Xiquilpa and Toluca Basin. |
| 1488 | The king attended dedication of Great Temple in Tenochtitlán. No sacrificial victims were Tarascan. |
| 1489 | Ahuitzotl attacked Oztoman after this border settlement refused to acknowledge tributary status to the Aztecs. The entire population of Oztoman and several neighboring communities were killed or dispersed; the settlements were repopulated with settlers from the Triple Alliance capitals. Tarascans established a series of fortifications at strategic points from the Lerma to the Balsas basins. Tarascans were settled at some, and all had direct control from the Tarascan capital. |
| 1490–1491 | Aztecs expanded into Guerrero to the Pacific coast and moved north along the coast. Hassig sees this as an attempt to encircle the Tarascans (1988:211). |
| 1499 | Tarascans attacked fortified Oztoman, and Aztecs responded with additional buildup of population and fortifications in region. |
| 1502 | Motecuczomah Xocoyotl (Moctezuma II) was crowned *tlatoani* in Tenochtitlán. Durán indicates that the king attended, but was brought in secret. |
| 1515 | Aztecs attacked from the Toluca Basin under Moctezuma II, with the great Tlaxcalan general, Tlahuicole, in command. This was the first direct attack on Tarascans since Axayacatl's defeat. The Aztecs failed to |

Table 8.1    *Continued*

|  | take any sites but attacked along line including Taximaroa, Maravatio, Acámbaro, Ucareo, and Zinapécuaro. A major Aztec defeat took place between Maravatio and Zitácuaro (La Rea insisted that even in 1639 the bones from the battles were still visible; in Beaumont 1932). |
|---|---|
| 1519–1520 | Continued Tarascan harassment along southern border, with repeated attacks against Oztoman. |
| 1519–1521 | Aztec requests for help against the Spaniards in a series of embassies to Tzintzuntzan. At least two embassies were ignored, and the Aztec ambassadors were killed and sacrificed. In all cases the embassy traveled to the Tarascan frontier settlement of Taximaroa, where they were detained until a messenger was sent to Tzintzuntzan and permission was received from the king allowing safe passage, under escort, to the Tarascan capital. A Tarascan party did go to Tenochtitlán in 1520 at Moctezuma II's request. The king, Zuangua, was suspicious that the Aztecs would use a Tarascan alliance to defeat the Spaniards and then turn on them, or that Moctezuma would simply sell the Tarascan soldiers to the Spaniards as sacrificial victims. Zuangua blamed their misfortunes on the fact that "they merely sang songs to their gods, instead of carrying wood to their temples to keep the fires burning" (Warren 1985:28; RM 1956:243–44; RM 1980:304 ff.). |
| 1521 | *Summer.* When Tenochtitlán was surrounded by the Spaniards another embassy was sent. The Tarascans sent the Aztecs back, agreeing to consider the request for help. As soon as the Aztecs left messengers were dispatched to capture three Otomí, who were then questioned about the truth of the Spanish seige. *Late August to November.* Following the fall of the Aztec capital to Cortés, some Tarascans and Matlatzincas from the Taximaroa-Charo region were brought to Tenochtitlán. Cortés returned them to Tzintzuntzan with gifts and messages to the king. An offer of an Aztec escort was rejected in favor of an escort of Tlaxcalans (Warren 1985:30), indicating again the distrust of Aztec intentions as well as Tarascan knowledge of central Mexican politics. |

region as part of the mission of the fortifications of Oztoman. The northern border region was of great value to the Tarascans, containing major obsidian deposits and sacred thermal springs.

In a larger framework, the most active sections of the border controlled access to the Lerma and Balsas River systems, and the Tarascans prevented Aztec penetration of either. This effectively prevented further Aztec penetration to the west and northwest along major trade routes.

Over time, Aztec actions were both defensive, preventing Tarascan movement into the Toluca Basin, and offensive, finding alternative means of reaching the trade center at Zacatula. Hassig sees this as a policy of encirclement by the Aztecs. If that is so, it was clearly only a partial success, as only one of the Tarascan borders was effectively closed to further expansion by the Aztec actions. Other parts of the Tarascan border remained stable due to the inabilities of the Tarascan central government to field armies and retain control of increasingly distant populations to the north, west, and south.

The Tarascan frontier with the Aztecs was clearly a closed border. While it was only 160 km from the border settlement of Taximaroa to Tenochtitlán, and messengers could move between the two capitals (Tzintzuntzan and Tenochtitlán) within four days of travel (Gorenstein and Pollard 1982), clearly movement was strongly restricted. Aztec messengers had to present themselves at the official "ports of entry" and await permission to pass into the Tarascan domain, under Tarascan escort. Safety was clearly the enforcing principle, and the continuing hostilities along the border bred distrust of spies, who might precede raids or major campaigns. The movement of Tarascans within Aztec territory was probably also difficult, as Tarascan was not a language spoken within the Aztec domain, and speakers would be quite noticeable. On both sides, one solution was to use Otomí or Matlatzinca messengers and spies, but this meant that communication between the elite of these states was indirect and intermittent.

## ECONOMIC EXCHANGE

The available ethnohistoric and archaeological data indicate only two classes of economic interaction between the Tarascan and Aztec domains. The first, and primary, class includes goods acquired by Tarascan and Aztec long-distance traders. Tarascan long-distance merchants traveled to the borders of the Tarascan state, including Zacatula on the Pacific coast and Taximaroa on the frontier with the Aztecs, to acquire materials utilized by the elite of Tzintzuntzan. These included green obsidian from central Mexico and the Llano Grande of Jalisco, and a range of raw materials that would have come from central and southern Mexico, including jade, onyx, serpentine, pyrites, and copal. There is, however, no indication that Tarascan long-distance merchants went beyond the borders of the Tarascan domain, nor that Aztec merchants (*pochteca*) entered Tarascan territory. Exchanges made at frontier settlements, such as Taximaroa, may have been directly between Tarascan and Aztec merchants, or Tarascan merchants may have dealt with Matlatzinca or Otomí traders at these places. Studies of obsidian artifacts from Postclassic-period Apatzingán (in the southwestern portion of the state) conducted in the early 1970s (Hester, Jack, and Benfer 1973) suggested that most of the obsidian used came from Aztec territory

(Pachuca, Hidalgo, and Guadalupe Victoria, Puebla). However, as this determination was based on the distribution of only three trace elements (Sr, Rb, Zr), it is quite possible the artifacts were made of obsidians from Magdalena, Jalisco, and Zináparo, Michoacán, respectively. All green obsidians, whether from Pachuca, Pizarrín, or Magdalena, had to be imported and distributed by the long-distance merchants, but it would be quite unusual for the gray-black obsidian, used in far greater quantities, to have moved in local marketing networks from Aztec-held territory through the entire Balsas Basin to reach Apatzingán.

Sahgún (1950–1969, Book 10, pp. 66–67) indicates that maize and chili from Michoacán were sold in the large Aztec market at Tlatelolco. Given the need for these products in central Michoacán and the distances involved in their transport, the only region of Michoacán from which such exports would have come is the frontier region, especially the eastern portion of the Lake Cuitzeo basin. This region, in the northeast of the Tarascan domain, was productive enough to export basic commodities and close to the Aztec-controlled upper reaches of the Lerma River. Exchange across the frontier was probably carried out by the non-Tarascan groups occupying both sides of the border, especially Otomí and Matlatzinca communities.

## PROTOHISTORIC ETHNIC STEREOTYPES

One result of restricted communication across military borders was the ease with which each government could develop negative stereotypes of their enemies. Much of what Sahagún was told about the Tarascans probably falls into this category, but because of the detail and authority with which his informants spoke, his words have entered the Mesoamerican literature as truth about the Tarascans. Part of Sahagún's report (1950–1969, Book 10, pp. 188–89) is paraphrased in table 8.2.

There are a number of patterns suggested by the views recorded by Sahagún. First, most of the characteristics of dress and adornment relate to battle dress, reinforcing the view that the primary contact between these peoples was in battle. Many of the faults fall in the traditional category of complaints about "foreigners" where there is limited contact (the food is bad, their houses are different, their lip plugs are too big). The informants reveal that they are totally unfamiliar with Tarascan religion, or they would not confuse the word *taras* (term for a statue or figurine) with the major deities. Some of these inaccuracies, like the statement concerning the lack of human sacrifice, suggest second- or third-hand sources of information (or wishful thinking?) and are simply wrong. Of interest is that the centrality and power of the Tarascan king was clearly recognized, although the informants clearly omit any reference to Tarascan warriors or the

Table 8.2    Aztec Views of the Tarascans

They were called Michoaque (singular Michoa), from the fact that fish in plenty came from there. They were called Quaochpanme (singular Quaochpa) because they shaved their heads—all men and women, even old women.

Their land had all manner of food: maize, amaranth, beans, chia, gourds, fruit.

The men's clothing included sleeveless jackets, bows, woven-reed quivers, animal-skin clothing (ocelot, wolf, lynx, fox, deer), yellow fan-shaped things, squirrel skins headgear, *ayoquan* feather capes (heron?).

Their houses were good, but made of straw huts.

They were artisans (*tolteca*), featherworkers, carpenters, cutters, woodworkers, painters, lapidaries.

The women worked well with cotton thread, were good embroiderers, and made cross-weave capes.

The men made wonderful sandals.

They prepared food all at once for several days, or up to a week.

Their faults included that they wore no breech clouts—only a *cicuilli*, or long sleeveless shirt; their lip-plugs were very big, as well as the holes in their ears and lips for them; the women wore only a shirt, reaching only to above the knees; the people were unskilled with food.

The name of their god was Taras, and they are now called Tarascos. This god is Michoacatl in Nahuatl and Coatl in Chichimeca. Birds and rabbits were sacrificed to him. They did not sacrifice people, but kept captives as slaves.

The Tarascan ruler was shown obedience and sent tribute by his subjects. "He was the equal of him who was the ruler of Mexico."

inability of the Aztecs to penetrate Tarascan territory. While the king may have been seen as "equal" to the Aztec ruler, and despite the praise of artisans, politically they were considered "barbarians." Perhaps to rationalize the difficulty of obtaining Tarascan prisoners, Tlacaelel is said to have reminded the *tlatoani* (Aztec king) of the limit of the gods, including Quetzalcoatl, to accept barbarian offerings (Durán in Davies 1987:232). The "barbarian" offerings included sacrificial victims from the Yopis, Huaxtecs, and Tarascans.

Less specific information is available on the Tarascan view of the Aztecs. The king had several Nahuatl interpreters (RM 1980:239, 296, lamina xliii), sending four to Tenochtitlán at one time. They were used as messengers (*uaxanoti*) and spies, and they were housed within the king's court. The Tarascans acknowledged Mexico as the only other kingdom they viewed as politically significant: "It is a long time since these two kingdoms, Mexico and Mechuacan, were appointed." (RM 1980:297–99). They knew the Aztecs referred to them as fellow Chichimecs, but while the Aztecs referred to the Tarascans in their origin legends and histories, the Tarascans did not refer similarly to the Aztecs. Perhaps most pervasive was the belief that the Aztecs wanted to conquer them (RM 1980:297).

An interesting note about these stereotypes is the depth to which they became embedded, and reinforced, long after both states were ceded to the Spaniards. Van Zantwijk has recorded modern Nahua peasants' echo of the condescension implicit in the Protohistoric: "They [Tarascans] are a poor lot and badly in need of someone to put things in order" (Van Zantwijk 1967:185). Modern Tarascans of Ihuatzio seen to be quoting from the 1541 RM when they assert that "Aztecs are bad people; they used to come to Tzintzuntzan and Ihuatzio and other places in Michoacán, and they ate the people"; "Aztecs are proud and domineering people"; and "Aztecs always try to dominate other people, they are not to be trusted" (Van Zantwijk 1967:185).

The continual military hostilities between these two powers resulted in the emergence of a territorial frontier marked by restricted flow of people and information. Communication was dominated by military or diplomatic information, and it was often (if not usually) passed through neutral parties (e.g., Otomí or Matlatzinca) living in the frontier zone. This limited interaction fostered the creation of ethnic stereotypes, which would have served to rally support for military action and further decrease social interaction. One result can be seen in the material record, in which the Tarascan sphere is marked by distinctive forms of architecture, art, religion, artifact types, and manufacturing processes that abruptly stopped at the eastern border.

### THE EMERGENCE OF A WEST MEXICAN CIVILIZATION

Despite the general acknowledgement that the Tarascan state was indeed a variant of Mesoamerican civilization, it has long been viewed as an anomaly. The dominant language is not related (or only remotely related) to other indigenous Mesoamerican languages; the primary temple architecture, the *yácata*, is unique; ceramic forms and decoration and frequency of pipes are distinct; Tarascan clothing omitted some basic highland garments; and Tarascan metallurgy differs from other contemporary Mesoamerican states in technology, style, and some of its functions.

The often bewildering combination of traits that were shared with other Postclassic societies, traits that were unique to Michoacán, and traits that appear to represent later survivals from earlier times in distant regions has led to the characterization of the Tarascans as "an alien, barbarian people, almost untouched by Classic culture," who had "received a veneer of civilization from the Puebla-Mixteca culture and a tardy admixture of mainly theological influence from the Aztecs" (Krickeberg 1968:58). However, whether these imports are seen as Aztec, Toltec (e.g., Piña Chan 1982), Teotihuacano (e.g., Corona Núñez 1957), Mixtec (Chadwick 1971), or even Andean in origin, they are interpreted as indicators of a fundamental, unchanging relationship between central Mexico and the west. This relationship is one of core:periphery, donor:recipient, and Mesoamerican:barbarian.

To those who adopt this simplistic model of Mesoamerican prehistory, the true anomaly of Tarascan civilization is not the unusual traits enumerated above, but the emergence of this powerful empire in a periphery. Not surprisingly, a common "explanation" for the anomaly is "greater contact with central Mexico," stimulating secondary-state development. Apart from the inadequacies of this model to deal with what is already known of West Mexican prehistory (e.g., Weigand 1985), there is a confusion about the nature of secondary-state formation. As Gailey (1985:36) points out, states that emerge in societies that are developing class relations for the first time, as I believe the Tarascan state was, are undergoing a process quite different from that of states emerging from the political fragmentation of previous states. The salient questions are not whether trait x or y was imported, but how and why ethnic, class, and gender relations were transformed.

## POLITICAL UNIFICATION

At the present time, we have only limited archaeological and ethnohistorical information to use in understanding these processes. The RM remains the primary source of data but represents a biased, elite, and politically censored view of earlier basin society and the history of political unification. It does suggest that the consolidation of the Pátzcuaro Basin took place in the context of competition from adjacent polities (map 8.2). Within the basin there were several autonomous, internally ranked societies. Each was associated with one central place, a ruling elite, and a specific patron deity. Sometime during this period (A.D. 1000–1300) the lake basin assumed its sixteenth-century water distribution. That is, the water level of the lake reached the 2,045m–2,055 m level determined for the Protohistoric period. Whether this occurred due to soil erosion filling the lake floor or slight increases in precipitation, it meant major changes in the distribution and quantity of irrigable land, the quantity of harvestable fish, and the distribution and quantity of marsh resources (Pollard 1979, 1982b; Gorenstein and Pollard 1980). These shifts would have affected the basin polities differentially. Some would have lost agricultural land but gained significantly in marsh and lake resources (especially those based on the islands); others would have lost most of their irrigable land; and some would have been unaffected. The resulting disputes among their elites for access to

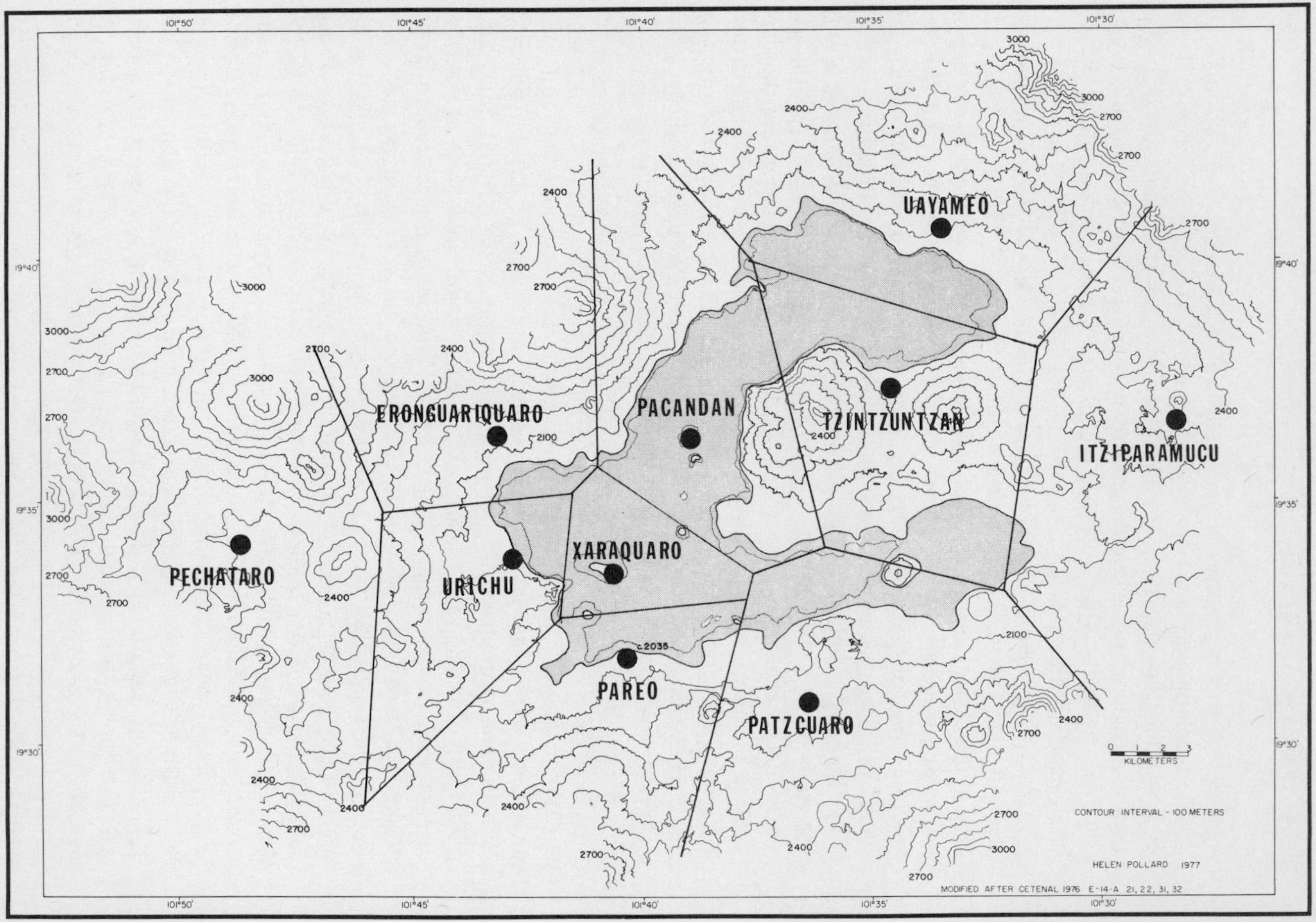

Map 8.2. Pre-protohistoric Polities of the Pátzcuaro Basin

Within the map:

UAYAMEO

ITZIPARAMUCU

TZINTZUNTZAN

PACANDAN

XARAQUARO

PAREO

PATZCUARO

ERONGUARIQUARO

URICHU

PECHATARO

CONTOUR INTERVAL – 100 METERS

HELEN POLLARD 1977

MODIFIED AFTER GETENAL 1976 E-14-A 21, 22, 31, 32

KILOMETERS

these shifting resources, perhaps made more difficult by the arrival of migrants, forms much of the historic action in the RM.

In addition, outside of the basin there were autonomous, ranked societies, which recognized relatively fixed territories. These polities are described in the RM as traditional enemies or allies of various Pátzcuaro Basin polities and were linked to them by marriage exchange within the elite and by economic exchange. Those mentioned most often surrounded the basin to the south, west, and north. The apparent lack of buffer zones between them and the Pátzcuaro Basin may have been a projection of Protohistoric concepts of territory to this earlier time, or a true indication of regional population growth. Of greatest importance to this process, according to the RM, was the expansion of Corínguaro, a polity immediately to the southeast of the Pátzcuaro Basin. Sometime during the thirteenth century Corínguaro expanded to control a territory from Tiripetío (on its west), north to Xénguaro, east to Guayangareo (now Morelia), and southeast to Etúcuaro (RM 1980:140–41). Whether it is historically accurate or not, according to the legendary history the formation of an alliance between Corínguaro and one of the basin polities served as the stimulus (or rationalization) for the consolidation of the two largest basin polities. This was rapidly followed by the incorporation of the remaining independent basin polities. In the RM this incorporation took place under the leadership of Taríacuri, ruler in Pátzcuaro. His tactics included alliances with basin and nonbasin polities through strategic marriages; military actions isolating other polities, particularly the island-based ones; and military conquest of the eastern basin, including Tzintzuntzan. In this early part of the unification process, the formerly independent elite appear to have retained their distinct ethnicity, patron deities, and ties to commoners. The new religious center at Ihuatzio was explicitly founded to join the worship of Taríacuri's patron god, Curicaueri, and the islanders' patron deity, Xarátanga, in a symbolically "neutral" place. In the following years distinctions arose, and formerly independent elite became subservient to leaders in Pátzcuaro, then Ihuatzio, and finally Tzintzuntzan.

## SOCIAL STRATIFICATION

The emergence of a hierarchical society appears to have taken place as part of the political unification of the Pátzcuaro Basin. Initially it seems to have been the product of military raids conducted under the *uacúsecha* leadership of Taríacuri on communities outside of the basin. Warriors who participated were rewarded. Taríacuri's mechanism of changing a group of independent leaders of autonomous polities into a hierarchically integrated social elite is most vividly expressed in this appeal to join his military expeditions: "I am making you a Lord if you do this [attack other villages], for you are not a Lord but of lowly class and a beggar" (RM 1980:108-9). By defining power as something that came from association with him, he was using the successes of the first raids to redefine social prestige and economic power. The material expression of these political shifts can be seen in the bringing of the Curicaueri cult to Tzintzuntzan, previously a sacred home of Xarátanga. Taríacuri comes to the heart of Xarátanga's home bearing a hummingbird (*tzintzu*), an aggressive symbol of war. As military campaigns shifted from raids to political conquest, the rewards shifted from booty and prestige to direct access to land and labor. The new society was not just socially differentiated, but truly stratified.

## GENDER STRATIFICATION

Tarascan society in the early sixteenth century was also gender stratified, although the evidence available suggests this stratification was incomplete and relatively recent. Kinship was bilateral, but inheritance of administrative, religious, and economic positions was primarily patrilineal, by sons, brothers, and nephews. Access to land was also patrilineal, although ultimate ownership was claimed by the king.

Among the higher elite, marriage was arranged by the king, with the consultation of the groom and the bride's father (RM 1980:260-62). The bride's family supplied her personal effects, including jewelry and tools, especially those associated with her primary duties to her husband— cooking, spinning, and weaving cloth. The groom's acceptance of the bride formalized his acceptance of loyalty to the king because the bride was ceremonially considered the king's daughter.

Among the remaining elite, marriage was arranged between the groom and the bride's father after consultation with the women of the bride's household (RM 1980:263-66). The priest who performed the ceremony reminded the bride of her duty to her family and her husband, and particularly warned her to be faithful. The groom was admonished not to abuse his wife, even if she committed adultery. Finally, the bride's father was shown the agricultural fields the couple were given, and the fathers exchanged gifts.

Among commoners marriage was arranged between the two families. The bride was admonished by her father not to commit adultery, for both she and her parents could be killed. Some marriages were contracted between parents when the parties were children. Divorce could take place when a woman refused to weave blankets for her husband or when a wife committed adultery. There are numerous examples in the RM of women simply leaving their husbands and returning to their family home (e.g., 1980:109). And men who left their wives for another woman, and then left that woman, could be put in jail (1980:272). Residence was generally patrilocal or virilocal, but men also moved to their wives' houses if "they were poor."

A gendered division of labor existed among both elite and commoners, but the divisions appear to have been far less flexible among the elite. For example, in describing the prehispanic copper mines, informants indicated that families had been moved to the mining centers and given access to land to support themselves. When word came from the king that copper was needed, everyone, both men and women, would quarry the ore (Warren 1968).

Thus, among the elite, gender was equated with succession, inheritance, and reproduction. Women held all the positions within the king's palace, under the control of the principal wife (*ireri*). These women were daughters of the nobility who became wives of the king or were given in marriage by the king to other members of the elite. Among commoners, there was substantial gender parallelism. Women spun and wove cloth, processed food, marketed goods, and performed a wide range of significant economic roles within and outside the household.

The reduction in status of the Cuerauáperi cult (the mother goddess) and the Xarátanga cult (the moon goddess), both of which were associated with female symbols of power, seems to have coincided with a reduction in women's autonomy. With the rise of the Curicaueri cult, state power became synonymous with maleness, fire, hunting, and warfare. It is possible that the traditional role of creator, ascribed to Cuerauáperi in one origin myth, was replaced by the second myth, in which Curicaueri is the creator of the mother goddess, who then creates humans. We know that inferring social changes from myth is very difficult because the relationship between the gender of deities and the relative power of genders in society is, at best, indirect. Nevertheless, it must be pointed out that one of the official reasons for attacking a community included rule by women (RM 1956:107). The excuse was that such rule would violate the divine laws, as women could not carry out the necessary ritual to Curicaueri (López Austin 1976:228). This suggests that at some point elite women could become political leaders, a role later denied them.

Despite the indications of gender stratification, it should be pointed out that at least symbolically Tarascan women, and femaleness in general, occupied a relatively high status. Two of the three major deities were female, and large numbers of elite women were among their ritual specialists. Of the eleven major celebrations for which we have information, seven were dedicated to one or both of these female deities. Finally, women as wives, aunts, and daughters occupy prominant roles in the legendary history of the state, as do the female deities in controlling major forces of nature. This may indicate the relatively recent emergence of gender stratification, or it may represent a variant possible in other early states.

## CLASS AND FACTIONAL RESISTANCE

The unification of political power that accompanied the emergence of class and gender hierarchies was neither accomplished nor maintained without resistance. Local elites were removed or incorporated into the new society, but always at the expense of their ethnic heritage and autonomy. Commoners lost whatever traditional claims to land and water they had, as all resources were considered the king's. They also were further removed from the process of choosing their village leaders, as previous bonds of kinship were replaced at the king's prerogative. This portion of the larger evolution of kin-based societies into tributary states is only poorly documented in the ethnohistoric data. Protohistoric-period Tarascan elites were interested in presenting history as a divinely ordained transformation to their subjects and later to the Spaniards. Despite this wish, it is possible to detect evidence of commoner and elite resistance to *uacúsecha* control.

Among commoners, resistance can be documented primarily by the attention paid to the punishment of rebels. On the installation of a new village leader, the king's representative and a higher priest made it clear that disobedience to the chosen *angámecha* (*caciques*) would result in death (RM 1980:256). Commoners were to support their leaders by providing food and service, follow their leaders into battle, and worship the god Curicaueri. The celebration of Hanciuanscuaro, dedicated to Curicaueri, was the time of triumph over those who threatened the kingdom, enemies within and without. This celebration consisted of a symbolic war during which communities would reaffirm their loyalty to the state by lighting fires to Curicaueri and sending warriors and their deity statues to Ihuatzio and Tzintzuntzan (Hurtado Mendoza 1986:144–47). On the other hand, village leaders were admonished to rule fairly and support and protect their commoners (RM 1980:256; Lagunas 1983:22). Complaints from commoners about the behavior of *angámecha* were a primary reason for the king to replace village leaders, at least in principle. In the years after the Spanish conquest there is little to indicate the nature of commoner resistance. Either the emergence of *purépecha* identity within the state had effectively reduced opposition, or the overwhelming hardships of the early Colonial period made Tarascan rule less oppressive by comparison.

Among the elite, however, the existence of competition for maintenance of local control and conflict over rights of succession form the main body of Tarascan legendary history. In the RM, as the *uacúsecha* leaders begin their armed struggle for control of the Pátzcuaro Basin, Taríacuri defended his imposition of power because specific community leaders had violated the divine order. Violations that "demanded" conquest included rulers with physical handicaps (e.g., blind), rulers whose people did not obey them enough, female rulers (since they could not perform all the required cult activities), entire communities that are impious, rulers who were always drunk, rulers with lewd and impious daughters, bad successors of dead rulers, and rulers who broke the divine order by unnecessary wars (López Austin 1976:228; RM 1980:139–48). López Austin (1976:228) points out that this last "affront" was seen as a breach of the divine order only because these wars were being fought against the *uacúsecha*. The actual incorporation of these elite was accomplished by a combination of military defeat, assassination, intermarriage, and alliance. The rewards for acquiescence included the booty of the early raids. The penalties for resistance included death for leaders and their people.

Factional competition after the emergence of the unified state, particularly after A.D. 1450, is unknown. While this lack of evidence may be a product of the nature of the documentary record, what is striking is the unanimity of the documents, whether Tarascan, Aztec, or Spanish, acknowledging the loyalty of the nobility to the king. The threat of factions within the royal family, however, must have been continuous. According to the RM, when a king became elderly or sick, he would name his successor, and that person, usually a son, would begin to assume power before the king's death (RM 1980:274–78). After the funeral for the dead king, the highest council of ministers would gather to formally endorse the named successor from among the king's brothers and sons (RM 1980:279–86). The process is portrayed as mechanical and friendly. Yet upon the death of King Zuangua in 1520, probably from smallpox, the eldest of his sons was persuaded to kill his brothers to reduce the possibility of conflict (RM 1980:308). The absence of mention of Zuangua's brothers at this time suggests that they too had been killed at the time of Zuangua's succession. What was apparently a successful policy to reduce power struggles within the ruling dynasty became a major handicap after the Spanish conquest. With the murder of Tangáxuan II (Zuangua's eldest son) in 1530, the only potential heirs to the throne were the king's boys, who were placed under a Spanish regent. The effective power of the native nobility thus ended barely four years after the first friars arrived (1526) and just nine years after the empire was formally ceded to Cortés (1521).

## THE TARASCAN KINGDOM AS AN ARCHAIC STATE

The Tarascan kingdom is an example of secondary-state development among societies that were previously unstratified. While it exhibits charac-

teristics common to premodern complex societies that are highly centralized and rapidly expanding, it cannot be understood apart from its historical and ecological context.

Within the constraints of Mesoamerican geography and history, Tarascan
civilization represented significant innovation in the structure of political
power and territorial control, particularly in the fortified frontier maintained against the Aztec Empire. As one variant of archaic states it was
characterized by a primate capital with only weakly developed urbanism
elsewhere; full-time craft specialists who were associated with the royal
palace; household- and workshop-level production serving local and regional markets; a geopolitical core that was spatially and demographically
small relative to the territory under control, yet dependent on territorial
tribute for basic resources; an ethnically homogeneous economic heartland
surrounded by multiethnic communities along the military frontiers; and
an extremely high degree of centralization of administrative and judicial
functions, reinforced by the interweaving of state and religious authority.

When the productive resources of the Tarascan core are compared to
those of other Postclassic Mesoamerican cultural heartlands, some of the
characteristics can be viewed as adaptive responses or solutions to stresses
felt during the Early Postclassic (table 8.3). These stresses may have
included resource shifts within the Pátzcuaro lake basin and population
movements into central Michoacán. In table 8.3, general characteristics of
four Postclassic political cores have been compared (Basin of Mexico, Valley
of Oaxaca, central Quiché, Pátzcuaro Basin). While all are considered
highland, they are noteworthy for their differences. The Pátzcuaro Basin is
distinguished by the relatively low risk of its agriculture and the small
amount of class 1 (irrigable) land. The population levels at which stress,
when it occurred, would be sufficient to stimulate change would have been
relatively high in populations within and adjacent to the basin proper,
which may be part of the reason for the slow pace at which basin elites
actively seized and held their neighbors' lands. Minor fluctuations in
rainfall and rates of soil erosion in earlier centuries could have led to out-
migration and/or economic specialization. The RM indicates that by the
Early Postclassic, populations were meeting such environmental stresses by
means such as selling oneself as a slave to another society, increased economic
specialization in lacustrine resources (especially fishing), and raiding/
seizing irrigable lands. Such responses stimulated dependence upon markets and increased rates of social differentiation, and rewarded those elites
who could effectively organize large raiding parties. In the absence of large
quantities of irrigable land or other intensifiable agricultural resources,
economic risk could be reduced only by seizing additional resources outside

Table 8.3 Agrarian Ecology of Postclassic (Late Horizon) Centralized Polities

| | Basin of Mexico (Sanders, Parsons, and Santley 1979) | Valley of Oaxaca (Kirby 1973) | Pátzcuaro Basin (Gorenstein and Pollard 1983) | Central Quiché (Carmack 1981; Brown 1982) |
|---|---|---|---|---|
| Area (sq km) | 7,000 | 3,600 | 928 | 750 |
| Lake area (percent basin area) | 1,000 (14.3) | — | 136 (14.6) | — |
| Area cultivated (percent basin area) | 2,500 (36.0) | 800 (22.0) | 421 (45.0) | 345 (46.0) |
| Current annual rainfall* (average mm) | 450–1500 (most agricultural land: 600–1,000) | 400–800 | 900–1,250 | 1,200–1,500 |
| Class 1 land: irrigated, 2000+ kg/ha yield (percent basin area) | 1,080 (15.4) | 210 (6.0) | 5.3 (0.6) | — |
| Class 2 land: lakeshore, no fallow; irrigated; 1200–2000 kg/ha yield (percent basin area) | 332 (5.0) | 200 (5.5) | 119 (13.0) | 84 (11.0) |
| Agricultural risk | Moderate to high | High | Low to moderate | Low |
| Class 1 and 2 land with low risk (percent basin area) | 425 (6.0) | 210 (6.0) | 124.3 (13.6) | 84 (11.0) |

*Sources*

*Mexico.* Sanders, Parsons, and Santley 1979:table 9.3. Class 1 includes chinampas, permanent, and seasonal irrigated land. Class 2 includes lakeshore, high water table, floodplain, and upper alluvium lands. Low risk includes all class 1 minus seasonally irrigated lands.

*Oaxaca.* Kirby 1973:fig. 27 for A.D. 900 to contact. Class 1 includes irrigated lands with 2,000 kg/ha yield from bar graphs. Class 2 includes lands with yields of 1,200–2,000 kg/ha. Low risk includes only those irrigated permanently and with good floodwater.

Table 8.3  *Continued*

*Pátzcuaro*. Gorenstein and Pollard (1983:146–47). Class 1 and 2 categories used intact. Low risk includes all Class 1 and 2.

*Quiché*. Brown (1982:36); Carmack (1981:table 4.3). Class 1 includes all land irrigated (none). Class 2 includes all land in "flat" zone. Total cultivated includes all land in "flat" and "hilly" zones. Low risk includes all Class 1 and 2 land.

*Rainfall probably was greater during Postclassic.

the Pátzcuaro Basin. With a large enough labor supply to mount effective campaigns, but not large enough to colonize other regions, the basin elite tapped into existing local community networks and focused them into a central tributary hierarchy. The brilliant transformation of raiding into conquest, credited to their culture-hero, Taríacuri, provided the economic basis for the expansion of the size and power of the elite.

But ecological potential alone cannot explain the emergence and structure of the Tarascan state. While the prehistory of western Mexico is still poorly understood, it is clear that during the Classic period parts of Michoacán were incorporated into the economic and/or political periphery of Teotihuacan. By the Late Classic, central Michoacán was located between the economic centers of Teuchitlán to the west in Jalisco, and the Matlatzinca centers in the Toluca Basin to the east. During the Epiclassic period (A.D. 700–900), some portions of Michoacán were still part of the economic periphery of central Mexico. Indeed, during this time the northeast, including the Cuitzeo Basin, may have become more directly tied to Toltec economic networks. Between A.D. 1000 and 1200, the Teuchitlán polity to the west and then the Toltec polity to the east lost their political centrality, triggering population movements and political instability. It is probable that for the first time since the Late Preclassic period, large portions of Michoacán were not part of the hinterlands of empires to the east or west.

The precise means by which Michoacán was transformed from a Mesoamerican periphery into a Mesoamerican core has yet to be understood. Indeed, even the basic chronology of this transformation has yet to be determined. The study of this particular archaic state, or premodern civilization, highlights the parallel processes of change associated with state emergence while demonstrating what Stephen J. Gould has referred to as the "contingent" nature of evolution.

Taríacuri's legacy was a new Mesoamerican civilization, as unique and valuable a contribution to humanity *for* its uniqueness as *purépecha* culture is today. But the means by which Tarascans negotiated for power among themselves and their neighbors reflect commonalities of social change. As modern Tarascans redefine their relationship to the Mexican state, they are continuing this process of negotiation, building upon their prehistoric and historic heritage, and still wrestling with the problems of agricultural development and powerful neighbors to the east.

# APPENDIX 1

# TZINTZUNTZAN
# ARCHAEOLOGICAL SURVEY

THE following list of sites corresponds to the numbers found on the detailed survey map (map 2.1). Sites were defined by concentrations of artifacts that were isolable as spatial units, and then consecutively numbered. Due to the aims of the survey, an effort was made to separate site areas whenever feasible. Roads, walls, field terraces, and gullies were used to arbitrarily separate the surface into smaller collection units. A grid plan was not used due to the irregular topography, high degree of soil erosion, and time available for field research. There is no implication that as single entities they necessarily represent structural or functional units of the Protohistoric settlement.

In general, sites are located in recently plowed fields where artificial disturbance of the soil has been great. Natural disturbance in the form of soil erosion has been extensive. Finally, modern residents dig in the fields for "idols," which they sell in the local market to tourists. Several such holes were pointed out to me along the slopes of Cerro Tariácuri, as they were to Carl Lumholtz at the turn of the century (1902). These holes and others located near Ojo de Agua appear to have been burials in the rear of residential terraces.

At many sites there appears to be a distributional association between artifact concentrations and basalt stone occurrence. In some fields these stones have been piled up in the center; similar stones are used as field dividers and walls throughout the region. Illustrations in the RM (1956) suggest they are the remains of Proto-historic building foundations (see chapter 3).

Sites were classified according to density of artifact concentration as follows: light, 5–20 artifacts per m sq; medium, 20–60; heavy, 60 and above. These classifications were based on visible artifacts and do not reflect absolute numbers of artifacts on or below the surface. The red clay base of most sites (*charánda* soil) clung to artifacts and thus often obscured them. The classification is only intended as a general guideline. Concentrations that varied within one site are noted by dual terms, such as light-medium; those with fewer than 5 artifacts per m sq are denoted on the map as *artifact scatters*.

The presence of glazed historic and modern pottery in many fields has not been included in the site descriptions. While in some cases it may reflect later habitation, in general it is a product of mixing when manure (taken from town houselots) is dumped onto fields. After one season of plowing, the sherds become completely mixed with in situ deposits.

At the end of each site description, there is a letter corresponding to the type of urban zone in which the site has been placed:

Ri   Residential type i (low-status residential)
Rii   Residential type ii (high-status residential)
Riii   Residential type iii (middle-status residential)
Li   Lithic workshop type 1 (manufacturing: blades)
Lii   Lithic workshop type 2 (manufacturing: nonutilitarian)
Liii   Lithic workshop type 3 (manufacturing: scrapers)
Pi   Religious—primary (public zone)
Pii   Religious—secondary (public zone)

*Tz-1.* Rectangular plowed terrace 3.0–5.0 m above level of main platform (Tz-25). An undressed basalt stone retaining wall separates this terrace from the platform below. Artifacts: light-medium. Pi.

*Tz-2.* Located within area of Tz-25. Large plowed field behind Yacatas 1 and 2. Artifacts: light. A low rise 30.0 m in diameter and 1.0 m high in center may indicate the remains of a structure. Pi.

*Tz-3.* Within plowed field at north edge of terrace upon which Tz-1 is located. 100.0 m by 50.0 m artifact concentration with heavy basalt stone concentration. Artifacts: medium. Soil is reddish brown clay found throughout sites 1–12, 25, and 26 on Cerro Yaguarato. Tests indicate depth of deposit averages 0.30 m. Pi.

*Tz-4.* Part of Tz-7. Western edge of large plowed field. This is a light artifact concentration over a 6 m by 5 m area. Originally it was defined as a separate unit when a circular structure was found. Subsequent excavation revealed it to be a wheat-threshing floor of late Colonial or recent age.

*Tz-5.* Large sloping field immediately above terrace upon which Tz-1 and Tz-2 are situated. Artifacts: medium. Obsidian concentration heavier than average. Li.

*Tz-6.* Portion of large terraced field. Artifacts: light-medium. Pi.

*Tz-7.* Large field incorporating Tz-4. Artifacts: light-medium, obsidian heavier than ceramic. Pi.

*Tz-8.* Large field on same terrace as Tz-9 and Tz-6. Artifacts: medium, heavy in obsidian flakes, blades and scrapers, and ceramic pipes. Pi.

*Tz-9.* Northern continuation of Tz-8. Artifacts: medium, heavy in obsidian flakes, blades, and cores. The remnant of a cobbled road runs between Tz-8 and Tz-9, and Tz-10. Heavier than usual basalt stone concentration. Pi.

*Tz-10.* Rectangular terrace above Tz-8 and Tz-9, 250 m north-south and 50 m east-west. Artifacts: medium heavy, heavy on northern end of terrace. Two square-based undressed basalt stone piles are located in the center of the terrace. The terrace has been plowed up to the bases of these structural remnants. Any facing that may have been on them is gone; they are heavily overgrown and damage by tree roots, and stone removal reveals a rubble core.

They are the Yácatas 6 and 7 described by Ramón Gali (1946:57–59) with the following dimensions (recorded by Gali and verfied by me):

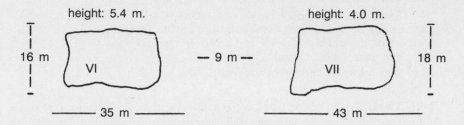

height: 5.4 m.          height: 4.0 m.

16 m    VI      — 9 m —        VII      18 m

——— 35 m ———        ——— 43 m ———

Foster (1948:25) presumed that one was a Colonial chapel. The resemblance of both to the reconstructed platforms at Ihuatzio (Acosta 1939) and the depiction of two structures in similar locational orientation to the main platform (Tz-25) on the third Beaumont map (Seler 1908) suggest that they are in fact associated with the structures of prehispanic Tzintzuntzan. Published references: Gali (1946), Marquina (1964). Lii and Pi.

*Tz-11.* Located in large plowed field immediately southwest of main platform (Tz-25). Artifacts: medium-heavy. Unusually large number of pipe fragments in eastern section. There may be a 30–50 cm depth of deposit, but continual plowing has disturbed the site. There is extensive gullying surrounding the site. Riii.

*Tz-12.* In a large plowed field south of Tz-11 is the heaviest surface concentration of artifacts for the entire survey zone. The area of Tz-12, Tz-13, and Tz-14 was separated into three different sites on the basis of a stone field marker and natural gullying. Unlike the previously described sites, the natural inclination of the land is small, and no artificial terracing is found. The artifact concentration at Tz-12 is very heavy, and at Tz-13 and Tz-14 is medium. The obsidian is particularly well represented by blades and finished tools such as scrapers, notched tools, and small projectile points. The ceramics include large quantities of pipes and pipe fragments, polychrome sherds, and miniature vessels. Ground stone artifacts such as mano and metate fragments were present. A depth of 30 cm is the estimated maximum depth of the deposits. Rii.

*Tz-13.* See description Tz-12. Rii or Riii.

*Tz-14.* See description Tz-12. Riii. A portion of this site was paved over to form the parking area for the Zona Arqueología after this survey was completed. It is not known how many of the adjacent sites were disturbed.

*Tz-15.* Located along the steep slope of Cerro Taríacuri above the second platform (Tz-29, Santa Ana), this site occupies several narrowly terraced fields. Artifacts: light-medium. Rii.

*Tz-16*.  Located east of Tz-15, it occupies a 200 m by 100 m area of terraced fields on a curving knoll of Cerro Taríacuri. Artifacts: heavy, with signs of potholing in rear portions of fields. Several metate fragments were noted. Rii.

*Tz-17*.  In a series of terraced fields adjacent to Tz-16 are heavy and medium artifact concentrations. The artifacts are particularly heavy in polychrome sherds and light on pipes and pipe fragments. The depth of deposit varies and goes up to 50 cm. There has been much potholing in this site. It is probably the location of the Santa Ana test pit by Noguera (1931). Tz-85 is almost contiguous with the upper extension of the site. Rii.

*Tz-18*.  Located at the base of the Santa Ana platform retaining wall (Tz-29), this 50 m by 20 m heavy artifact concentration is noteworthy in several respects. In the immediate area are no more than scatters of artifacts, although this site is small and heavy in concentration. There is little obsidian and few pipes or pipe fragments, but unusual ceramic shapes and decorations. Rii.

*Tz-19*.  In this plowed field behind the modern cemetery is a light-medium artifact concentration, heaviest in the southwest portion. Ri.

*Tz-20*.  Large plowed field separated from Tz-19 by remnants of early Colonial cobbled road. Artifacts: medium-heavy. Riii.

*Tz-21*.  Small plowed field with few decorated sherds. Artifacts: light-medium. Ri.

*Tz-22*.  Together with Tz-23 there is a medium-heavy and heavy artifact concentration in plowed fields along the slope of Cerro Tariácuri immediately behind the church courtyard. Only 10 cm of deposit noted. Riii.

*Tz-23*.  See Tz-22. Riii.

*Tz-24*.  Located on the steep slope of Cerro Tariácuari, this 150 m by 15 m site contains a medium artifact concentration. It is heavy in obsidian, particularly flakes, with some decorated pottery. The site curves around a knoll to face a gully. The soil is gravelly yellow clay. There is no depth of deposit. Lii.

*Tz-25*.  Tz-2 and Tz-26 included in this zone. Commonly called the main platform or central plaza of Tzintzuntzan, it constitutes the Zona Arqueología of the Instituto Nacional de Antropología e Historia (INAH). The author did no primary research at this site except to verify measurements and locations of published material. A map was made at this time, although subsequent work by INAH has altered some parts (see below). Previous publications of the excavations by INAH should be consulted for detailed descriptions of the site and their excavations: Noguera 1931; Acosta 1939; Rubín de la Borbolla 1939, 1941, 1944; Gali 1946; Marquina 1964; Piña Chan 1963, 1977; Cabrera Castro 1987).

The site consists of a large artificial platform, 450 m by 250 m, built on to the lower slope of Cerro Yaguarato. It is of rubble on the inside and faced with stacked tabular basalt. There is no visible facing on the top of the platform, although occasional patches of tabular basalt suggest it was faced (or paved). The sides of the platform were probably vertical or steeply stepped. The front of the platform drops in steps 0.9 m high and 0.2 m wide. After three such steps from the top, there is a 2.1

m wide step which is superimposed over the remaining steps. On the center front of the platform is a ramp which extends in a series of sloping terraces toward the northwest. At the top of the ramp on the south side is the remains of a square structure 3.8 m square; on the north side is a reconstructed room 4.8 by 5.7 m containing a rectangular stone ring 0.8 m by 0.6 m and 0.15 m high. Adjacent to this room is a reconstructed stairway (six steps, 13 m wide) on one side of the ramp.

There are five stone platforms or *yácatas* located along the east side of the platform surface. They consist of rubble core mounds faced with dressed basalt slabs (*xanamu*). On several of these slabs are petroglyphs of spirals, circles (bull's-eyes), and eccentrics. Slabs used in the facing of the Colonial churches of Tzintzuntzan also have such designs. The *yácatas* are believed to have originally been rectangles with stairs facing toward the center of the platform; on the west side are circular extensions giving "T" or keyhole shapes to the wholes. The facing of the bodies are of twelve stone steps, each approximately 1.0 m high and 0.3 m wide. At least four and maybe five superpositions are visible on Yácata 5 and Yácata 2, although Cabrera Castro (1987:536) suggests that these are not true superpositions but part of the construction technique. The maximum dimensions of Yácata 5 are 65.75 m long, 42.6 m wide, 22.1 m wide for the rectangular portion alone, 38.9 m diameter of circular section, and 13 m high. It was reconstructed by the INAH from 1939 to 1945. Since then Yácata 1 has been reconstructed under Román Piña Chan (1964) and portions of Yácatas 2, 3, and 4 under Rubén Cabrera Castro (1977–1978). Yácata 3 was almost completely destroyed by Trespena in 1852, and Yácata 2 was severely damaged by Hartford in 1888, making accurate reconstruction very difficult.

A tunnel into and under Yácata 5 revealed the facing of another *yácata*, called 5-A, beneath it. The walls of several superimposed structures were excavated adjacent to Yácata 5 (Edificio A and Edificio C), and small test pits revealed burials around the base of this *yácata*. In the 1977–1978 excavations portions of an earlier platform edge and substructure of Yácata 3 were revealed (Cabrera Castro 1987:538–43). The bases of these were found resting on the original rocky surface of Cerro Yaguarato. The earlier structure had a circular portion, indicating that it was probably in the *yácata*-shape, although the smaller size of the overall platform may mean that there were not five temple structures at this earlier time. While few of the results of excavations since 1946 have been published (including field seasons in 1956, 1962–1964, 1968, and 1977–1978), Marcia Castro-Leal (1986) and Rubén Cabrera Castro (1987) have summarized some of the material. By 1968, forty-four burials had been excavated, including two clusters of multiple burials and several offering caches (according to Cabrera Castro, only forty-one had been excavated). During the 1977–1978 season, seventeen additional burials were excavated. Most of these were found adjacent to the base of the *yácatas*, and many were disturbed, possibly due to early Colonial looting.

Northeast of Yácata 5 are excavated remains of Edificio B ("El Palacio"), a series of rooms of dressed and undressed stone walls. A patio within contained two columns and a slightly raised central platform that contained several burials. Within the walls have been found other burials, and a piece of sculpture was located in the southwest zone. An ossuary was located off the northeast side of the platform, as well as a series of terraced rooms.

Low rises in the platform surface (less than 1.0 m high) were located along the rear edge of the plaza. Piña Chan (personal communication, 1970) agrees that they probably indicate structural remains. Tz-26 is one such rise that exhibits a high concentration of stone over the surface. In 1977–1978 this area was excavated under Cabrera Castro and designated Edificio E. The remains of five rooms were found, and, although the contents have yet to be studied, Cabrera Castro (1987:549) suggests they may have been storerooms for materials used in temple activities.

At the time of the 1942 aerial photographs, the plaza was entirely under cultivation. In 1970 half of the plaza was covered by trees with no visible artifacts. The town soccer field has been relocated from adjacent to the churchyard to the main plaza directly behind the *yácatas*. Pi.

*Tz-26.* See description Tz-25. Pi.

*Tz-27.* Land immediately surrounding chapel in barrio of Ojo de Agua. Artifacts: light. Deposits of up to 1 m are visible in barrancas and ditches between the paved road and the chapel. Pii.

*Tz-28.* The site appears to be an erosional remnant between the paved road and a cobbled road, 75 m by 25 m. Artifacts: medium. Riii.

*Tz-29.* Artificial platform 300 m east-west by 125 m north-south. Referred to as Santa Ana platform owing to presence of remains of a Colonial chapel of Santa Ana on its surface (founded 1525). A portion of the front face has been cleared and reveals a stepped surface of stacked basalt such as is found on Tz-25. There is a light artifact concentration on the surface. Two stone piles of no recognizable shape are located on the platform. One bears a cross and remains of mortared walls, indicating it is the chapel remains. The platform is depicted on the Beaumont map adjacent to the Santa Ana chapel and labeled "Yácata del Rey." During the 1968 field season, under Román Piña Chan, Colonial-period ceramics were found adjacent to the structure believed to be the remains of the Santa Ana chapel. It was at this time that the two mounds were cleared and clearing of the face of the platform was begun. Rii.

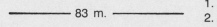

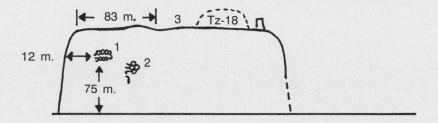

1. rubble 2 m high
2. remains of chapel
3. four stepped faces
   0.9 m high (each)

*Tz-30.* Medium artifact concentration, 50 m diameter, in plowed field; probably an extension of Tz-20. Riii.

*Tz-31.* In large field adjacent to modern town on flat land below slope of Cerro Tariacuri. Artifacts: medium. Ri.

*Tz-32.* Medium-heavy artifact concentration in terraced field above Tz-31. Potholes appear against a stone wall at the south end of the site. A small test pit of 15 cm by 15 cm was made in the north center of the field next to the wall separating it from another field. Ri.

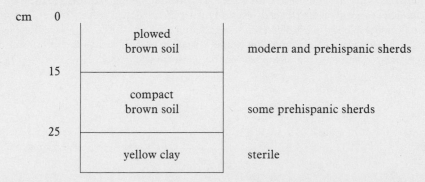

*Tz-33.* Light-medium artifact concentration in plowed field adjacent to Tz-32 and Tz-34. Ri.

*Tz-34.* Light artifact concentration in two plowed and terraced fields. Ri.

*Tz-35.* Light artifact concentration in west portion of two terraced fields directly above Tz-34. Ri.

*Tz-36.* Light artifact concentration similar to Tz-24. Unusually high proportion of obsidian, especially large flakes. Ri.

*Tz-37.* Light artifact concentration in several terraced fields above Tz-35. Ri.

*Tz-38.* Light-medium artifact concentration in several terraced fields. Ri.

*Tz-39.* Light-medium artifact concentration in several terraced fields. Ri.

*Tz-40.* Light artifact concentration. Probably continuation of Tz-38. Ri.

*Tz-41.* Medium artifact concentration in terraced field. More pipes and pipe fragments and decorated sherds than in adjacent sites. Pii.

*Tz-42.* Medium artifact concentration in small field and scrub land near quebrada. Heavy concentration of obsidian, especially scrapers. The field has a fairly steep slope. Liii.

*Tz-43.* Light-medium artifact concentration in field immediately above Tz-42. Contains greater proportion of obsidian then ceramics. Metate fragment noted. Ri.

*Tz-44.* Light artifact concentration in terraced field. Ri.

*Tz-45.* Light artifact concentration in terraced field. Ri.

*Tz-46.* Light-medium artifact concentration in lower fields above modern town. Extensive gullying around site probably has altered extension. Ri.

*Tz-47.* Medium artifact concentration in fallow field. Heavy stone concentration of basalt cobbles. The soil is rapidly eroding. Ri.

*Tz-48.* Light artifact concentration in large plowed field. Some obsidian and basalt, but ceramics predominate. Ri.

*Tz-49.* Light-medium artifact concentration in large rectangular field. Besides the stone wall separating the field above, there is a retaining wall at the rear of part of the field. The slope of Cerro Tariácuri becomes increasingly steep at this portion of the survey zone. Ri.

*Tz-50.* Light artifact concentration in field above Tz-49. Ri.

*Tz-51.* Light-medium artifact concentration located in field at base of steeply inclined slope above Tz-50. Ri.

*Tz-52.* Medium-light artifact concentration at western limit of survey zone. Sherds are small, and there is limited quantity of basalt and obsidian. Ri.

*Tz-53.* Medium-heavy artifact concentration in plowed fields and eroded scrub land. Adjacent to the spring at Ojo de Agua. Considerable potting by local inhabitants. Several holes still containing human bones were pointed out by one inhabitant. A similar hole, more than 1 m deep, was located within the garden plot of this informant immediately below the designated area of Tz-53. Appear to be many burial depressions rather than a midden deposit. This may be the San Bartolo barrio referred to by Foster (1948) and the local informant. The informant, whose primary language (and his parents' only language) is Tarascan, indicated that the entire zone around the chapel of Ojo de Agua has been heavily collected for "idolos." Only small quantities of obsidian were noted. Pii.

*Tz-54.* Light-medium artifact concentration in plowed field adjacent to Tz-53. See description above. Ri.

*Tz-55.* Light-medium artifact concentration in entire large field immediately above Tz-54. Ri.

*Tz-56.* Medium-heavy artifact concentration in sloping area of field and scrub. Only a few centimeters of depth to the deposits noted. Large quantity of pipe and pipe fragments. Pii.

*Tz-57.* Medium artifact concentration in two remnant fields in heavily eroded area. Ri.

*Tz-58.* Light artifact concentration in heavily gullied fields. Ri.

*Tz-59.* Medium-heavy artifact concentration in large field and eroding scrub vegetation zone. The yellow-brown soil may contain up to 10 cm of artifact depth. A small test pit immediately adjacent to a looter's hole revealed sterile soil almost immediately, suggesting that the many signs of potholing over the site reflect small burials, rather than uniform deposition. Very heavy in ceramics, especially polychrome. Riii.

*Tz-60.* Small light artifact concentration in heavily eroded area. Only 5 cm deposit noted. Ri.

*Tz-61.* Medium and heavy artifact concentration in series of plowed and terraced fields. The concentration is heaviest along the eastern portions of the site. Li.

*Tz-62.* Medium-light artifact concentration in heavily eroded area. The artifacts are eroding out of the surface as the soil washes away. Adjacent to this site artifacts were seen mixed in a 45 cm layer in the wall of an arroyo. This layer rests immediately upon a red clay base. Ri.

*Tz-63.* Medium-heavy artifact concentration in fallow field. Little obsidian or basalt noted. Riii.

*Tz-64.* Light-medium artifact concentration in plowed and terraced field. Riii.

*Tz-65.* Light artifact concentration at eastern end of plowed and terraced field. Riii.

*Tz-66.* Two large mounds of rock and clay are located in adjacent fields with light artifact concentrations. Because the mounds are very much destroyed, their shape is difficult to determine. They appear to be very similar however to the mounds of Tz-10. There is no exterior facing. As a result of the "mining" of one mound, the interior structure of carefully stacked, tabular basalt stones is visible. Within the west mound, a clay layer 30 cm from the top was noted. They are located within 100 m of the northern edge of the main platform (Tz-25) and may be in association with it. The third Beaumont map (1932) shows two structures in this relationship to the platform. Pi.

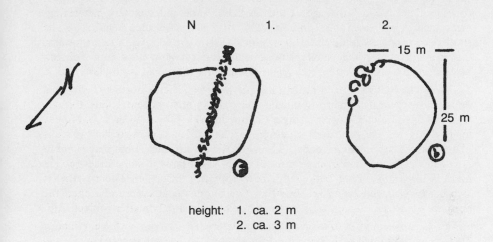

height:  1. ca. 2 m
         2. ca. 3 m

*Tz-67.*  Light-medium artifact concentration in plowed field adjacent to Tz-66. Ri.

*Tz-68.*  Medium artifact concentration in two fields below Tz-67. Ri.

*Tz-69.*  Light artifact concentration north of Tz-68 in northern zones of same fields. Riii.

*Tz-70.*  Medium artifact concentration in large, eroded, uncultivated zone surrounded by deep gullies. There is more obsidian than in the previously described sites (Tz-60–68), and very little decorated pottery. Ri.

*Tz-71.*  Light artifact concentration in portion of eroding land adjacent to Tz-70. Ri.

*Tz-72.*  Medium artifact concentration in plowed field 100 m north of main platform (Tz-25). Ri.

*Tz-73.*  Light artifact concentration in plowed and terraced field. Ri.

*Tz-74.*  Light artifact concentration in plowed field. Ri.

*Tz-75.*  Medium artifact concentration in heavily eroded fallow and plowed fields. Up to 5 cm depth of deposit visible. Li.

*Tz-76.*  Medium artifact concentration in plowed field below cobbled road crossing zone. Ri.

*Tz-77.*  Light and medium artifact concentration distributed over series of terraced fields above Tz-12. Most of the area is uncultivated and covered with heavy scrub vegetation. Wherever there has been soil erosion, and thus no vegetation cover remains, medium concentrations of ceramic and lithic artifacts are visible on the clay base. Depth of deposit is estimated to be about 30 cm. Riii.

*Tz-78.*  Located above Tz-77, this site begins on the south end of the terrace on which

Tz-10 is situated and, although crossed by several arroyos, continues up the slope of Cerro Yaguarato without significant break in artifact concentration. The artifact concentration is medium throughout with much basalt, decorated pottery, metate fragments, and a few dressed stones in field walls, which may have come from Tz-10. The site appears to end at the top of the knoll, which levels off before sharply rising towards the mountain summit. Vegetation changes to a pine forest at this point. Depth of deposit may extend 20–30 cm. Petroglyphs reported from here (Cabrera Castro 1987). Riii.

*Tz-79.* Light artifact concentration in upper portion of fields northeast of chapel remains. Particularly rich in decorated pottery. Heavy rock concentrations. Excavations by INAH under Rubén Cabrera Castro, in 1977–1978, appear to have been made at this site. The excavated structure, termed Edificio F, consisted of two stone platforms containing four rooms. Three of the rooms were occupied contemporaneously, and their remains consisted of three contiguous stone bases (60 cm high) facing a stone paved patio with a hearth/altar in the center. This hearth was slab-lined, 20 cm high, and 72 cm by 90 cm. One burial was excavated adjacent to the entrance to room 3. Some Colonial remains indicate occupation after contact. Riii.

*Tz-80.* Light-medium artifact concentration in eroded area below chapel remains. Surface similar to that of Tz-77 and extremely thick with scrub vegetation. Riii.

*Tz-81.* Light artifact concentration in large plowed field on slopes of Cerro Tariácuari below Santa Ana platform (Tz-29). Ri.

*Tz-82.* Light-medium artifact concentration in eroded area adjacent to Tz-83. Riii.

*Tz-83.* Light-medium artifact concentration in terraced and plowed field below Tz-29. Riii.

*Tz-84.* Medium-light artifact concentration in small field above Tz-29. Rii.

*Tz-85.* Medium-heavy artifact concentration above Tz-29; particularly heavy in decorated pottery. The surface scatter continues down the slopes of Cerro Tariácuari to mesh with Tz-17. Compared to other sites in the adjacent slopes, this site and Tz-17 are unusually low in their numbers of pipes and pipe fragments. Rii.

*Tz-86.* Medium artifact concentration located on extreme southwest corner of platform of Santa Ana (Tz-29). Extends along slope connecting two terraces. Artifacts: medium with low obsidian quantities and much decorated pottery. Rii.

*Tz-87.* Medium-heavy artifact concentration in a plowed field below Santa Ana. Evidence of recent potting in back wall. Ri or Riii.

*Tz-88.* Medium-light artifact concentration in fallow field above Tz-87. Riii.

*Tz-89.* Medium artifact concentration in plowed field above Tz-88. Riii.

*Tz-90.* Medium artifact concentration in plowed and terraced field adjacent to Santa Ana platform (Tz-29). A deep quebrada runs between this site and Tz-86 and Tz-29. The remains of a cobbled road become indistinguishable from the quebrada at this point. Decorated pottery concentrated in northern end of site. Rii.

*Tz-91.* Medium-heavy artifact concentration in plowed and terraced field above Tz-90. Very heavy in polychrome and minibowl ceramics. Rii.

*Tz-92.* Medium-heavy artifact concentration in south end of plowed field between Tz-90 and Tz-91. Artifact scatter between these sites all along slope of Cerro Tariácuri. Ri.

*Tz-93.* Series of plowed and fallow fields in which are clusters of heavier artifact concentrations, especially in association with basalt stones. Artifacts: medium-light. In the area marked "A" is a heavy concentration of obsidian blades associated with some decorated pottery. The obsidian collection from this site comes from this area. The site is somewhat sloped here; it levels off just behind this area. At the crest of this rise are indications of recent looting of burials. Immediately behind these holes are the remains of a wall. About 15 cm is exposed, and another 15 cm was uncovered. Only about 1.5 m in length was visible. The wall is of unmortared stacked basalt, similar in composition to the platform retaining walls at sites Tz-25 and Tz-29. The wall contained two steps, each 15 cm high. Metate fragments were noted. Where not eroded, the deposit may extend to 10 cm in depth. Riii (Tz-93A is Li).

*Tz-94.* Medium-light artifact concentration in series of plowed and eroding fields below Tz-93. Probably continuation of Tz-93. Some heavy artifact clusters noted within area of site. Ri.

*Tz-95.* Small light artifact concentration in center of large plowed field on slopes of Cerro Yaguarato. The only stones in the adjacent fields are clustered here. Some recent potting holes are in the rear of the terrace. Ri.

*Tz-96.* Large light artifact concentration in plowed field. Ri.

*Tz-97.* Light-medium artifact concentration above Tz-96 near survey limit of Cerro Yaguarato. Unusually high numbers of obsidian scrapers with some decorated pottery and pipes and pipe fragments. Liii.

*Tz-98.* Medium artifact concentration in heavily eroded area south of Tz-97. Ri.

*Tz-99.* Medium artifact concentration in fallow and eroded field south of Tz-98. Adjacent to a wide, deep aroyo, the site is almost an erosional remnant above the remaining fields. An extremely high concentration of obsidian debitage almost forms a pavement of obsidian for 2 m sq. Li.

*Tz-100.* Medium artifact concentration in several plowed fields. Ri.

*Tz-101.* Light-medium artifact concentration in scrub vegetation south of Tz-100. There is a higher proportion of obsidian than ceramic artifacts, especially wherever the vegetation cover has been eroded. Ri.

*Tz-102.* Light-medium artifact concentration in unplowed area. The site is located on a small rise between two arroyos, in a very eroded zone. Ri.

*Tz-103.* Light-medium artifact concentration on eroded scrub vegetation. Located south of Tz-102. Ri.

*Tz-104.* Light artifact concentration in large plowed field adjacent to paved road. It also is immediately contiguous to the cobbled road, which parallels the paved one at this point. The concentration of artifacts is medium in the west end of the site; wherever the soil cover is lost, obsidian and ceramics are visible. Riii.

*Tz-105.* Heavy artifact concentration in several plowed fields southeast of Tz-104. Very heavy in obsidian debitage, flakes, and use of red obsidian. Deposit estimated to 15 cm. Lii.

*Tz-106.* Light artifact concentration in plowed fields just below beginning of pine vegetation. Ri.

*Tz-107.* Medium-heavy artifact concentration in long narrow plowed field separated from Tz-106 by small gully. Several manos were noted. Ri.

*Tz-108.* Light-medium artifact concentration in two large plowed fields below Tz-105. A cluster of basalt stones is in the fields. Behind the site there is a small cave. A small test pit was put in the cave entrance, but no refuse was located. In the southwest part of the site are two large basalt boulders covered with petroglyphs. The motifs appear similar to those reported from the main platform *yácata* facing stones (Acosta 1939) and from an arroyo adjacent to the main platform (Gali 1946). Ri.

*Tz-109.* Medium artifact concentration in long narrow plowed field located between paved road and cobbled road southwest of Tz-108. Ri or Riii.

*Tz-110.* Light artifact concentration in plowed field. Clusters of basalt stones are in the field. A small collection was made from an erosional remnant just north of the site and labeled Tz-110A. The deposit may be 15 cm deep, although the extensive erosion in the entire zone makes such estimates highly unreliable. Ri.

*Tz-111.* Light artifact concentration in two plowed fields and adjacent arroyo. In the northeast corner of the lower field are bone fragments that might be human. Local tradition (as recounted by one farmer) considers this site the location of an early chapel and the beginning of the prehispanic San Juan barrio. Pii.

*Tz-112.* Medium-heavy artifact concentration in large flat plowed field. The paved road crosses the site, which is especially heavy in pipes and pipe fragments and polychrome pottery. Riii.

*Tz-113.* Light artifact concentration in plowed field separated from Tz-112 by large arroyo. Ri.

*Tz-114.* Light-medium artifact concentration in plowed field above Tz-113. Clusters of basalt stones were noted. Ri or Riii.

*Tz-115.* Heavy artifact concentration located in eroded area west of Cerro Colorado. In a 3 m sq area is an obsidian pavement containing both red and gray-black obsidian. Lii.

*Tz-116.* In a very eroded area west and south of Cerro Colorado is a light artifact concentration. Scrub vegetation mixed with arroyos made it very difficult to judge the concentration of artifacts, which included pipes and pipe fragments, obsidian flakes and blades, and polychrome pottery. Local farmers ascribed this area to the San Lorenzo barrio of the early Colonial period. During the survey two different red clay mines, still in use, were located in this zone. During the 1970s Cerro Colorado was mined for gravel deposits used in road construction, and more than half of the hill was destroyed. Ri.

*Tz-117.* Light-medium artifact concentration in large flat plowed field south of Tz-112. It was arbitrarily separated from Tz-112, although the artifacts evince a continuous distribution. There are six possible structural remnants at this site. Structure 1 consists of a large rubble pile, which rises on its north side more than 2 m above the field level. Trees and brush are growing on top. It measures 15 m east-west and 10 m north-south. It appears very similar to the remains of sites Tz-10 and Tz-66. Structures 2–6 are low rises covered with rocks. They rise from 0.6 m to 0.9 m and have approximately 15 m diameters. Because of the slope of the plain from Cerro Colorado to the lake, from these features one can see the main platform on approximately eye level. Pii.

*Tz-118.* Light-medium artifact concentration in plowed field surrounded by arroyos east of Tz-117. Riii.

*Tz-119.* Medium artifact concentration with heavy clusters toward southwest end of site. Probably continuation of Tz-112 and Tz-117. Contains large amounts of obsidian, pipes and pipe fragments, and polychrome pottery. Riii.

*Tz-120.* Light-medium artifact concentration in plowed field south of Tz-119. Riii.

# APPENDIX 2

# TZINTZUNTZAN
# THE CERAMIC ARTIFACTS

AS part of the surface survey of Tzintzuntzan in 1970, ceramic collections were made from 88 of the 120 sites recorded (fig. A.2.1). Some sites, such as the two large artificial platforms (Tz-25, Tz-29), had been previously entirely stripped of artifacts. Under the terms of my permit with INAH, and with a small field budget, a deliberate effort was made to keep the size of the collections small.

This limitation, plus the greatly disturbed nature of the sites, led to a decision to use nonrandom sampling that would maximize information about possible temporal and social variation. Considering the small samples that were to be made, it was felt that random collections could easily miss significant variance. An effort was made to collect examples of the range of artifacts in roughly the proportion of their occurrence at the sites by eyeballing. Artifacts that might be particularly diagnostic, especially decorated pottery, were then added to the collections. The result has been an overrepresentation of polychrome and rim sherds, although plainware was collected from all sites. This, combined with the relatively small sample sizes, makes statistical analysis of the collection impossible.

To derive the maximum information from the collection, two classificatory procedures were undertaken. The first, an analytic classification, involves the isolation of modes (Rouse 1960). A mode is a "selected attribute or cluster of attributes which display significance in their own right" (Sabloff and Smith 1969:279). The second is a form of taxonomic classification that has been utilized extensively in Mesoamerica, the type-variety system, in which wares, groups, types, and varieties are distinguished by the sharing or lack of sharing of similar states of particular attributes. The attributes utilized include ware: paste composition and surface finish; types: vessel form and decorative technique; varieties: minor variations in vessel form, decorative technique, or decorative style; and group: closely related types sharing vessel form and surface color. Due to the size of the collection, only wares and groups were named and described in detail.

In the analysis of this collection the first attribute which divided material was the paste, followed by the surface finish, particularly slip color, and then decoration and vessel forms. Due to the small size of the collection and the fragmentary nature of the sherds, the presence/absence of slip and the color of slip was not sufficient to create new wares, but only to distinguish groups within wares. In this way sherds that have come from the same vessel, only part of which was slipped, or from vessels that had polychrome decoration on only a portion of the surface, would not be separated. This means that several of the wares listed below include similar polychrome decoration,

Fig. A.2.1. Tzintzuntzan polychrome pottery.

for example, but on vessels made of different pastes. A common form of ceramic analysis in Mexico uses the paint and slip color as the primary attributes to distinguish wares, with rather large ranges of paste variation in each one. To make my analysis comparable to other studies, I have indicated, where possible, the equivalent name for the ceramic groups defined by Castro Leal (1986) in her study of material from test pits 36 and 37 (adjacent to Yácata 2 on the main platform, Tzintzuntzan) and from the burials excavated at the same time (1962–1964), and from Moguel Cos (1985) in her analysis of ceramics collected during the surface survey of the Pátzcuaro and Zirahuen basins as part of the Salvage Gasoducto project. Their analyses combine portions of the modal and taxonomic classifications used here. However, it means that some of their types, such as "polychrome," cross-cut several different ceramic groups. In addition, given the extremely small size of the Moguel Cos sample (fewer than 2,600 sherds for more than one hundred sites in two lake basins) and the restricted sample of the Castro-Leal study (from the main ceremonial platform) it is not surprising that several wares and groups are not represented at all in these other studies.

The various wares and groups presented below are believed to have composed the range of ceramic variation represented at Protohistoric-period Tzintzuntzan (1450–1520). The dating of these materials is based upon three separate lines of evidence: the published ceramic study by Castro-Leal (1986) based on stratified material from INAH excavations on the main platform (Tz-25); the widespread distribution of ceramic wares and types collected in the surface survey, in which most groups are represented at most sites; and the depiction of ceramic vessel forms and decoration in illustrations of the RM (1956, 1980). In addition, the one spatially restricted ware (Querenda White) has been cross-dated to the Protohistoric period at Acámbaro (Gorenstein 1985), and the identifiable nonlocal sherds are also dated to this period. The test pits used in Castro Leal's study were 50–60 cm in depth. They contained five stratified layers, representing perhaps successive modifications of the main pyramid platform. No clear pattern of ceramic change can be discerned, and most types are present in all layers. Several of the groups undoubtedly are continuations of material produced from at least the Late Postclassic, as early as 1300, but until systematic excavations away from the building fill on the main platform are undertaken and published, it is most reasonable to view the pottery as part of one ceramic complex.

# WARE

*Paste Attributes*
Color range (based on Munsell Soil Color Chart)
Texture (percent of inclusions): sparse <15 percent; moderate, 15–30 percent; heavy, >30 percent
Size of particles: fine, 0.01–0.25 mm; medium, 0.26–0.50 mm; coarse, 0.51–1.00 mm
Hardness (Moh's scale)
Firing (even-uneven)
Fracture (straight, irregular, friable)
Inclusions: types identified by I. M. Drew (then of the Sackler Laboratory, Columbia University). She concluded that except for sherd material, all inclusions are natural to the clay (personal communication, 1971).

*Surface Finish Attributes*
Slip (presence or absence; thickness; condition)
Color range (based on Munsell Soil Color Chart)
Hardness (Moh's scale)
Texture (smooth, rough, grainy)
Polish (matte, lustrous, highly lustrous, none)

*Group*
Decorative technique (see modal analysis below)
Vessel form (see modal analysis below)

*Ceramic Modes*
1. *Paste composition.* Eleven local wares defined; see description under typological analysis.
2. *Vessel form.*
   2.1 *bowls*

2.1.1 *convex wall bowls* Have a round/flat base; with/without supports; if with, are usually hollow-tripod supports up to 4.0 cm diameter at juncture with bowl. One tetrapod example. Rims are direct; lips are rounded, squared, and tapered. Diameters at the lips range from 15 to 45 cm; the 40–45 cm ones have a simple vertical handle or lug. Walls range from 0.4 cm to 1.2 cm thick.

2.1.2 *outsloping wall bowls* Walls are inclined outward in a straight line, probably associated with a flat base. Lips are beveled and tapered with diameters from 30 cm to 35 cm and walls from 0.4 cm to 0.6 cm thick.

2.1.3 *everted rim bowls* Have a pronounced bending out and extension of the rim; bases were probably rounded; lips are tapered or rounded. Diameters 12–25 cm and walls 0.4–0.7 cm thick.

2.1.4 *incurved rim bowls* An extreme form of convex wall bowl with the rim of a *tecomate*. Bases are rounded with/without basket handles. Lips are squared or bolstered (thickened); diameters at the lip are 10–30 cm and walls 0.8–0.9 cm thick.

2.1.5 *composite silhouette bowls* There is a sharp change in the curvature about 1.25 cm from the lip creating a shouldered vessel; with/without basket handles; some with a small convex protrusion between the shoulder and the lip. The bases are rounded; lips are rounded; diameters 10–12 cm and walls 0.2–0.6 cm thick.

2.1.6 *miniature bowls* They are a distinctive feature of the assemblage. They have rounded bases and tripod supports; diameters 3–6 cm, heights 2–3 cm, and walls 0.2–0.6 cm thick.

    2.1.6.1 *everted rim miniature bowls* Includes types A, B, and C of Moedano (1941:30).

    2.1.6.2 *convex wall miniature bowls* Includes type D of Moedano (1941:30).

    2.1.6.3 *flange wall miniature bowls* A small protrusion encircling the vessel 1.0 cm below the lip. Includes type E of Moedano (1941:30).

Smith and Hirth (1988) refer to Moedano's (1941:30) suggestion that the miniature bowls were used to anchor the spindles in the spinning of cotton yarn. The miniature bowls from Tzintzuntzan, both those excavated by INAH and those collected during my surface survey, are all 3–6 cm in diameter, considerably smaller than those from Morelos (6–9 cm diameters). In addition, most of these bowls are decorated on the interior bottom, something which led Moedano to insist that at least one of his types (type D) must have been used in ritual, not cloth production. I have examined all bowls from the 1972 survey collection and have not been able to document any indication of use wear on the interior bottom. While Tarascan has words for cotton (*xurata*) and spindle (*uixucata*), I have not been able to document a sixteenth-century word comparable to the Nahuatl term *tzaoalcaxitl* for the bowl used in anchoring a spindle (Gilberti 1975, from 1559). The distribution of miniature bowls and spindle whorls in the survey do not support (or completely rule out) the spinning association of the bowls:

| Low-status residential | 4 minibowl sherds | 1 spindle whorl |
| High-status residential | 20 minibowl sherds | 4 spindle whorl |
| Middle-status residential | 1 minibowl sherds | 0 |
| Primary public zone | 3 minibowl sherds | 2 spindle whorl |
| Secondary public zone | 2 minibowl sherds | 3 spindle whorl |

2.2 *brasero* Possibly an *apaxtle* (Noguera 1965:fig. 17). A straight-walled or inslanting open vessel. Probably flat-bottomed, with small appliqué pellets on the exterior surface and rim edge. Pellets: 1.0 cm diameter, 0.3 cm thick; vessel is 40 + cm in diameter, with walls 1.2 cm thick.

2.3 *sieve* Convex wall vessel with random punctures 1.0–1.5 cm apart. Vessel surface was smoothed on the outside but left with the clay pushed up around the holes on the inside. Walls are 1.2 cm thick, no diameter estimate possible.

2.4 *graters* Shallow convex vessels with punctate depressions in interior. Depressions are 0.3–0.5 cm in diameter, 0.3 cm deep, and >1.0 cm apart. They are found with/without supports, lips are rounded; 20 cm in diameter with walls 0.6–0.8 cm thick.

2.5 *plates*

2.5.1 *convex wall plates* A slight curvature on round/flat based vessels; no supports; lips are tapered or rounded. Diameters range from 10–12 cm and 15–25 cm, with walls 0.45–0.60 cm thick. There may be large and small plates, which could be distinguished in larger collections.

2.5.2 *flat base plates* Similar to a *comale* or griddle; square or rectangular slabs with supports. Edges are flattened on the sides but not raised above the level of the vessel floor. Noted a slight rise and thickening toward the edge, although one example has a downslope and thinning toward the edge. Slabs are 1.5 cm thick; one is ca. 8 by 8 cm and another is ca. 15 by 15 cm.

2.6 *jars*

2.6.1 *everted rim jar* Often referred to as an *olla*. Several kinds of rim eversion have been recognized, but the small sample size makes classifying difficult. Probable varieties include: even curve with/without stirrup handles; sharp curve, large jar (20–25 cm diameters, Castro-Leal 1986, using material from excavations on the main platform extends this to 17–29 cm); sharp curve, small jar (6 cm diameter); elongated neck, even curve rim; elongated neck, sharply everted rim (almost a bottle, called a *florero*); interior thickening with an even curve.

Bodies are globular or shouldered; lips are rounded, tapered or bolstered; vessels are with/without supports; and diameters range from 6 cm to 35 cm at the lip.

2.6.2 *incurved jars* Often referred to as a *tecomate*. Neckless, round-based jars; lips are squared; diameters at lip are 20–32 cm, and walls are 0.5–0.6 cm thick.

2.6.3 *miniature jar* A small everted rim jar with a spherical body; maximum diameter is 3.5 cm; diameter at orifice is 1.5–2.0 cm; walls are 0.3 cm thick.

2.6.4 *ripple wall jar* A small jar with an undulating wall that forms a series of horizontal bands around the vessel body. Only body sherds represented in this collection. Examples are in the Lumholtz collection (American Museum of Natural History, New York) and illustrated in Ross (1939), and in the INAH collection from excavations at Tz-25 (Tzintzuntzan).

2.7 *spouted vessels* This is a category of closed vessel that takes many forms in the ceramic complex. Listed below are those represented in this collection. Body sherds are often unassignable to a particular shape.

2.7.1 *handled teapot* A solid handle with a separate spout and orifice in the center top. It resembles a modern teapot.

2.7.2 *spout handle* A hollow-handled vessel with an orifice (or two) in a handle. May also have a separate spout. Bodies may be globular, shouldered, or almost flanged. This category was tabulated on the number of spout-handle sherds.

2.7.3 *loop handle* The handle is attached to the lip of an everted rim orifice in the center top. They may be miniature in size.

2.7.4 *animal effigy* Locally called *patojas*. Vessels in the shape of an animal, usually a bird of some kind (not necessarily a duck, however).

2.8 *supports*

2.8.1 *small supports* Supports less than 4.0 cm long and probably associated with miniature bowls.

    2.8.1.1 *spider support*

    2.8.1.2 *conical support*

    2.8.1.3 *flat oblong support*

    2.8.1.4 *foot-claw support*

    2.8.1.5 *flared support*

    2.8.1.6 *hollow cylindrical support*

    2.8.1.7 *solid foot support*

2.8.2 *regular supports* Supports that are generally longer than 4.0 cm.

    2.8.2.1 *solid conical support*

    2.8.2.2 *solid spider support*

    2.8.2.3 *hollow rattle cylindrical support*

    2.8.2.4 *hollow rattle wide top support*

    2.8.2.5 *hollow nub support*

    2.8.2.6 *drilled cylinder support*

    2.8.2.7 *large hollow support* attached to convex wall bowl

    2.8.2.8 possible annular base

3. *Surface finish and decoration*

    3.1 *slip* and *paint* Colors used refer to:

    red        2.5YR/4/6,8        10R/4/4,6,8        10R/5/6.8

| white | 2.5Y/8/2 | 2.5YR/N2,5/0 | 5YR/8/1,2 |
|-------|----------|--------------|-----------|
|       | 10YR/7/1 | 10YR/8/1,2,3 |           |
| cream | 2.5YR/5/6,8 | 2.5YR/6/6,8 | 5YR/5/4,6 |
|       | 5YR/6/4,5,6 |            |           |
| pink  | 10YR/5/3 |              |           |
| black | 10YR/2.5/0 |            |           |

3.1.1 *unslipped*
   3.1.1.1 *unpainted*
   3.1.1.2 *painted*
      3.1.1.2.1 *red*
      3.1.1.2.2 *white*
      3.1.1.2.3 *red, white, and cream*
      3.1.1.2.4 *negative on red and white*
3.1.2 *slipped*
   3.1.2.1 *unpainted*
      3.1.2.1.1 *red*
      3.1.2.1.2 *cream*
      3.1.2.1.3 *pink*
      3.1.2.1.4 *white*
      3.1.2.1.5 *gray*
   3.1.2.2 *painted*
      3.1.2.2.1 *white-on-red slip*
      3.1.2.2.2 *negative-on-red slip*
      3.1.2.2.3 *red-on-white slip*
      3.1.2.2.4 *red-and-white-on-white slip*
      3.1.2.2.5 *negative-on-red-on-white slip*
      3.1.2.2.6 *red-on-pink slip*
      3.1.2.2.7 *red-and-white-on-pink slip*
      3.1.2.2.8 *red-on-cream slip*
      3.1.2.2.9 *white-on-cream slip*
      3.1.2.2.10 *red-and-white-on-cream slip*
      3.1.2.2.11 *negative-on-red-and-white-on-cream slip*
      3.1.2.2.12 *negative-on-cream*
      3.1.2.2.13 *white-on-all-over-red-on-cream* The vessel is slipped and then painted over the entire slip in red.
      3.1.2.2.14 *all-over-red-on-cream* (includes mode .13)
      3.1.2.2.15 *red, white, and black-on-cream*

3.2 decorative technique

3.2.1 *appliqué conical pellets* Called *al fresco* by Moedano (1941:26).

3.2.2 *modeled corrugation* Produces a ripple effect (see 2.6.4)

3.2.3 *excision* A technique by which small areas are gouged out of the vessel surface.

3.2.4 *incision* On interior bottom of bowls. A technique by which a narrow depressed line is cut by means of a sharp instrument. This technique is not common among the sherds but is more frequent on the stems of pipes.

3.2.5 *negative decoration* This includes all sherds with negative irrespective of slip or paint; also called resist. Involves the covering of the vessel with a temporary protective material, followed by a coat of darker color and the removal of the protective material from selected surfaces. This is a frequent technique on polychromes in this collection.

3.3 decorative motifs

3.3.1 red and white vertical dashes (interior jar rim or everted rim of miniature bowl)

3.3.2 red band (1.0–1.5 cm wide, on interior and/or exterior jar or bowl)

3.3.3 "X" motif

3.3.4 "S" band

3.3.5 "Z" band

3.3.6 double spiral on bowl

3.3.7 thin parallel lines, red on white slip

3.3.8 line of white dots

3.3.9 white neck band on everted rim jars

3.3.10 white or red lines on interior rim

3.3.11 hatching, red lines on zoned white paint

3.3.12 checkerboard, red on white

3.3.13 spiral with ticks or lines

3.3.14 combination of 1 and 7. Thin lines on vertical dashes, some dashes ending in upward curve.

3.3.15 motifs on handles

3.3.15.1 1.5 cm wide handle; white dots on a red band

3.3.15.2 2–3 cm wide handle; double spiral (3.3.6) and/or zoned curvilinear and parallel lines surrounding the spiral

3.3.15.3 2–3 cm wide handle; "Z" band with dots

3.3.15.4 solid red handle, any size; slip or paint

3.3.16 motifs on small supports (minilegs)

3.3.16.1 parallel vertical red lines

3.3.16.2  parallel vertical white lines
3.3.16.3  parallel horizontal white lines
3.3.16.4  lower exterior painted red
3.3.16.5  lower exterior painted white
3.3.16.6  alternate red and white vertical lines

Table A2.1    Type-Variety Analysis
(in order of decreasing frequency)

| Ware | Groups |
|------|--------|
| Tariácuri Brown | Santa Ana |
| | San Juan |
| | Cucuchucho |
| | La Vinata |
| | Tziranga |
| | Las Granadas |
| Tarerio Cream | Jarácuaro |
| | San Andres |
| | Pastorela |
| | Copujo |
| Yaguarato Cream | San Pablo |
| | Cocupao |
| | Santa Fé |
| Sipiho Grey | Pacandan |
| | Janitzio |
| | Yunuén |
| | Tecuena |
| Patambicho Red | Ajuno |
| | Huecorio |
| | La Playa |
| Tecolote Orange | San Jerónimo |
| | Urandén |
| Tariácuri Coarse | San Pedro |
| | Oponguio |
| | Puacuaro |
| Yaguarato Coarse | San Bartolo |
| | Uricho |
| Querenda White | Ojo de Agua |
| Sanabria Red | Tócuaro |
| | Nocutzepo |
| Ichupio Coarse | Arocutín |

*Ware: Tariácuri Brown*
(frequency: 389 sherds)

*Paste* 1. color: 5YR/4/4,6 yellowish red; 7.5YR/4/4 brown; 2. texture: medium compact with medium-fine size inclusions and high percentage of inclusions; 3. hardness: 3–4; 4. inclusions: basalt, quartz; some have a bit of red, which is an iron oxide or sherd material; 5. firing: even firing; thicker pieces tend to have a gray core; some clouding; 6. fracture: straight.

*Surface* 1. slipped; medium thick and uniform application; often the color of the clay; 2. hardness: 2–4; 3. texture: smooth; many eroded sherds; 4. polish: lustrous to highly lustrous; 5. color: cream (Santa Ana), red (Cucuchucho), white (Tziranga), unslipped (Las Granadas), gray (San Juan), pink (La Vinata).

*Santa Ana Group* The vessels are covered with a uniform application of cream slip (5YR/6/4,6; 5YR/5/4 reddish brown).

Vessel forms: 1. bowls (convex wall, outsloping wall, incurved rim, composite silhouette, and miniature); 2. plates; 3. grater; 4. everted rim jars; 5. spouted vessels of all types.

Decoration: 1. red and white on cream; 2. red on cream; 3. negative, red and white on cream; 4. plain cream slip; 5. red and/or white bands, wavy lines, dots, dashes, and circles; 6. double spiral; 7. "Z" band; 8. "X" motif; 9. ripple modeled (mode 3.2.2).

Remarks. Decorative motifs are often in one color paint on top of the paint of another color; they are usually found on the interior and upper exterior of bowls; spouted vessels contain motifs on their entire upper (and sometimes lower) exteriors; red bands are commonly associated with interior and exterior lips of everted rim jars; white bands are often on the necks of everted rim jars; and the double spiral and "Z" bands are on spout handles and solid handles of spouted vessels. Includes types "Blanco y rojo sobre cafe" and "Policromo" (Castro-Leal 1986:110–11).

*Cucuchucho Group* The vessels are covered with a uniform application of red slip (2.5YR/4/6,8).

Vessel forms: 1. bowls (convex wall, outsloping wall, incurved rim); 2. everted rim jars; 3. spouted vessels.

Decoration: 1. white on red; 2. negative on red; 3. white dots, curvilinear lines; 4. excision (almost fluting); 5. ripple modeled.

Remarks. Most sherds have no decoration. Includes "Rojo pulido" and "Rojo pulido con decoracion negativa" (Castro-Leal 1986:87–98), and "Policromo Tarasco blanco-negro/rojo" (Miguel Cos 1985).

*Las Granadas* The vessels are unslipped and easily confused with the Santa Ana Group because the body surface color is close to the cream slip.

Vessel forms: 1. everted rim jars; spouted vessels.

Decoration: 1. red and white paint; 2. red, white, and cream paint; 3. white and red bands, dots, parallel lines, curvilinear lines; 4. double spiral; 5. "Z" band; 6. cross-hatching.

Remarks: Includes "Policromo" (Castro-Leal 1986:111).

*Tziranga Group*  The vessels are covered with a thin and unevenly applied white slip (2.5Y/8/2).

Vessel forms: 1. bowls (convex wall, miniature); 2. spouted vessels.

Decoration: 1. red on white; 2. red and white on white; 3. negative on red on white; 4. plain white slip; 5. red and/or white bands, stripes, dots, dashes; 6. double spiral.

Remarks: The motifs are on the interior and upper exterior of bowls and the bodies of spouted vessels. Includes "Rojo sobre blanco" (Castro-Lean 1986:109).

*San Juan Group*  The vessels are covered with a medium thin gray slip (10YR/5/2, 10YR/3/1).

Vessel forms: bowls (convex wall and composite silhouette).

Decoration: none.

Remarks: May include "Negro pulido" (Castro-Leal 1986:82).

*La Vinata Group*  The vessels are covered with a thin pink slip (10R/5/3 weak red). It tends to be unevenly applied, and the clay may be visible below.

Vessel forms: everted rim jars.

Decoration: 1. red and white on pink; 2. red on pink; 3. red and white bands, circles, dots, curvilinear lines.

Remarks: All rims have red painted bands on the interior and exterior lips.

*Ware: Tarerio Cream*
(frequency: 293 sherds)

*Paste* 1. color: 2.5YR/5/4,6 and 2.5YR/4/8 red; 2. texture: the paste is very compact, with medium-large size inclusions, and medium-sparse percentage of inclusions; 3. hardness: 3–4; 4. inclusions: quartz sand, basalt, iron oxide, sherds, lime; well balanced with the basalt occasionally heavier; 5. firing: many incomplete with dark cores with a grey-green tint and a fair amount of clouding; 6. fracture: even, straight.

*Surface* 1. slipped; medium thick; 2. hardness: 2–4; 3. texture: smooth, unslipped surfaces often grainy (wiped); 4. polish: lustrous, highly lustrous (grainy surfaces are matte); 5. color: cream (Jarácuaro), red (Pastorela), unslipped (San Andres), and white (Copujo).

*Jarácuaro Group*  The vessels are covered with a uniform cream slip (5YR/5/4,6), which is the same color as the fired clay and often difficult to detect.

Vessel forms: 1. bowls (convex wall, outsloping wall, composite silhouette, miniature); 2. plates; 3. everted rim jars; 4. spouted vessels.

Decoration: 1. red and white on cream; 2. negative on red and white on cream; 3. red on cream; 4. white on cream; 5. red and white lines, dots, bands, dashes, curvilinear lines, spirals; 6. cross-hatching; 7. "Z" bands.

Remarks: The negative technique is used to form the full range of motifs, including bands, dots, lines, etc.); the slip and decoration often stop midway down the exterior of bowls and the interior and exteriors may be of different paint colors; the everted rim jars usually have red bands at the rim. Includes "Blanco y rojo sobre cafe" and "Policromo" (Castro-Leal 1986:110–13), and "Policromo Tarasco rojo-blanco/naranja" (Miguel Cos 1985:104).

*Pastorela Group* The vessels have a thick, often eroding, red slip (10R/4/6, 2.5YR/4/6).

Vessel forms: 1. bowls (convex wall, incurved rim, miniature); 2. everted rim jars; 3. spouted vessels.

Decoration: 1. black on red; 2. white on red; 3. white and black thin parallel and curvilinear lines, dots, bands.

Remarks: Most sherds are undecorated. May include "Rojo pulido" (Castro-Leal 1986:87).

*San Andres Group* The vessels are unslipped and smoothed.

Vessel forms: 1. graters; 2. everted rim and incurved jars.

Decoration: 1. red on unslipped; 2. red bands.

Remarks: none.

*Copujo Group* The vessels are covered with a medium thick white slip (10YR/8/1,2).

Vessel forms: 1. bowls (convex wall); 2. everted rim jars.

Decoration: 1. red on white; 2. negative on red on white; 3. negative and red lines, dashes, dots, bands.

Remarks: Includes "Rojo sobre blanco" (Castro-Leal 1986:109).

*Ware: Yaguarato Cream*
(frequency: 259 sherds)
Note: With a larger sample, this ware may prove to be part of the range of Tariácuri Brown Ware.

*Paste* 1. color: 5YR/6/6, 5YR/5/6, 7.5YR/8/4, 2.5YR/6/6, reddish yellow; 2. texture: fine, compact paste with medium-fine size inclusions, medium-heavy percentage of inclusions; 3. hardness: 3–4; 4. inclusions: basalt, iron oxide, some clear quartz; the basalt is predominant inclusion; 5. firing: some gray cores, several blackened surfaces and firing clouds; 6. fracture: fairly straight.

*Surface* 1. slipped; 2. hardness: 2–3; 3. texture: smooth; 4. polish: lustrous, highly lustrous; 5. color: cream (San Pablo), pink (Cocupao), red (Santa Fé).

*San Pablo Group* Vessels are covered with a medium thick cream slip (5YR/5/4, 5YR/6/4,5). Often the slip is covered with an allover paint.

Vessel forms: 1. bowls (convex wall, outsloping wall, everted rim, incurved rim, composite silhouette, miniature); 2. plates; 3. everted rim and incurved jars; 4. spouted vessels.

Decoration: 1. red and white on cream; 2. red on cream; 3. negative on red and white on cream; 4. allover red on cream (often the cream shows through); 5. red and white lines, bands, curvilinear lines, circles, dots; 6. negative bands, lines, and dots; 7. zoned white paint; 8. double spiral; 9. "Z" band; 10. checkerboard.

Remarks: Negative decoration is used on both interior and exterior of bowls; everted rim jars usually have red bands on the interior and exterior lip and white bands on the exterior necks. Includes "Blanco y rojo sobre cafe" and "Policromo" (Castro-Leal 1986:110–11) and "Policromo Tarasco negro-rojo/naranja" (Miguel Cos 1985).

*Cocupao Group* Vessels are covered with a thin, unevenly applied pink slip (10R/5/3, 5YR/7/3).

Vessel forms: 1. bowls (convex wall); 2. everted rim jars.

Decoration: 1. red and white on pink; 2 red on pink; 3. white on pink; 4. red and white vertical dashes, bands and lines; 5. zoned white paint; 6. "Z" bands.

Remarks: Includes "Policromo" (Castro-Leal 1986:111).

*Santa Fé Group* Vessels covered with a medium thick red slip (10R/4/6).

Vessel forms: 1. convex wall bowls; 2. everted rim and ripple wall jars.

Decoration: 1. white on red; 2. white dots and lines; 3. modeled corrugation.

Remarks: Most sherds are undecorated.

*Ware: Sipiho Grey*
(frequency: 185 sherds)

*Paste* 1. color: 5YR/5/2,3,4 reddish grey; 2. texture: moderately compact with medium coarse inclusions, medium percentage of inclusions; 3. hardness: 3–4; 4. inclusions: iron oxide, possibly sherds, lime; coarse size inclusions of a gray color predominate; 5. firing: some gray cores, although most are complete; 6. fracture: straight.

*Surface* 1. slipped; 2. hardness: 2.5–3; 3. texture: smooth, unslipped surfaces are grainy; 4. polish: lustrous, unslipped surfaces are matte; 5. color: cream (Pacandan), red (Yunuén), unslipped (Janitzio), white (Tecuena).

*Pacandan Group* Vessels are covered with a thin cream slip (5YR/5/4,6).

Vessel forms: 1. bowls (convex wall, everted rim, incurved rim, miniature); 2. plates; 3. grater; 4. everted rim jars; 5. spouted vessels.

Decoration: 1. red and white on cream; 2. negative, red and white on cream; 3. red on cream; 4. white on cream; 5. red, white, and negative parallel lines, curvilinear lines, bands, dots and circles; 6. zoned white paint; 7. zoned red paint; 8. modeled vertical fluting.

Remarks: Negative is often found on the rim lip of convex wall bowls. May include "Blanco sobre cafe" and "Policromo" (Castro-Leal 1986:97–111).

*Yunuen Group* Vessels are covered with a red slip (10R/5/6, 10R/4/6).

Vessel forms: 1. bowls (convex wall, everted rim); 2. everted rim jars; 3. spouted vessels.

Decoration: 1. black on red; 2. black parallel lines; 3. incision.

Remarks: Most sherds are undecorated; parallel incised grooves on interior of open vessel body sherds, possibly a type of grater.

*Janitzio Group* Vessels are unslipped with zoned paint.

Vessel forms: 1. bowls (convex wall); 2. grater; 3. everted rim jars.

Decoration: 1. red on unslipped surface; 2. white on unslipped surface.

Remarks: none.

*Tecuena Group* Vessels are covered with a medium thin white slip (5YR/8/1).

Vessel forms: 1. bowls (convex wall, everted rim).

Decoration: 1. negative on red paint on white; 2. red on white; 3. negative dots, circles, lines; 4. red bands and lines.

Remarks: Negative is usually on rims and lip edge. Includes "Policromo Tarasco rojo-blanco/bayo (Miguel Cos 1985:105).

*Ware: Patambicho Red*
(frequency: 130 sherds)

*Paste* 1. color: 5YR/4/3,4; 5YR/5/4, reddish brown; 2. texture: a medium compact paste with fine inclusions, medium-light percentage of inclusions; 3. hardness: 3–4; 4. inclusions: basalt, some lime, possibly some sherd; has a nondistinctive quality — a light brown base with black, white, and red inclusions; 5. firing: generally even, although many dark cores; 6. fracture: straight.

*Surface* 1. slipped; 2. hardness: 2.5–3.0; 3. texture: smooth; 4. polish: lustrous and highly lustrous; 5. color: cream (Ajuno), red (Huecorio), unslipped (La Playa), may include gray/black.

*Ajuno Group* Vessels are covered with a medium thick cream slip (2.5YR/5/8, 2.5YR/6/8, 5YR/6/6).

Vessel forms: 1. bowls (convex wall, outsloping wall, everted rim, incurved rim, miniature); 2. grater; 3. everted rim jars; 4. spouted vessels.

Decoration: 1. red and white on cream; 2. red on cream; 3. negative on red and white on cream; 4. negative on cream; 5. red and white parallel lines, curves, spirals, dots, circles; 6. negative bands and parallel lines; 7. "Z" band; 8. modeled fluting.

Remarks: Polychrome bowls tend to have decoration on the interior and upper exterior. Includes "Rojo sobre anaranjado" and "Policromo" (Castro-Leal 1986:90–111).

*Huecorio Group* Vessels are covered with a medium thick red slip (10R/5/8, 10R/4/8).

Vessel forms: 1. bowls (convex wall, miniature); 2. spouted vessels.

Decoration: 1. white on red; 2. white lines.

Remarks: none.

*La Playa Group* Vessels are unslipped.

Vessel forms: 1. miniature bowl; 2. jar.

Decoration: 1. red and white paint on unslipped surface; 2. negative on white with red on unslipped surface; 3. red, white, and negative lines, dots, dashes, and bands.

Remarks: none.

*Ware: Tecolote Orange*
(frequency: 125 sherds)

*Paste* 1. color: 2.5YR/5/8, 2.5YR/6/8, 2.5YR/4/8 (orange); 2. texture: a very compact paste with fine inclusions, light percentage of inclusions; 3. hardness: 3–4; 4. inclusions: quartz sand, iron oxide, basalt all in small amounts; many sherds have so few inclusions they appear to be a homogenous paste; closest of all the pastes to the modern; 5. firing: generally complete, some green-gray cores; 6. fracture: straight.

*Surface* 1. slipped; 2. hardness: 2.5–3; 3. texture: smooth; 4. polish: lustrous, although many are badly eroded; 5. color: red (San Jerónimo), white (Uranden). Many sherds are too eroded to tell if they had been slipped or not. Some have traces of red and white, but it is not possible to tell if they had been slipped or painted.

*San Jerónimo Group* Vessels are covered with a medium thick red slip (2.5YR/4/6,8, 10R/4/6).

Vessel forms: 1. bowls (convex wall, everted rim, outsloping wall, miniature); 2. plates; 3. everted rim jars; 4. spouted vessels.

Decoration: 1. white on red; 2. black on red; 3. zones white on interior and portions of supports.

Remarks: Most sherds are undecorated; large number of miniature bowls. Includes "Rojo pulido" and "Blanco sobre rojo" (Castro-Leal 1986:87–107).

*Uranden Group* Vessels are covered with a white slip (10YR/8/1).

Vessel forms: 1. bowls (convex wall, composite silhouette, miniature); 2. plates; 3. jars.

Decoration: 1. red on white; 2. negative on red on white; 3. red and negative lines, beads, dashes, circles, and dots.

Remarks: Includes "Rojo sobre blanco" (Castro-Leal 1986:109).

*Ware: Tariácuri Coarse*
(frequency: 93 sherds)

*Paste* 1. color: 5YR/3/4, 5YR/4/6,8 (reddish brown); 2. texture: a medium-loose compact paste with medium-coarse inclusions, heavy percentage of inclusions; 3. hardness: 2.5–4; 4. inclusions: basalt, limonite, which are large and angular; 5. firing: even, some darkened cores; 6. fracture: generally even, some friable.

*Surface* 1. slipped; 2. hardness: 2–3; 3. texture: smooth or grainy; 4. polish: smooth surfaces are lustrous, grainy are matte; 5. color: cream (San Pedro), red (Oponguio), unslipped (Puácuaro).

Note: the following groups include "Tipo domestico con engobe y pulido" (Castro-Leal 1986:81) and "Monocromo: Pasta Gruesa Tardia" (Miguel Cos 1985:100).

*San Pedro Group* Vessels are covered with a medium thick, easily eroded, cream slip (2.5YR/6/6, 2.5YR/5/4).

Vessel forms: 1. bowls (convex wall); 2. everted rim jars.

Decoration: 1. red on cream; 2. white on cream; 3. white squares, dashes, cross-hatching; 4. zoned red on handles and rims.

Remarks: Generally sherds are undecorated; open vessels often are unslipped on the exterior.

*Oponguio Group* Vessels are covered with a medium thick red slip (10R/4/6).

Vessel forms: 1. convex wall bowls; 2. plates (flat based); 3. everted rim jars.

Decoration: 1. stamping (heavily eroded).

Remarks: Most sherds are undecorated, many have unslipped portions.

*Puácuaro Group* Vessels are unslipped. These may be portions of vessels from the other groups.

Vessel forms: 1. bowls (convex wall, incurved rim); 2. sieve.

Decoration: none.

Remarks: none.

*Ware: Yaguarato Coarse*
(frequency: 92 sherds)

*Paste* 1. color: 10YR/6/4,6 (yellowish brown); 2. texture: a compact paste, with medium size inclusions, heavy percentage of inclusions; 3. hardness: 3–4; 4. inclusions: basalt, limonite, some quartz; 5. firing: often have black cores, some smudging; 6. fracture: even, some friable.

*Surface* 1. slipped and slipless; 2. hardness: 3–4; 3. texture: usually smooth where slipped, rough or grainy where unslipped; 4. polish: rims usually lustrous, others matte; 5. color: cream (San Bartolo), red (Uricho).

Note: The following groups include "Tipo domestico con engobe y pulido" (Castro-Leal 1986:81) and "Monocromo: pasta gruesa tardia" (Miguel Cos 1985:100).

*San Bartolo Group* Vessels covered with a medium-thin cream slip (2.5YR/6/6), generally very eroded.

   Vessel forms: 1. bowls (convex wall); 2. brasero; 3. everted rim jars.

   Decoration: 1. red on cream; 2. white on allover red on cream; 3. white band on jar neck; 4. appliqué pellets on exterior and lip edge of the brasero.

   Remarks: none.

*Uricho Group* Vessels are covered with a medium thick red slip, many are eroded (10R/4/6).

   Vessel forms: 1. everted rim jars.

   Decoration: 1. white on red; 2. white dots.

   Remarks: none.

*Ware: Querenda White*
(frequency: 81 sherds)

*Paste* 1. color: 7.5YR/7/6, 5YR/6/6, 7.5YR/6/4 (yellow-brown); 2. texture: very compact paste; I. M. Drew commented that the example she examined was fired to almost a glassy state; fine size and sparse percentage of inclusions; 3. hardness: 3.5–4; 4. inclusions: iron oxide, possibly some sherd, occasionally basalt; 5. firing: almost glassy in some cases; a large gray/green core is characteristic; 6. fracture: even, straight.

*Surface* 1. slipped and slipless, the sherds are heavily eroded; 2. hardness: 3–4; 3. texture: smooth, whether slipped or not; 4. polish: one uneroded is lustrous, the rest unclear; 5. color: red (Ojo de Agua) or slipless.

*Ojo de Agua Group* Vessels are covered with a thick red slip (10R/5/8, 10R/4/6).

   Vessel forms: 1. bowls (convex wall, everted rim); 2. jars (everted rim, incurved rim).

   Decoration: 1. white on unslipped area; 2. white bands.

   Remarks: Most common is slipped allover or on exterior and interior rim only; collection includes large number of vessel supports, especially those with a rattle leg; several of the forms in this group are either absent or rare in all other groups. The closest relationship in vessel form, especially the supports, includes Cojumatlan Tan and Cojumatlan Polychrome. I have identified sherds identical in paste, surface, vessel forms, and decoration from surface collections at Taximaroa, Michoacán, Zitácuaro, Michoacán, and Cerro Chivo, Acámbaro, Guanajuato. There the group (and ware) are dated to the Protohistoric period (Gorenstein 1985). This ware may be "Rojo erosionado" (Miguel Cos 1985:107). I have identified an identical paste, but with a different surface finish and with incised decoration, in the collections from Zacapu (CEMCA project) currently dated to the Epiclassic (A.D. 950).

*Ware: Sanabria Red*
(frequency: 57 sherds)

*Paste* 1. color: 2.5YR/5/6, 2.5YR/4/6 (red); 2. texture: a medium compact paste with fine size inclusions, medium percentage of inclusions; 3. hardness: 3.5–5; 4. inclusions: basalt, rounded pebbles of iron oxide, small amounts of quartz, lime and possibly sherd; 5. firing: generally even, some clouding; 6. fracture: even.

*Surface* 1. slipped, thin and uneven application; 2. hardness: 2–3; 3. texture: smooth; 4. polish: lustrous and highly lustrous; 5. color: cream (Tocuaro), red (Nocutzepo).

*Tócuaro Group* Vessels are covered with a thin, unevenly applied cream slip (2.5YR/5,6/6).

Vessel forms: 1. bowls (convex wall, miniature); 2. everted rim jars.

Decoration: 1. red and white on cream; 2. red on cream; 3. white on cream; 4. negative on red and white on cream; 5. red and white bands, lines, dots, circles, curvilinear lines; 6. negative lines and dots; 7. "Z" bands.

Remarks: The lower exterior of the convex wall bowls are often not polished or slipped. Includes "Rojo sobre anaranjado" (Castro Leal 1986:90).

*Nocutzepo Group* Vessels are covered with a medium thin, unevenly applied red slip (10R/4/7).

Vessel forms: 1. bowls (convex wall, everted rim); 2. plates.

Decoration: 1. white on red; 2. white spirals, dots, and bands.

Remarks: The vessel surfaces are highly lustrous; most are undecorated. May include "Blanco sobre rojo" (Castro-Leal 1986:107).

*Ware: Ichupio Coarse*
(frequency: 40 sherds)

*Paste* 1. color: 5YR/5/3, 10YR/6/3, 2.5YR/5/4 (reddish brown); 2. texture: a compact paste, often with a scaling or layering quality, medium-coarse size inclusions, and medium-light percentage of inclusions; 3. hardness: 2.5–4; 4. inclusions: mostly glass (obsidian?), angular, with some basalt; 5. firing: many black-gray cores, which are up to 50 percent of the thickness of the vessel wall, some clouding; 6. fracture: straight, some friability due to the coarseness of the inclusions.

*Surface* 1. slipped, medium thick; 2. hardness: 2.5–5; 3. texture: slipped surfaces are grainy or smooth, unslipped surfaces are rough; 4. polish: rim interiors are lustrous, exteriors are matte (even if slipped); 5. color: cream (Arocutin).

*Arocutín Group* Vessels are covered with a thick cream slip (2.5YR/5,6/6).

Vessel forms: 1. everted rim jars.

Decoration: 1. red on cream (allover paint on interior or exterior).

Remarks: Often only the rim is slipped. Appears to be the same as "Tipo Burdo con engobe sin pulir" (Castro-Leal 1986:80).

*Miscellaneous (identifiable nonlocal)*

Cholula Polychrome. One body sherd from Tz-18; it matches the description in Noguera (1965) and was confirmed by Gordon Ekholm (personal communication 1971).

Texcoco Black-on-red. One rim sherd of a convex wall plate from Tz-18; it matches the description in Tolstoy (1958) and was confirmed by Gordon Ekholm (personal communication 1971); a black spiral on a red slip.

*Miscellaneous (other)*

Black and red on white slip; an outsloping or everted rim bowl; paste similar to Querenda White, but may belong to Ihuatzio Ware (see pipe analysis). From Tz-18 and associated with the Cholula Polychrome and Texcoco Black on Red.

Black thin lines on red slip body sherd; surface is extremely lustrous and the paste is close to Ihuatzio Ware (see pipe analysis); from Tz-78.

Red slipped everted rim jar body sherd; the paste has large coarse pebbles (1 cm and larger) as inclusions; from Tz-62.

## OTHER CERAMIC ARTIFACTS

### I. *Pipes*

A model analysis was made of the pipe fragments in the collection. Fragments were first divided into bowls, bits, and stems. Attributes of form were distinguished, and then those of decorative motif and technique associated with each form were tabulated.

Paste and surface finish attributes were analyzed and categorized into ware units, most of which fell easily within those established for the ceramic wares. These ware units have not been correlated with the vessel form and decorative motifs. A great percentage of the pipe fragments were too burned to permit ware classification (109 of 329). An attempt was made to correlate the assignable fragments, but preliminary results indicated the variability of form and decoration within wares to be as great as that between wares. In any case, the numbers involved became absurdly small.

*Wares*

1. Tecolote Orange (179). Includes some examples with a higher percentage of basalt inclusions than in the ceramics; grades imperceptibly to a higher level.
2. Yaguarato Cream (17). Most are white slipped with plain tubular stems.
3. Sipiho Grey (4). All were large pipes, unslipped or slipless; 3 of the 4 had incised designs on the stem. A grainy surface finish.
4. Patambicho Red (5). All white slipped.
5. Sanabria Red (2).
6. Ihuatzio Fine (13). a. color: 10YR/7/2,3 (light gray, very pale brown); b. inclusions: sherds, basalt; c. hardness: 3–4; d. texture: medium compact, grainy, size inclusions: fine, percentage inclusions: light; e. firing: appears complete, but pipe use has distorted this; f. fracture: straight.

Red or white slipped, smooth texture, and lustrous polish; Most stems are plain tubular, occasionally incised.

*Bowls*
1. thin walled, beveled lip (7). An out-curving silhouette on the exterior and straight on the interior, with a sharp eversion at the rim (see illustrations). A rounded or tapered lip with the interior surface beveled. Diameter at the lip 3–4 cm.
   Red or cream slipped, lustrous surface, no exterior modeling or applique.
2. thin walled, conical bowl (3). Type A (Moedano 1941:36). Associated with a thin stem and two straight supports. Two examples have everted rims with modeled exterior band below the rim. 3.0, 3.75 cm long and 3.5–4.0 cm in diameter (Type 3G, Porter 1948:234). (Rubín de la Borbolla 1944:131 and illustration from burial in Tz-25 adjacent to Yácata 5.)
   White slipped. Two contain exterior appliqué, one has parallel incised horizontal lines on the exterior.
3. thick modeled (1). Type B (Moedano 1941:36, illustration p. 37, fig. 6, row 3, no. 3). Walls are 0.4 cm. thick. Convex wall bowl with two supports indicated. 3 + cm high. The exterior has vertical undulating modeled "ribbing." (Type 3F, Porter 1948:234).
   White slipped.
4. bulbous base (4). Type B (Moedano 1941:36, illustration p. 37, fig. 6, row 3, nos. 1, 2; row 4, nos. 1, 2). It is either a bulbous base for a thinner bowl above (e.g., 1) or a thickening of the stem with two supports attached here, upon which a bowl is placed. (Type 3F, Porter 1948:234).
   Red slipped. A flat stipple on the bulber portion done while the clay was wet; appearance of a corncob.
5. small, conical supports (4). 2.0–2.5 cm long, 0.6–1.0 cm in diameter at attachment. Red and cream slipped.

*Bits*
1. plain (8) Squared. The stem is ended and rounded, then smoothed. Generally associated with thinnest stems—0.4–0.6 cm. diam. Associated with round, twisted and flat cross-sections.
2. ground around (7) After the clay had dried the bit end is ground and tapered. Generally associated with wider stems.
3. beveled (5) Same as above but ground only on two opposite sides to form a beveled profile.

*Stems*
A. Circular cross section
   Diameter: 0.8–2.0 cm; most 1.0 cm.
   1. white slipped (50)
   2. white slipped with incision (1); parallel "nicks"
   3. gray (blackened) (13)
   4. gray with pattern burnish (2); thin parallel lines
   5. red slipped (38)
   6. red slip with line incision (1)

    7. red slip with pattern burnish (1)
    8. cream slipped (29)
    9. cream slipped with red paint (3)
  10. unslipped (2)
  11. unslipped with pattern burnish (1)
  12. unslipped with vertical incision (2)

B.  Twisted stem
    While the clay was wet it was twisted.
    1.  Simple twist (circular or oval cross section)
       Diameter: 1.0–2.0 cm.
      a.  white slipped (1)
      b.  red slipped (5)
      c.  cream slipped (9)
      d.  slipless, brush incision (3) shallow parallel lines
      e.  unclassifiable (2)
    2.  Incised twist four.
       Cross section is squared or deeply "winged." The incising can be fairly shallow or so deep and broad as to be almost excision.
       Diameter: 0.6–1.75 cm.
      a.  white slipped (11)
      b.  red slipped (9)
      c.  cream slipped (10)
      d.  unclassifiable (11)
    3.  Incised twist three.
       Same as above, but with only three lobes. Some are fairly uneven in the division of the three wings.
       Diameter: 1.0–2.0 cm.
      a.  white slipped (7)
      b.  unclassifiable (3)
    4.  Twisted and incised.
       This differs from (2) and (3) in that the incising bears no relation to the twisting. Rather than following the degree of surface twist, the incising is unrelated to the form of the stem. It generally consists of several parallel lines curving around the stem. In one example, the incising is so deep as to create "wings" or lobes, as in the previous groups. However, in general the cross section remains circular, with only small indentations.
      a.  white slipped (10)
      b.  red slipped (7)
      c.  unclassifiable (11)
    5.  Twisted and scalloped (5)
       A four-wing twist with scalloping (a modeled edge produced by alternate pressing of the clay) located on two noncontiguous corners. All specimens burnt, possibly cream or white slipped.

C. Oval cross section.
   Vary in size from 1.0 cm by 0.8 cm to 2.5 cm by 2.0 cm (width/height).
   1. cream slipped (5)
   2. pink slipped (1); for color see type-variety analysis.
   3. red slipped (5)
   4. unclassifiable (4)
   5. Pattern burnished, unslipped (1)
   6. stamp incised, unslipped (4)
      Stamps include lunates, in random or parallel lines. Often zone incised (see
      Rubín de la Borbolla 1939:118).
   7. incised short lines, unslipped (4); nicks in parallel rows along the stem
   8. incised parallel wavy lines (2); brush or stick-like marks; 1 white slipped.
D. Miscellaneous
   1. scalloped (1)
      As on the scalloped incised four, but all the way around the stem. 1.5 cm diam-
      eter. Incised lines push up the ridge between them. Burnt, no surface
      determination.
   2. corncob
      Modeled and incised. Looks like a corncob. The center portion (around the
      "kernels") has been excised. Red slipped.

II. *Spindle Whorls*
Eleven spindle whorls were found during the surface survey. A classification of so
few is difficult due to the great diversity of form and decoration. Therefore,
I have simply grouped similar specimens on the basis of form and then described
the range of decoration within this group. As can be seen, with nine groups for
eleven specimens, little in the way of analytical classification was accomplished.
See "ceramic modes 2.1.6 miniature bowls" for the distribution within the survey
zone.

1. Biconvex (2)
   Disc shaped with convex surfaces on both the upper and lower facies. See Moedano (1941:fig. 2, line 1, nos. 4 and 5). Tz-117. Red paint. 2.5 cm diameter at widest, 0.9 cm height through the hole, 0.3 cm hole diameter. Tz-73. Eroded, possibly red paint. 2.5 cm diameter at widest, 1.15 cm height through hole, 0.35 cm
   hole diameter.
2. Truncated convex upper surface, flat lower (1)
   Disc shape with flat bottom and convex upper. However, the area immediately
   around the hole on the upper surface is flattened as though pressed with a finger in
   shaping. Close to Moedano (1941:fig. 2, row 2, no. 1). Tz-75. Burnt and eroded.
   No decoration visible, 2.6 cm diameter, 0.9 cm height, 0.3 cm hole diameter.
3. Truncated cylinder (1)
   Flat upper and lower surfaces. There are traces of red paint on all surfaces, including
   the sides. On the lower surface are crude incised lines in the shape of windmill sails.
   Possibly white paint was in the incised grooves. Moedano (1941:fig. 2, row 1, no. 1).

Tz-120. 2.35 cm diameter at widest, 2.1 cm diameter at upper surface, 0.7 cm height, 0.4 cm hole diameter.

4. Flattened spheres (2)

Similar to biconvex, but the sides are flattened. Gives a bead-like appearance. See Moedano (1941:fig. 2, row 2, no. 5). Tz-111. Traces of white paint all over. 1.5 cm diameter, 1.2 cm height, 0.3 cm hole diameter. Tz-17. Grainy surface. Traces of red paint all over. 1.3 cm diameter, 1.0 cm height, 0.3 cm hole diameter.

5. Bell shape (1)

A sphere with a flared base (see Moedano 1941:fig. 2, row 3, nos. 1, 2). Smoothed surface, lustrous base. Tz-53. Traces of red paint. 2.1 cm diameter at base, 1.35 cm diameter at break before flare, 1.25 cm height, 0.3 cm hole diameter.

6. Modified bell shape (1)

Similar to bell shape except that the base is slightly convex, and rather than a sphere, a true cylinder. Five incised lines around the cylindrical portion contain traces of white paint, as does the top of the piece. Tz-12. 1.8 cm diameter at base, cylinder 1.3 cm in diameter, 1.4 cm height, 0.3 cm hole diameter.

7. Modeled truncated cone (1)

A roughly conical shape with a convex base. A series of constructions forming circles in the body of the piece. See Modeano (1941:fig. 2, line 3, nos. 5, 7, 8, 9). Tz-84. Traces of red paint on the entire surface. 1.4 cm diameter at widest, 0.9 cm diameter at top, 0.35 cm hole diam., 1.5 cm height.

8. Composite form (1)

See Moedano (1941:fig. 2, row 3, no. 6). One end of example broken; orientation questionable. Tz-16. 1.3 cm diameter at widest. 0.9 cm diameter at other shoulder, 1.2 cm height (incomplete), 0.3 cm hole diameter.

9. Incised black polished fragment (1)

See Moedano (1941:fig. 2, row 4, no. 2). A deeply incised and well executed incision. Highly lustrous. A spiral motif is indicated curling along the sides of a circular or oval form (unable to tell). Tz-16. If symmetrical, 2 + cm diameter, 0.3 cm hole diameter.

III. *Other*

1. Bead or pendant (1)

Conical shape with a rounded bottom. A hole is drilled through the center of the cone, as if it had been strung. The lower portion is painted red, the upper painted white. It is smoothed and polished. Tz-12: 2.15 cm height, 1.90 cm maximum diameter.

2. Figurine fragment (1)

If placed on the flattened surface this object looks like a duck. Attachments are indicated in positions suitable for another wing, a head, and a tail. It is similar in overall shape to a spouted vessel from Tzintzuntzan in the Museum of Fine Arts, Montreal. Tz-110. Traces of red and white paint. Body: 2.6 cm long, 1.7 cm high.

## Key to colors on painted sherds

Cream

White

Red

Negative black

Note: Stippling is used to represent cream slip or paint only when there are two or more colors. Otherwise it is used to illustrate form.

## Decorative techniques

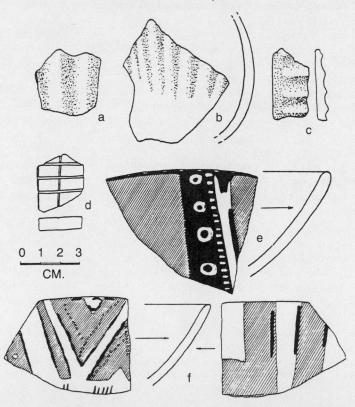

0 1 2 3
CM.

1. Decorative techniques. a–c modeled corrugation; d. excision; e–f. negative.

# Decorative motifs

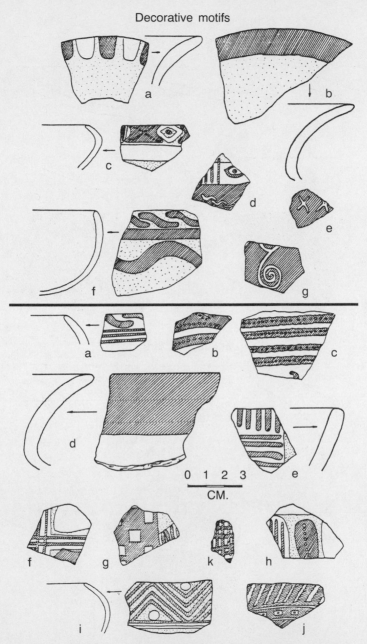

2. Decorative motifs. upper page: a. red and white vertical dashes; b. red band; c, e. "X" motif; d. "S" band; f. "Z" band; g. double spiral. lower page: a. thin parallel lines; b–c. line of white dots; d. white neck band; e. thin parallel lines; f, k. hatching; g. checkerboard; h. thin lines on vertical dashes; i–j. miscellaneous.

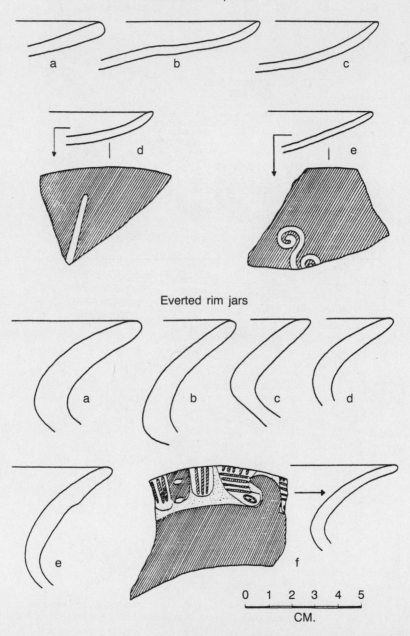

Convex wall plates

a   b   c

d   e

Everted rim jars

a   b   c   d

e   f

0 1 2 3 4 5
CM.

3. Convex wall plates. Everted rim jars. f. red and white vertical dashes with thin parallel lines.

## Miniature bowls

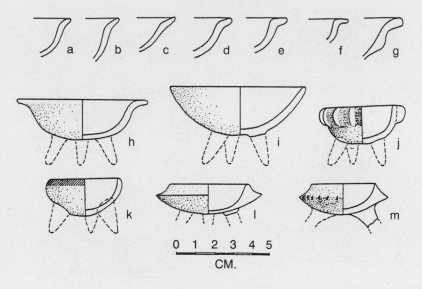

## Spindle whorls and miscellaneous

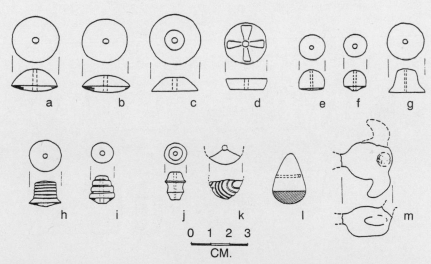

4. Miniature bowls. a–h. everted rim miniature bowls; i–k. convex wall miniature bowls; l–m. flange wall miniature bowls.

Spindle whorls and miscellaneous. a–b. biconvex; c. truncated upper and flat lower surface; d. truncated cylinder; e–f. flattened spheres; g. bell shape; h. modified bell shape; l. modeled truncated cone; j. composite form; k. incised fragment; l. bead or pendant; m. figurine fragment.

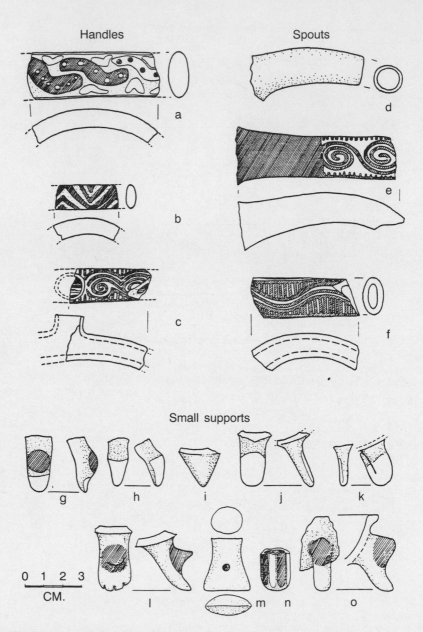

5. Handles. a–b. solid handles; c. spout handle.

Spouts. d. red polished spout; e–f. spout/spout handle with double spiral or zoned curvilinear motifs.

Small supports. g–h. spider support; j–k. flat oblong support; l. foot-claw support; m. flared support; n. hollow support; o. solid foot support.

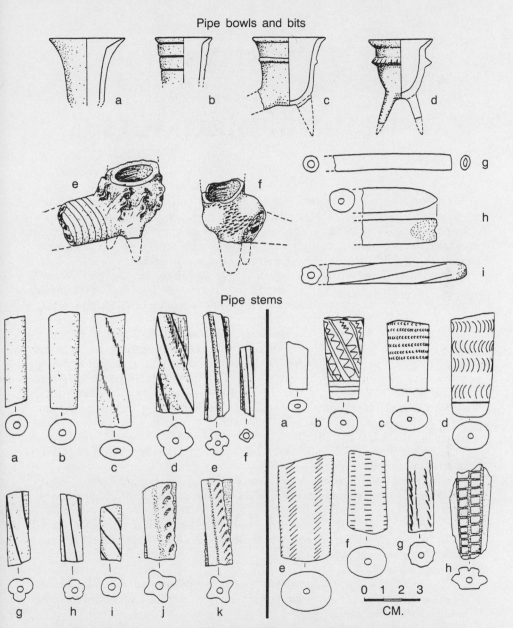

Pipe bowls and bits

Pipe stems

6. Pipe bowls and bits. a–b. thin walled, beveled lip; c–d. thin walled, conical bowl; e. thick modeled; f. bulbous base; g. plain bit; h. beveled bit; i. ground around bit.

Pipe stems. (a) a–b. circular cross section; c. simple twist; d–f. incised twist four; g. incised twist three; h–i. twisted and incised; j–k. twisted and scalloped. (b) a–f. oval cross-section; b. pattern burnished; c–d. stamp incised; e–f. incised; g. scalloped; h. corncob.

# APPENDIX 3

# TZINTZUNTZAN
# **THE LITHIC ARTIFACTS**

ALONG with the ceramic artifacts collected in the 1970 surface survey of Tzintzuntzan was a similar collection of lithic artifacts. The sample, while small, was designed to be representative of the range of lithics in the Protohistoric assemblege. Unusual concentrations of specific artifacts, such as prismatic blades, scrapers, or cores, were more heavily collected, making the overall sample a nonrandom one. However, because the artifacts were often completely covered with the local red clay (*charánda*), it was often only after washing that the type was known. To the extent that much of the lithic material was thus collected somewhat blindly, it is probably representative of Tarascan lithic use at Tzintzuntzan.

At the time of the original collection and analysis (1970–1972) only a few lithic analyses had been published for the ceramic periods of Mesoamerica, and none, in any systematic way, for Michoacán. While that has changed with regard to Mesoamerica, only the current work by CEMCA (as yet unpublished) in the Zacapu Basin represents any systematic analysis of lithics in Michoacán. In the present study artifacts were classified primarily according to the method of manufacture and raw material. The following attributes were utilized:

1. chipped or ground stone
2. basic morphological units: core, flake, blade, unifacially retouched artifact, bifacially retouched artifacts
3. secondary morphological units: core platform preparation; proximal, medial, and distal blade fragments; fine or crude blade; scraper or drill; projectile point or biface
4. retouch: method (pressure, percussion), location, kind (e.g., straight, concave); use retouch was not recorded due to the nature of obsidian, which constituted almost 90 percent of the collection
5. raw material

The definition of the basic morphological units follows standard Mesoamerican usage (Tolstoy 1971). For increased clarity, terms that may have alternate meanings have been listed below.

*Retouch.* Whenever the term is not otherwise qualified, it refers to straight retouch.

Straight, concave, and notched retouch follow Tolstoy (1971).

*Denticulate Retouch.* A series of notches; scalloped (Tolstoy 1971).

*Medial Retouch.* Straight retouch along the center ridge of a thick blade or polyhedral flake; the angle of retouch is 90° or greater.

*Corner Retouch.* One corner of a blade end is retouched, giving a pointed end or rounding off the blade end with one side.

*Sides.* Lateral edges; the longer edges of a rectangular object.

*Ends.* Shorter edges; usually the striking edge and distal side from striking edge.

*Proximal End.* End with the striking platform, bulb of percussion.

*Distal End.* End opposite that of impact, furthest from proximal end.

*Unilateral Retouch.* Retouch along one of the sides.

*Bilateral Retouch.* Retouch along both of the sides.

*Unifacial Artifact.* Retouch on one face only.

*Bifacial Artifact.* Retouch from two facies at a single point; the edge is thus formed from two convex surfaces.

## RAW MATERIAL

*Gray-black obsidian.* 921 artifacts (89 percent)

The color of the obsidian varies from a translucent gray to opaque black. Of the 335 samples of gray-black obsidian analyzed by XRF (1987–1990), 314 are attributed to the Zinapécuaro-Ucareo source. The remainder (<6 percent) are attributed to Zaragoza (3) and Tozongo (2), Puebla, Balvandeda (7), Jalisco, and an unknown source (9).

*Red obsidian.* 48 artifacts (4.6 percent)

Includes pieces that are a solid red color and those that are banded red-black. All those that have been trace element analyzed are attributed to the Cerro Zináparo, Michoacán, source.

*Green obsidian.* 35 artifacts (3.3 percent)

The 25 artifacts tested with trace element analysis (XRF 1987–1990) represent a variety of sources in Jalisco (Amatitan, LaMora Teuchitlan, Llano Grande) and central Mexico (Tulancingo-Pizarrin, Pachuca) and two unknown sources.

*Basalt.* 26 artifacts (2.5 percent)

The basalt in the collection is probably of local origin because the substructure of the region is basalt. The small quantity clearly reflects a preference for obsidian, even though it had to be imported into the basin. Despite its rarity of use for small tools and jewelry, basalt was the primary building material, used for rubble cores of mounds and facing stones.

*Vesicular volcanic.* 11 artifacts (1.05 percent)

The stone described here was ground and used primarily for metates and manos. Modern ground stone comes from Turicuaro and is of a fine-grained andesite from the nearby summit of Kanakuarani (Cerro de la Corona) (West 1948:71). The artifacts are of a darker, scoriacious material. Modern ground stone was distinguished in the survey principally on stylistic grounds, although cleaning and breaking indicated that the stone itself was different. Foster (1948:135) indicates that metates had been made at Patambicho and Cuanajo of local stone during this century. As Patambicho is adjacent to Tzintzuntzan within the basin, and Cuanajo is just outside the basin, it is probable that the ground stone used during the Protohistoric was available locally.

*Chert.* 6 artifacts

This category includes white chert (5 artifacts, 0.4%) and red chart (or jasper) (1 artifact). The stone probably came from central Michoacán, as there are known sources in several zones. Clearly they were not selected for tool production, although a variety of nonobsidian stones are included in the personal jewelry and ritual objects found in the burials on the main ceremonial platform.

# CORES (59)

*Polyhedral blade core*

Called fine (Tolstoy 1971) or fluted core; all gray-black obsidian.

1. *Ground Platform*
   a. *Unretouched* (7). No entire cores. Five of the seven appear to have had crude blades removed after the core broke (or at least stopped functioning as a prismatic blade core). Striking platform: 1.6–3.5 cm diameter, 2.0 mode. Longest fragment 6.5 cm.
   b. *Retouched* (2). Straight retouch along distal edge along break. One includes a notch thus formed. The other was ground for 1.5 cm from the platform after blades had been removed. Grinding was stopped after ridges between blade scars were removed. The core then broke and was retouched along the break. Possibly the core was to be ground into a disk 1.5 cm high but broke in process. Tz-12. Striking platform: 2.5 cm diameter, both. One 6.5 cm long until break.
2. *Prepared Platform* (2)
   Could also be called *secondary cores* because both were prepared and used from both ends. Both have prismatic blade scars made before the core was prepared to presently observed platforms. Very possibly were large ground platform cores that were reprepared by flaking, not grinding, and used again. Suggests maximal use of core material. 2.5 cm and 4.0 cm diameter. 4.0 cm length.
3. *Core Fragments* (no visible platform)
   a. *Unretouched* (17). Includes several distal ends of bullet-shaped cores. Diameter at time of break ca. 2.5–5.0 cm. Mode: 3.0 cm.
   b. *Retouched* (18). Straight retouch along breaks. On medial core fragments this may be on both ends. Includes unifacial and bifacial edges.
   c. *Reused* (7). Seven cores may have been reused as crude blade cores from the end opposite their original striking platform. Difficult to separate from percussion retouch poorly done. Diameter 1.5–4.5 cm. Mode: 3.0.

*Crude core* (6)

Unprepared striking platform. Called crude core (Tolstoy 1971), although same as conical and hemiconical core used by MacNeish et al. (1967). Four of the six still have some cortex. Three of basalt have flakes removed on both faces; may have served also as small ovoid bifaces. Mode: 4.0 cm diameter. One gray obsidian, straight retouch along two edges. No dimensions. Two predominantly red obsidian. Much cortex visible. Large chunks: 6–7 cm long axis, 2 and 4 cm height.

## FLAKES (212)

No core preparation was noted, although this by no means indicates they are from unprepared cores. Many of the flakes are without bulbs, or not enough of the platform remains.

*Lamellar shaped*
1. Unretouched
   a. *Gray Obsidian* (76). All thin, largest 8 cm × 5 cm. Mode: 4 cm diameter. Larger flakes, 4 cm + wide concentrated at Tz-89, Tz-90, Tz-93, Tz-99, Tz-105, Tz-108, Tz-115.
   b. *Red Obsidian* (31). Smaller than above. Largest 4 cm. Mode: 2–3 cm. Many chips (1 cm or less). Larger flakes at Tz-93, Tz-115.
   c. *Green Obsidian* (12). Size same as red obsidian. Mode: 3 cm.
   d. *White Chert* (5). Size same as red obsidian.
   e. *Basalt.* (4) Size same as gray obsidian.
2. Straight Retouch
   Includes good percussion or pressure. While the amount of retouch varies, in no case is the flake modified very much. Flakes are thin, and mode diameter is 3–4 cm, with red obsidian 2–3 cm.
   a. *Gray Obsidian* (33)
   b. *Red Obsidian* (7)
   c. *Green Obsidian* (7)
   d. *Basalt* (3)
3. Notched Retouch
   Same as above except for three large flakes (4 cm +) of gray obsidian.
   a. *Grey Obsidian* (17)
   b. *Red Obsidian* (2)
   c. *Green Obsidian* (1)
4. Denticulate Retouch (9)
   All gray obsidian. Within size range of straight retouched flakes noted above.

*Polyhedral flakes*
1. Unretouched
   Cylindrical, but appear to be products of the production of other flakes; one bulb.
   a. *Gray Obsidian* (1)
   b. *Green Obsidian* (1)
2. Medial Retouch
   a. *Gray Obsidian* (2). One has notch also.
   b. *Green Obsidian* (1)

## BLADES (630)

*Crude Blade* (117)
Made from conical or hemiconical nuclei, not parallel-sided blades. Suggest random striking pattern from the core. Some, however, may be the preliminary flakes (of a blade form) removed from a core in the process of forming a polyhedral fine blade

core. These are suggested by the larger blades (width greater than 3 cm) with cortex visible. 3.5–7.5 cm long, mode 5–6 cm; width, 2.0–5.0 cm, mode 2.5–3.0 cm. Most fall within the "macroblade" category.

1. *Unprepared striking platform*
   a. *Unretouched*
      *Gray obsidian* (19). Larger: Tz-99, Tz-105, Tx-107, Tz-109.
      *Green obsidian* (2)
   b. *Distal and Retouch*
      Percussion or poor pressure.
      *Gray Obsidian* (1)
   c. *Unilateral Notched Retouch*
      *Gray Obsidian* (3)
      *Red Obsidian* (1)
   d. *Unilateral Straight (Pressure)*
      *Gray Obsidian* (3)
      *Red Obsidian* (1)
   e. *Bilateral Retouch*
      One straight, one notch
      *Gray Obsidian* (2)

2. *Ground Striking Platform*
   Struck after previous fine blades had been removed. Possible reuse of core after no longer yielding fine blades. Unilateral straight retouch; one notched. All gray obsidian (5).

3. *Blade Fragments*
   No striking platform visible, or bulbs, but unable to tell platform condition.
   a. Unretouched
      *Gray Obsidian* (24)
      *Red Obsidian* (3)
      *Green Obsidian* (1)
   b. Unilateral Straight Retouch (Pressure)
      *Gray Obsidian* (16)
      *Red Obsidian* (1)
   c. Bilateral Straight Retouch
      *Gray Obsidian* (17). Pressure, possible good percussion.
   d. Unilateral Notched Retouch
      *Grey Obsidian* (12)
   e. Bilateral Denticulate Retouch
      *Gray Obsidian* (4)
   f. Medial Retouch
      *Grey Obsidian* (2). One with notch.

*Prismatic blade* (514)
Called fine blades. Presumably struck from polyhedral blade cores. Only one of these falls within the category of "macroblade," and this still has cortex on it, suggesting it

was one of the early blades removed from the core. The rest average 1–2 cm wide and 0.2–0.4 cm thick. Except for four green obsidian blades, all are gray obsidian.

1. *Ground Striking Platform*
   a. Unretouched (79)
      Gray. Length: 3.1–8.8 + cm. Almost all have distal ends broken off (a snap hinge is visible).
   b. Unilateral Straight Retouch (15)
      Gray. Only one is entire blade, rest snapped or broken distal end.
   c. Bilateral Straight Retouch (24)
      Gray. Pressure. Only two entire blades.
   d. Notched Retouch (one or both edges) (11)
      Gray. Five entire blades.
   e. One Edge Notched; Other, Straight (8)
      Gray. No entire blades.
   f. Concave Retouch (one edge) (5)
      Gray. No entire blades.
   g. One Edge Concave Retouch; Other, Straight (7)
      Gray. One entire blade.
   h. Denticulate Retouch (8)
      Gray. No entire blades.
   i. Medial Retouch (1)
      Gray. No entire blades.

2. *Unprepared striking platform* (11)
   Six are 2.5 cm or larger (one "macroblade"). Thicker than average, 0.5 cm and greater; five with visible cortex. It is probable that some or all of these were primary trimming blades in the production of the fine blades but before the platform was ground.
   a. Unretouched
      *Gray Obsidian* (3). Two entire.
      *Green Obsidian* (2). Both entire, 3.1 cm and 4.0 cm long.
   b. Notched Retouch (3)
      Gray. All entire.
   c. Unilateral Straight (2)
      Grey. Both entire.
   d. Denticulate Retouch
      Both edges. Gray. One macroblade.

3. *Distal end blade fragments* (90)
   No bulb or striking platform visible. All within range of fine blade size discussed above. While some are probably broken, most were probably snapped deliberately for use. Three features suggest this: (1) the presence of hinge fractures on most (the author experimented with several of her longer specimens and found that placing a blade on a hard surface and holding one side down while pulling back with the other

duplicates this hinge—on the other hand, simple dropping or breaking by pushing in with the thumbs on the center, as one breaks a twig, will produce an irregular edge with a marked bulb); (2) the high degree of standardization of size: 27 equal to or less than 3.5 cm long, 58 at least 4.0 but less than 6.0 cm long, 4 longer than 6.0 cm. Two clusters were noted, one at 3.0–3.5 cm and another at 4.5–5.5 cm; (3) the retouch (pressure) was done after most blades were their present size (including some on the proximal ends). They are all gray obsidian unless specified.

a.  Unretouched (9)
b.  Unilateral Straight Retouch (6)
c.  Unilateral Retouch at Proximal End (1)
d.  Bilateral Retouch (1)
    Including one notch.
e.  Distal End Retouch
    *Green Obsidian* (1)
    *Gray Obsidian* (25)
f.  Distal End Plus Unilateral Straight (16)
g.  Distal End Plus Unilateral Denticulate (2)
h.  Distal End Plus Bilateral Straight
    *Green Obsidian* (1)
    *Grey Obsidian* (14)
i.  Distal End Plus Bilateral (2)
    One side notched.
j.  Distal End Plus Bilateral (1)
    One side denticulate.
k.  Distal End Plus Bilateral (1)
    One side concave.
l.  Distal End Plus Bilateral (2)
    One side proximal.
m.  Distal End Plus Proximal End and Unilateral Straight (2)
n.  Distal End Plus Proximal End and Bilateral Straight (3)

4. *Medial blade fragments* (254)
   As the name implies, this category includes blade fragments that have been broken or snapped on both ends. Includes the category of truncated blades used by Tolstoy (1971) and snapped blades by MacNeish et al. (1967). Again, the same features suggesting that the distal end blades were intentional artifacts (and not just broken whole blades) apply here: the hinge fracture is present, the blades cluster in size (the same 3.5–5.5 cm), and the retouch was usually post-break. All blades are of gray obsidian.

   a.  Unretouched (84)
   b.  Unilateral Straight Retouch (40)
   c.  Unilateral Notched Retouch (11)
   d.  Unilateral Denticulate Retouch (2)
   e.  Bilateral Straight Retouch (38)

f.  Bilateral (9)
    One side notched; other, straight.
g.  Bilateral (4)
    Notched both edges.
h.  Bilateral (7)
    One edge denticulate; other straight.
i.  Bilateral (2)
    Denticulate both edges.
j.  Bilateral (6)
    One edge concave; other straight.
k.  One End Retouch (11)
l.  One End Plus Notched One Side (1)
m.  One End Plus Bilateral Straight (17)
n.  One End Plus Bilateral (5)
    One side notched; other straight.
o.  One End Plus Bilateral (1)
    One side notched; other denticulate.
p.  Both Ends Retouched Plus Unilateral (1)
    Notch one side.
q.  Both Ends Plus Bilateral Straight (1)
r.  Corner Retouch (9)
s.  Corner Plus Bilateral Straight (3)
t.  Corner Plus Denticulate (1)
    The two retouched edges bring one end of the blade fragment to a point. One
    end has corner retouch; the other has denticulated corner retouch. One side is
    straight and other concave retouched. Only degree separates this from
    unifacial perforator.
u.  "Chiconautla" Blade (1)
    Similar to so-named blade (Tolstoy 1971). Retouch appears broken; blade
    broken, not snapped. 7.1 cm to break. Retouch like saw tooth, small
    continuous notches. Opposite edge has fine even pressure retouch as backing
    (in fact is dulled for cutting). Also corner touch on specimen.

## UNIFACIALLY RETOUCHED ARTIFACTS

*Scrapers*

While certain artifacts were classified on their basic morphology in the "blade"
category, it was deemed necessary to repeat them in the present category. These
include fine blades with end retouch. MacNeish et al. (1967) has classed them with
end-scrapers, although Tolstoy (1971) has not. Placing them with the blades emphasizes the means by which the artifact was made, and the range of retouch modification. However, straight retouch on the sides of fine blades tends to produce edge
angles of 30° or less, while end retouch, like that of the following scrapers, is
consistently 50° or more. Studies have reinforced the utility of multiple classifica-

tions, as edge angles probably reflect functional patterns (i.e., scraping vs. cutting motions). This applies equally to notched, concave, and denticulate retouch.

A. Scraper Tools Listed in Other Sections
MacNeish et al. (1967), fine prismatic blade end-scrapers.
   1. *Distal End Fine Blades*
   All with end retouch. Letters e through n.
   2. *Medial Fine Blade Fragments*
   All with one or two end retouch. Letters k through q.
B. Other Scrapers (73)
   1. *Crude End of Flake* (5)
   MacNeish et al. (1967:36), crude percussion. 5.8–8.0 cm by 3.0–5.0 cm. Mode: 6.0–4.0 cm, 1.0–1.5 cm thick. No secondary retouch. Flaking along end opposite bulb and may also be flaked on one or both longer sides. One may fall in MacNeish group of "gouges." Angle: mode: 50° (one 90°). Large flat flake of basalt.
   2. *Simple End of Blade Scraper* (3)
   Long, crude blade of gray obsidian. Percussion and pressure retouch on cutting edge (opposite bulb) only. Very little modification of blade. 6.0–7.0 cm by 4.5 cm, 1.0–1.5 cm thick. Angle: 60–70°.
   3. *End and Backed Scraper* (14)
   Long crude blade of gray obsidian. Percussion and pressure retouch on cutting edge. Small, even pressure retouch (backing) along one or both lateral edges. Angle: 50–60°, one 90°. One with side notch. 4.5–7.0 cm by 3.0–5.4 cm, 1.0–2.5 cm thick.
   4. *End and Unilateral Scraper* (16)
   Crude blade or flake of primarily gray obsidian. One basalt example. Percussion and pressure retouch along cutting edge and one side. The other side may or may not be backed. Thus, the cutting edge is extended from the distal edge of the blade or flake to one side. 3.5–7.0 cm (mode 5.0), 2.5–5.0 cm (mode 3.5), 1.0–1.7 cm thick. The basalt example is the smallest, 3.5 cm by 2.5 cm by 1.0 cm. Angle: 30–70°, one 75° (basalt). The end angle is steeper than the side.
   5. *End and Bilateral Scraper* (21)
   Crude blade or flake of gray obsidian. Percussion with pressure retouch along the cutting edge and both sides. On many a striking platform is still visible, with little or no shaping of the butt. The platforms are keeled, although the variation is great on this point. Three fragments are placed within this type on the basis of the size, keeling, and retouch visible on the fragments. This category is somewhere between Tolstoy's (1971) crude and fine end of blade scrapers and MacNeish's (1967:42) fine ovoid plano-convex end-scrapers. One possible variant is very much like Tolstoy's fine end of blade scraper. As above, but made on a long blade with more even trimming. 4.6–5.5 cm by 3.0–5.5 cm by 1.0–1.2 cm thick. Mode 5 by 4 cm. Angle: 55–90°. Variant: 9.0 by 4.2 by 1.1 cm.

6. *Discoidal Scraper* (11)

Small flake of gray or green obsidian. Both with a ridge or partial keel and flat dorsal surface. Some may have been made from medial sections of polyhedral cores. Percussion and pressure retouch on all edges to form a roughly hemispherical contour. Ventral surfaces are flat to slightly convex. 3.5–4.2 cm diameter. 1.0–1.5 cm thick. Angle: 50–70°. Two with notches. Two green obsidian, nine gray obsidian.

7. *Thumbnail Scraper* (1)

See MacNeish et al. (1967:43). Thin flake with fine pressure retouch all around to give thumbnail outline. One example with flat ventral surface and fairly flat dorsal surface, green obsidian. 2.0 cm by 1.6 cm by 0.4 cm thick. Angle: 85°.

8. *Rectangular Scraper* (1)

Large thick flake trimmed by percussion and pressure to a rectangular shape. Commonly called chisel or scraper-plane. All four sides have steep angles— 80° or greater. 3.5 cm by 2.5 cm by 1.6 cm thick. Gray obsidian.

9. *Scraper-Denticulate* (1)

Probably an end and bilateral scraper that has been considerably modified to roughly a "tail," leaving the scraper unmodified but removing material along the sides to form a long concave surface on one side and a denticulate edge along the other. Gray obsidian. 3.5 cm by 3.5 cm (at head), 0.6 cm (at butt), 1.0 cm thick. Angle: 60° at head.

*Other Unifacial Artifacts* (23)

A. Simple Burin (2)

Single blow burins on thin crude blade fragment. Form sharp points. One green obsidian, one gray. 3.0 cm and 3.5 cm long, respectively; 2.0 cm and 2.5 cm wide, respectively. 0.4 cm thick.

B. Flake Graver (3)

See MacNeish et al. (1967:47). One made from prismatic blade core flake; others from thin flakes. Retouched to a point from the dorsal surface on one side and the ventral on the other. Gray obsidian, 6 cm, 4.5 cm, and 3.0 cm long.

C. Notched Artifact (11)

See MacNeish et al. (1967:47), spokeshave-like tools. From crude blades and flakes. Irregular in outline although generally longer than wide with the notch on one of the longer edges. One is notched on both longer edges; the other has a denticulate edge; two have pressure retouch on the side opposite the notch. One green obsidian, rest gray.

D. Perforator (1)

A fine blade fragment that has been finely pressure retouched to a point. In addition the sides have been retouched also. Differs from the medial blade category "t" by degree. Gray obsidian, 1.6 cm by 1.2 cm by 0.3 cm thick.

E. Drill (1)

Basalt flake which has been percussion retouched to form a long tapering point. The flake is 3.1 cm long, 1.8 cm of which is the point. 1.6 cm wide at base.

F. Irregular Crude Blades (2)

Catch-all category for two crude blades, which are finely pressure retouched around most of perimeter. Very thin, one a crude "eccentric," edges of which may have been utilized. One still has cortex. 7.0 cm and 7.5 cm. One gray and one green obsidian.

G. Large Trapezoidal Artifacts (2)

Large basalt flakes that have been percussion trimmed to a trapezoidal shape. One has a flake removed to thin the butt end, as for hafting. There is no abrasive wear, such as an object used in digging would receive, and the shape and location of retouch (the distal end and sides) suggest that the objects were hafted, probably as axes. Shapes similar to these are in plates 7 and 9 of the RM, one of which is described as illustrating the person chopping wood. 9 cm by 6.5 cm by 1.5 cm and 11 cm by 7 cm by 1.7 cm. Angle: 25° and 35°.

H. Lamellar Rectangle (1)

A large thin basalt flake has been percussion retouched forming essentially a square with a wide stem on it. 7.5 cm per side, with a stem 3.0 cm wide and 1.0 cm long. The ventral surface is flat and the dorsal slightly convex. Hafting would have been aligned as on a shaft. Angle: 20 degrees. Possibly a shovel, as suggested by the wear pattern and hafting possibilities.

## BIFACIALLY RETOUCHED ARTIFACTS

*Projectile Points* (15)

A. Large Stemmed (1)

Uneven percussion flaked. Only primary flakes removed. Basalt. Central ridge on one side of this crude blade. Broken stem, triangular shape. 5.5 cm + 4.4 cm tip to beginning of stem, maximum width 2.3 cm by 0.7 cm thick. Tz-73.

B. Large Convex Base, Notched Side (1)

Large flake of basalt. Percussion flaked. No secondary flaking, crudely, unevenly done. Broken tip. 5.7 cm, 4.7 cm tip to notch. 2.75 cm maximum width. 0.8 maximum thickness. Tz-63. Relations: Ensor (Tolstoy 1961).

C. Broken Lanceolate (1)

A percussion flaked basalt flake. No secondary trimming. Has a crude appearance. Presently not symmetrical although flaking indicates it was parallel flaked. Broken at the base. 5.1 cm by 2.0 cm maximum width, 0.6 cm thick. Tz-50.

D. Large Rounded Base (1)

A large flake with some secondary trimming. Gray obsidian. Triangular with a rounded base. 4.65 cm long, 3.1 cm maximum width, 0.5 cm thick. Tz-16.

E. Concave Base (1)

Fragment. Obsidian flake with pressure retouch. 3.5 + cm long. Tz-17.

F. Corner Notch (1)

Gray obsidian. Fine pressure flaked. Very pointed triangle with notched corners. Flat dorsal and ventral surfaces. 4.0 cm, 2.6 cm maximum width, 0.65 cm thick. Relations: like Apatzingan point in Kelly (1947:131, fig. 75, P). Tz-109.

G. Side Notch, Convex Base (1)
Broken fragment, reused as a knife. Gray obsidian. Pressure flaked, 0.5 cm thick. Tz-56.

H. Side Notch, Concave Base (2)
Pressure flaked gray obsidian on a thin blade. Shallow notches and concave base. 3.05 cm and 2.2 cm long, 1.0 cm maximum width, 0.3 cm thick. Tz-13, Tz-75. Relations: Apatzingan-Chila phase in Kelly (1947:131, fig. 75, K); Edgewood (?) in Tolstoy (1971:fig. 2q).

I. Thin Basal Notched (1)
Pressure flaked gray obsidian. On a thin blade. 3.0 cm long, 1.0 cm maximum width, 0.3 cm thick. Tz-12. Several of this shape on display in the Museo Michoacano, Morelia, from INAH excavations (1937–1941) at Tzintzuntzan.

J. Diamond-Shaped Basal Notch (1)
As above but maximum width midway between the point and the base. 3.1 cm long, 1.15 cm wide, 0.3 cm thick. Tz-43.

K. Small Concave Base (1)
Very thin finely pressure flaked gray obsidian. Tip broken. 2.0 cm long, 0.8 maximum width, 0.2 cm thick. Tz-119.

L. Side Notch (1)
Fine pressure gray obsidian fragment. Size: 3.5 + cm long, 1.9 cm maximum width, 0.6 cm thick. Tz-61.

M. Triangular (1)
Very fine parallel pressure flaking of this gray obsidian fragment. 2.7 + cm long, 1.8 cm maximum width, 0.5 cm thick. Tz-75.

N. Diamond Shaped (1)
White chert pressure flaked fragment. 2.15 + cm, 1.7 cm maximum width, 0.7 maximum thickness. Tz-77.

Basalt points appear larger and cruder than the obsidian. No pressure flaking is associated with them. In distribution they are restricted to the lakeshore. The differences between the basalt and other points may be temporal or functional in origin. The RM describes the use of several different types of points for deer, small mammal, and duck hunting, for example.

*Other Bifacially Retouched Artifacts*

A. Crude Ovoid Bifaces (2)
Fall within the larger end of MacNeish's category of this name (1967:89–90). They are basalt percussion flaked flakes. They may have served as cores for some small flakes. Amount of retouch and worn edge appearance of one suggest that they were primarily tools themselves. 9.2 cm by 7.5 cm by 2.3 cm and 8.0 cm by 6.5 cm by 2.5 cm. Angles: 30–40°.

B. Bifacial Disks and Ovoids (5)
See MacNeish et al. (1967:81). Bifacially retouched flakes of gray obsidian. They are smaller and better flaked (percussion, possibly some pressure) than above

category. Ovoid: 5.5–6.0 cm by 3.5–4.0 cm by 1.0–1.5 cm. Round: 4 cm diameter by 1.2 cm by 1.5 cm thick. Angles: 30–50°.

C.  Bifacial Drills (4)
All fragments of bifacially pressure retouched blades. While different shapes are suggested, they all are fragments, and reconstruction is difficult. 2.0–3.5 cm long, 0.8–1.7 cm wide. All gray obsidian.

D.  Bifacially Notched Tool (1)
Medium size, thick flake of gray obsidian, which was bifacially percussion flaked to form a large notch near the most acutely angled point of this triangular flake. 5.5 cm by 3.5 cm by 2.3 cm. May have served as a perforator.

E.  Lunate (1)
Small, bifacially pressure flaked object in the shape of a lunate. Gray obsidian. 2.0 cm long, 0.4 cm thick.

# GROUND AND POLISHED STONE

*Mano Fragments (11)*
Although metate fragments were located and recorded in the field, they were not collected. The mano fragments here are of vesicular volcanic stone (probably basalt). They are all rectangular, with a slight thinning in width towards the ends noted in two examples. Width: 6.5–8.0 cm (5.5 cm at thinned end). Thickness: 2.5–4.5 cm.

*Other*
A.  Ear/Lip Plug and Fragments (3)
Ground and polished gray obsidian. One almost entire lip plug 1.4 cm long cylinder, 1.1 cm diameter, 2.0 cm width of cross bar. A small depression in the cylinder. 0.4 cm diameter may have held a stone inlay as in the specimens in the Museo Michoacano, Morelia, taken from INAH excavations (1939–1941). Another fragment is 2.5 cm diameter, 1.0 cm long. One 0.7 cm diameter cylinder appears to have been unfinished when it broke.

B.  Hollow Cylindrical Fragment (1)
Gray obsidian with cortex still visible. 2.0 cm diameter of outer perimeter. Wall 0.5 cm thick.

C.  Unfinished Disks (2)
Two thin flakes of gray obsidian that have been ground on one side, and one ground on the edges. They apparently both broke before the disks were completed. 4.0 and 4.5 cm diameter, 0.5 cm and 0.7 cm thick.

D.  Oval Cylinder (1)
Also unfinished. Ground piece of gray obsidian, 3.0 cm long, 1.2 cm wide, 0.6 cm maximum thickness.

E.  Pendant Fragment (1)
A red chert piece shaped like a flat half moon and scalloped. Two holes (hanging? sewing?) are located along the straight edge. Polished.

F.  Trapezoidal Basalt Fragment (1)
A puzzle piece. 1.5 cm thick, 3.0 cm by 3.5 cm average size. Two squared, linear

grooves on both faces, 0.3 cm deep, and parallel to the sides of the stone. The edges parallel to the grooves are polished, but the ends of the stone (perpendicular to the grooves) are broken edges. The entire surface is polished.

# Cores

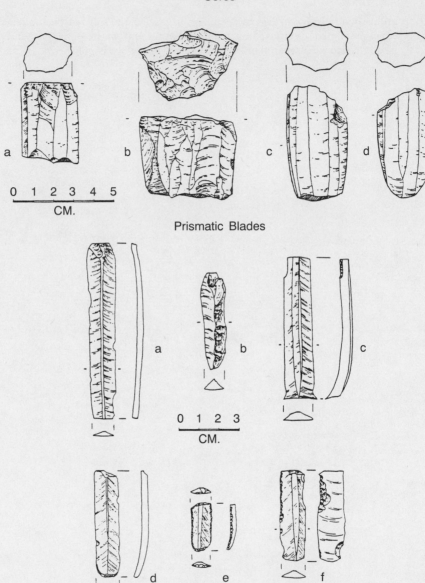

Prismatic Blades

1. Cores. a. ground platform; b. prepared platform; c–d. core fragments.
   Prismatic blades. a. ground platform, no retouch; b. ground platform, medial retouch; c. distal fragment, unilateral retouch; d. distal fragment, end retouch; e. distal fragment, all edges retouched; f. distal fragment, unilateral and concave retouch.

Unifacially retouched artifacts

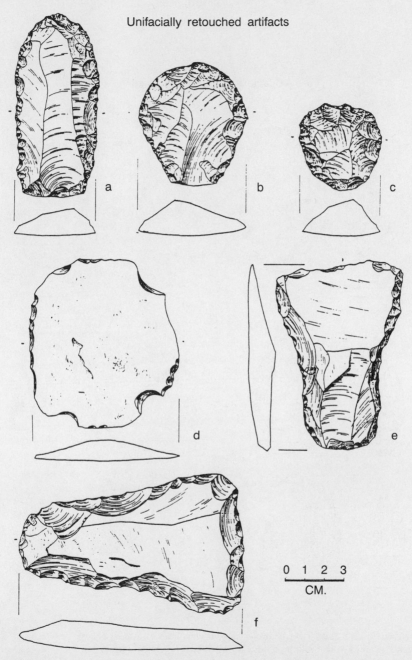

2. Unifacially retouched artifacts. a–c. scrapers; a–b. end and bilateral; c. discoidal. d–f. basalt tools. d. lamellar rectangle (shovel); e–f. large trapezoidal forms (axheads).

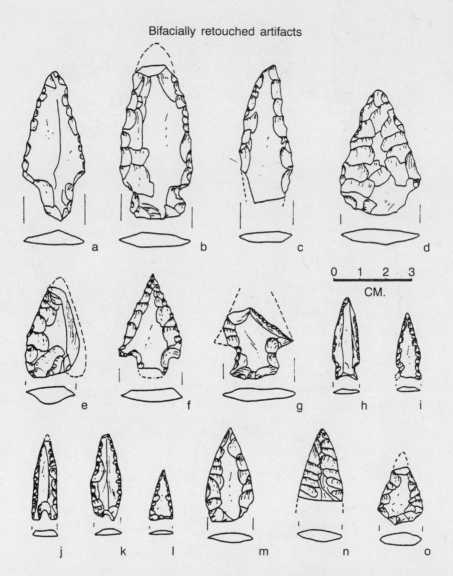

Bifacially retouched artifacts

0 1 2 3
CM.

3. Bifacially retouched artifacts: projectile points. a. large stemmed; b. large convex base, side notched; c. broken lanceolate; d. large rounded base; e. concave base; f. corner notch; g. side notch, convex base; h–i. side notch, concave base; j. thin basal notched; k. diamond-shaped basal notch; l. small concave base; m–o. fragments.

# BIBLIOGRAPHY

Acosta, Jorge
  1939  "Exploraciones arqueológicas realizadas en el estado de Michoacán durante los años de 1937 y 1938." *Revista Mexicana de Estudios Antropológicos* 3 (2):85–99.
Adams, Robert Mc.
  1979  "Late Prehispanic Empires of the New World." In *Power and Propaganda: A Symposium on Ancient Empires*, edited by M. T. Larsen, pp. 59–73. Akademisk Forlag, Copenhagen.
AGEM 1713, 1715, 1763
       Archivo General del Estado de Michoacán. Epoca Colonial. Títulos de Tierras y Aguas, legájo 1, tomo 1. Microfilm Collection Library of the National Museum, Mexico.
Aguilera Herrera, Nicolás, and Mauricio Aceves García
  1973  "Análisis de la carta de suelos del estado de Michoacán." In *Memoria del VI congreso nacional de geografía*, tomo 1, pp. 39–44. Gobierno del Estado de Michoacán, Uruapan, Michoacan.
Ancona, Ignacio, and staff of Instituto de Biología (Mexico)
  1940  "Prospecto biológico del lago de Pátzcuaro." *Anales del Instituto de Biología* 11 (2):415–502.
Anonymous
  1595, 1618–1610
       "Mandamiento del Virrey Velasco II para que los de Tzintzuntzan elijan sus autoridades. Lista de pueblos de su jurisdicción." Mexico 1595. Tzintzuntzan 1595 y 1618–19. Library of the National Museum of Anthropology, microfilm, Pátzuaro 114.
Anonymous
  1991  *Diccionario Grande de la Lengua de Michoacán.* Introducción, paleográfia y notas by J. Benedict Warren. Fimax Publicistas, Morelia. Two volumes.
Arnauld, Marie Charlotte
  1987  "Asentamientos lacustres prehispánicos en la cienega de Zacapu: Problemas arqueológicos y sedimentológicos." Paper presented at El Hombre y los Lagos en el Centro y Occidente de México, CEMCA, Mexico, D.F.
Barrett, Elizabeth
  1973  "Encomiendas, Mercedes, and Haciendas in the Tierra Caliente of Michoacán." *Jahrbuch für Geschichte Lateinamerikas* Band 10:71–112.
  1974  "Indian Community Lands in the Tierra Caliente of Michoacán." *Jahrbuch für Geschichte Lateinamerikas* Band 11:78–120.
  1975  *La cuenca del Tepalcatepec.* Vol. 1, *Su colonización y tenencia de la tierra.* SEP-SETENTAS 177. Mexico.

1981    "The King's Copper Mine: Inguaran in New Spain." *The Americas*
        38:1–29.
Barth, Frederic, ed.
    1969    *Ethnic Groups and Boundaries*. Little, Brown, Boston.
Beals, Ralph L., and Pedro Carrasco
    1944    "Games of the Mountain Tarascans." *American Anthropologist*
            46:516–22.
Beals, Ralph L., Pedro Carrasco, and Thomas McCorkle
    1944    *Houses and House Use of the Sierra Tarascans*. Institute of Social An-
            thropology 1. Smithsonian Institution, Washington, D.C.
Beaumont, Pablo
    1932    *Crónica de Michoacán* (1776–1780). Archivo General de la Nación:
            17–19, Mexico.           ɩ
Belshaw, Michael
    1967    *A Village Economy: Land and People of Huecorio*. Columbia Univer-
            sity Press, New York.
Beltrán, Ulises
    1982    *Tarascan State and Society in Prehispanic Times: An Ethnohistorical In-
            quiry*. Ph.D. diss., Department of History, University of Chicago,
            Chicago.
    1986    "Estado y sociedad tarascos." In *La sociedad indígena en el centro y oc-
            cidente de México*, edited by P. Carrasco, pp. 45–62. El Colegio de
            Michoacán, Zamora.
Berdan, Frances F.
    1982    *The Aztecs of Central Mexico: An Imperial Society*. Holt, Rinehart,
            and Winston, New York.
Blanton, Richard, and Gary Feinman
    1984    "The Mesoamerican World System." *American Anthropologist*
            86:673–82.
Blanton, Richard, Stephen Kowalewski, Gary Feinman, and Jill Appel
    1981    *Ancient Mesoamerica*. Cambridge University Press, Cambridge.
Blasques, L., and R. Lozano García
    1946    *Hidrogeología y minerales no-metálicos de la zona norte del estado de
            Michoacán*. Anales del Instituto de Geología 9. Universidad Nacional
            Autónoma de México, Mexico.
Borah, Woodrow, and Sherbourne F. Cook
    1960    *The Population of Central Mexico in 1548*. Ibero-Americana 43.
    1963    *The Aboriginal Population of Central Mexico on the Eve of the Spanish
            Conquest*. Ibero-Americana 45.
Brand, Donald
    1943    "An Historical Sketch of Geography and Anthropology in the Taras-
            can Region." *New Mexico Anthropologist* 6–7 (2):37–108.
    1951    *Quiroga, a Mexican Municipio*. Institute of Social Anthropology 11.
            Smithsonian Institution, Washington, D.C.

1980 "A Persistent Myth in the Ethnohistory of Western Mexico." *Tlalocan* 7:419–36.

Bravo Ugarte, Jose
1962 *Historia sucinta de Michuacán*. Vol. 1, *Michoacán: El estado tarasco*. Editorial Jús, S.A. Mexico.

Bravo Ugarte, José, ed.
1960 *Inspección ocular en Michoacán* (1799). Testimonia Histórica 2. Editorial Jús, S.A. Mexico.

Bray, Warwick
1984 "Fine Metal Jewelry from Southern Mexico." In *Festeschrift for J. L. Lorenzo*, edited by L. Mirambell and J. Litvak-King. Universidad Nacional Autónoma de México, Mexico, D.F., in press.

Brown, Kenneth L.
1982 "Prehistoric Demography Within the Central Quiche Area, Guatemala." In *The Historical Demography of Highland Guatemala*, edited by R. Carmack, J. Early, and C. Lutz, pp. 35–48. Institute for Mesoamerican Studies, SUNY Albany, no. 6.

Cabrera Castro, Rubén
1986 "El desarrollo cultural prehispánico del Bajo Río Balsas." In *Arqueología y ethohistoria del estado de Guerrero*, pp. 119–51. INAH y Gobierno del Estado de Guerrero, Mexico.
1987 "Tzintzuntzan: Décima temporada de excavaciones." In *Homenaje a Román Piña Chan*, pp. 531–65. Serie Antropológica 79. UNAM, Instituto de Investigaciones Antropológicas, Mexico.

Campbell, Lyle, Terrence Kaufman, and Thomas C. Smith-Stark
1986 "Meso-america as a linguistic area." *Language* 62 (3):530–70.

Carmack, Robert
1981 *The Quiché Mayas of Utatlán: The Evolution of a Highland Guatemalan Kingdom*. University of Oklahoma Press, Norman.

Carrasco, Pedro
1969 "Nuevos datos sobre los Nonoalca de habla Mexicana en el reino tarasco." *Estudios de Cultura Nahuatl* 8:215–21.
1982 "The Political Economy of the Aztec and Inca States." In *The Inca and Aztec States: 1400–1800*, edited by G. Collier, R. Rosaldo, and J. Wirth, pp. 23–40. Academic Press, New York.
1986 "Economía política en el reino tarasco." In *La sociedad indígena en el centro y occidente de México*, edited by P. Carrasco, pp. 63–102. El Colegio de Michoacán, Zamora.

Carta de Climas, Mexico
1970 14Q–V 1:500,000. CETENAL, Mexico.

Caso, Alfonso
1930 "Informe preliminar de las exploraciones realizadas en Michoacán." *Anales del Museo Nacional de Arqueología, Historia y Etnográfia* 6 (2): 446–52.

248                                                          BIBLIOGRAPHY

    1943   "The Calendar of the Tarascans." *American Antiquity* 9:11–20.
    1967   *Los calendarios prehispánicos*. UNAM, Mexico.
Castro-Leal, Marcia
    1986   *Tzintzuntzan, capital de los Tarascos*. Gobierno del Estado de Michoa-
           cán, Morelia, Mexico.
CETENAL
    1974   Vertical aerial photographs. 1:50,000. Comisión de Estudios del Ter-
           ritorio Nacional. Mexico, D.F.
Chadwick, Robert
    1971   "Archeological Synthesis of Michoacan and Adjacent Regions." In
           *Handbook of Middle American Indians*, edited by R. Wauchope, 11
           (2): 657–93. University of Texas Press, Austin.
Cohen, Abner
    1981   *The Politics of Elite Culture*. University of California Press, Berkeley.
Contreras Ramírez, J. Antonio
    1987   "La Presencia tarasca en el estado de Gto.: Fluctuación de fron-
           teras." Tésis para Licenciatura. Universidad Veracruzana, Xalapa,
           Veracruz.
Cook, Sherbourne F., and Woodrow Borah
    1960   *The Indian Population of Central Mexico: 1531–1610*. Ibero-Ameri-
           cana 44.
    1972   *Essays in Population History: Mexico and the Caribbean*. Vol. 1. Uni-
           versity of California Press, Berkeley.
    1974   *Essays in Population History: Mexico and the Caribbean*. Vol. 2. Uni-
           versity of California Press, Berkeley.
Corona Núñez, José
    1957   *Mitología tarasca*. Fondo de Cultura Económica, Mexico.
Correa, Pérez, G., and C. Reyna
    1973   "La vegetación del estado de Michoacán y su explotación." In *Memo-
           ria del VI Congreso Nacional de Geografía*, tomo 1, pp. 53–64. Gobier-
           no del Estado de Michoacán, Uruapan, Michoacán.
Crabtree, Don E.
    1968   "Mesoamerican Polyhedral Cores and Prismatic Blades." *American
           Antiquity* 33 (4): 446–78.
Craine, Eugene R., and Reginald C. Reindorp
    1970   *The Chronicles of Michoacan*. University of Oklahoma Press, Norman.
Davies, Nigel
    1987   *The Aztec Empire: The Toltec Resurgence*. University of Oklahoma
           Press, Norman.
De Buen, F.
    1944   "Los lagos michoacanos, II, Pátzcuaro." Sociedad Mexicana de His-
           toria Natural. *Revista* 5 (1–2): 99–125.
Diehl, Richard A., ed.
    1974   *Studies of Ancient Tollan: A Report of the University of Missouri Tula*

Archaeological Project. University of Missouri Monographs in Anthropology 1.

Dinerman, Ina
1972 "Community Specialization in Michocan: A Regional Analysis of Craft Production." Ph.D diss. Brandeis University, Waltham, Mass. University Microfilms, Ann Arbor.

Earls, J., and I. Silverblatt
1978 "Ayllus y etnias de la region Pampas-Qaracha, el impacto del imperio Incaico." In *El hombre y la cultura andina*, tomo 1, edited by R. Matos Mendieta, pp. 157–77. III Congreso Peruano, Lima.

Edmonson, Munro S.
1988 *The Book of the Year: Middle American Calendrical Systems*. University of Utah Press, Salt Lake City.

Eisenstadt, S. N.
1979 "Observations and Queries About Sociological Aspects of Imperialism in the Ancient World." In *Power and Propaganda: A Symposium on Ancient Empires*, edited by M. T. Larsen, pp. 21–34. Akademisk Forlag, Copenhagen.

Ekholm, K., and J. Friedman
1979 "'Capital,' Imperialism and Exploitation in Ancient World Systems." In *Power and Propaganda. A Symposium on Ancient Empires*, edited by M. T. Larsen, pp. 41–58. Akademisk Forlag, Copenhagen.

Enloe, Cynthia
1972 *Ethnic Conflict and Political Development*. Little, Brown, Boston.
1980 *Ethnic Soldiers: State Security in Divided Societies*. University of Georgia Press, Athens.

FAO-UNESCO
1975 *Soil Map of the World*. Vol. 3, *Mexico and Central America*. UNESCO, Paris.

Fernandez, Justino
1936 *Pátzcuaro*. Secretaria de Hacienda y Crédito Público, Mexico.

Flores de Aguirrezabal, Ma. D., and C. A. Quijada López
1980 "Distribución de objetos de metal en el occidente de México." In *Rutas de intercambio en Mesoamérica y norte de México* 2:83–88. XVI Mesa Redonda, Sociedad Mexicana de Antropología, Mexico.

Flores Mata, G., J. Jiménez López, X. Madrical Sánchez, F. Moncayo Ruiz, and F. Takaki Takaki
1971 *Mapa y descripción de los tipos de vegetación de la República Mexicana*. Dirección de Agrología, Mexico.

Foglio Miramontes, F.
1936 *Geografía económico agricola del estado de Michoacán*. Imprenta de la Cámara de Diputado, Mexico, D.F.

Foster, George M.
1948 *Empire's Children: The People of Tzintzuntzan*. Institute of Social

Anthropology 6. Smithsonian Institution, Washington, D.C.

1967  *Tzintzuntzan: Mexican Peasants in a Changing World.* Little, Brown, Boston.

1979  *Tzintzuntzan: Mexican Peasants in a Changing World.* Revised edition. Elsevier, New York.

Foster, Michael, and Phil Weigand, eds.

1985  *The Archaeology of West and Northwest Mesoamerica.* Westview Press, Boulder.

Freddolino, Marie Kimball

1973  *An Investigation into the "Pre-Tarascan" Cultures of Zacapu, Michoacan, Mexico.* Ph.D. diss., Yale University, New Haven. University Microfilms, Ann Arbor.

Friedrich, Paul

1984  "Tarascan: From Meaning to Sound." In *Supplement to the Handbook of Middle American Indians*, vol. 2, *Linguistics*, edited by M. Edmonson, pp. 56–82. University of Texas Press, Austin.

Gailey, Christine Ward

1987  *Kinship to Kingship: Gender Hierarchy and State Formation in the Tongan Islands.* University of Texas Press, Austin.

Gali, Ramón

1946  "Arqueología de Tzintzuntzan." *Anales del Museo Michoacano* 2 (4): 50–62.

García, Enriqueta

1973  *Modificaciones al sistema de clasificación climática de Koppen.* Instituto de Geografía, Universidad Nacional Autónoma de Mexico, Mexico.

García Alcaraz, Agustín

1976  "Estratificación social entre los tarascos prehispánicos." In *Estratificación social en la Mesoamérica prehispanica*, edited by Pedro Carrasco and Johanna Broda, pp. 221–24. Centro de Investigaciones Superiores, INAH, Mexico.

García de León, Porfirio

1977  "Recuperación de datos y fotografía aerea (aeroarqueología)." *Revista Mexicana de Estudios Antropológicos* 23 (1): 97–122.

Gerhard, Peter

1972  *A Guide to the Historical Geography of New Spain.* Cambridge University Press, Cambridge.

Gilberti, R. P., Fr. Maturino

1975  *Diccionario de la lengua tarasca o de Michoacán* (1559). Edicion facsimilar, Pimentel 1902, Balsal Editores, S.A., Morelia, Mexico.

1987  *Arte de la lengua de Michuacán* (1558). Introducción histórica con apendice documental y preparación fotográfica del texto por J. Benedict Warren. Fimax Publicistas Editores, Morelia, Mexico.

1990  *Diccionario de la lengua tarasca o de Mechoacán* (1559). Introducción y preparación fotográfica del texto por J. Benedict Warren. Fimax

Publicistas Editores, Morelia, Mexico.

Gil Flores, J.
1966    "Fertility Studies in Volcanic Soils of the Sierra Tarasca, Mexico."
        Ph.D. diss., Purdue University, Lafayette, Ind. University Micro-
        films, Ann Arbor.

González Crespo, N.
1979    *Patrón de asentamientos prehispánicos en la parte central del Bajo Bal-
        sas: Un ensayo metodológico*. Colección Científica 73. Departamento
        de Prehistoria, INAH, Mexico, D.F.

Gorenstein, Shirley
1985    *Acambaro on the Tarascan-Aztec Frontier*. Vanderbilt University Pub-
        lications in Anthropology 32, Nashville.

Gorenstein Shirley, and H. Perlstein Pollard
1980    "The Development of the Protohistoric Tarascan State." Report to
        the National Science Foundation and the National Endowment for
        the Humanities. Photocopied.
1982    "Tarascan Territorial Routes: Their Role in Politics, War and Econ-
        omy." Paper presented at the 81st Annual Meeting, American An-
        thropological Association, Washington, D.C.
1983    *The Tarascan Civilization: A Late Prehispanic Cultural System*. Van-
        derbilt University Publications in Anthropology 28. Nashville.

Gortaire Iturralde, A.
1971    *Santa Fé: Presencia etnológica de un pueblo-hospital*. Universidad
        Iberoamericana A.C., Mexico.

Greenberg, Joseph H.
1987    *Language in the Americas*. Stanford University Press, Stanford.

Grinberg, D. M. K. de
1988    'Relaciones metalúrgias en América prehispanica. Tecnologias metal-
        úrgicas tarascas." Paper presented at the 46th International Congress
        of Americanists, Amsterdam.

Hassig, Ross
1984    "The Aztec Empire: A Reappraisal." In *Five Centuries of Law and
        Politics in Central Mexico*, edited by R. Spores and R. Hassig, pp.
        15–24. Vanderbilt University Publications in Anthropology 30.
        Nashville.
1988    *Aztec Warfare: Imperial Expansion and Political Control*. University of
        Oklahoma Press, Norman.

Healan, Dan M., ed.
1989    *Tula of the Toltecs: Excavations and Survey*. University of Iowa Press,
        Iowa City.

Herrejón Peredo, Carlos
1978    "La Pugna entre Mexicas y Tarascos." *Cuadernos de Historia* 1: 11–47.

Hester, Thomas R., Robert N. Jack, and Alice Benfer
1973    *Trace Element Analysis of Obsidian from Michoacan, Mexico, Prelimi-*

nary Results. Contributions of the University of California Archaeological Research Facility 18.

Hosler, Dorothy
  1985    "The Cultural Organization of Technology: Copper Alloys in An-
          cient West Mexico." Paper presented at the 50th Annual Meeting of
          the Society for American Archaeology, Denver.
  1988a   "Ancient West Mexican Metallurgy: A Technological Chronology."
          *Journal of Field Archaeology* 15: 191–217.
  1988b   "Ancient West Mexican Metallurgy: South and Central American Or-
          igins and West Mexican Transformations." *American Anthropologist*
          90: 832–55.

Hurtado Mendoza, Francisco
  1986    *La religion prehispánica de los Purhépechas: Un testimonio del pueblo
          tarasco*. Morelia.

Hutchinson, G. E., R. Patrick, and E. Deevey
  1956    "Sediments of Lake Pátzcuaro Michoacán, Mexico." *Bulletin of the
          Geological Society of America* 67:1491–1504.

INEGI
  1985    *Sintesis geográfica del estado de Michoacán*. Instituto Nacional de Es-
          tadística, Geografía e Informática, Secretaría de Programación y Pre-
          supuesto, Mexico.

Ivanhoe, Francis
  1978    "Diet and Demography in Texcoco on the Eve of the Spanish Con-
          quest: A Semiquantitative Reconstruction from Selected Eth-
          nohistoric Texts." *Revista Mexicana de Estudios Antropológicos* 34
          (2):137–46.

Jacobs, Jane
  1969    *The Economy of Cities*. Random House, New York.

Julien, C. J.
  1983    *Hatunqolla: A View of Inca Rule from the Lake Titicaca Region*.
          Publications in Anthropology 15. University of California,
          Berkeley.

Kelly, Isabel
  1947    *Excavations at Apatzingan, Michoacan*. Viking Fund Publications in
          Anthropology 7. New York.
  1949    *The Archaeology of the Autlan-Tuxcacuesco Area of Jalisco: The Tux-
          cacuesco-Zapotitlan Zone*. Ibero-Americana 27.
  1985    "Some Gold and Silver Artifacts from Colima." In *The Archeology of
          West and Northwest Mesoamerica*, edited by M. Foster and P.
          Weigand, pp. 153–79. Westview Press, Boulder.

Kirby, Anne
  1973    "*The Use of Land and Water Resources in the Past and Present Valley of
          Oaxaca, Mexico*. Memoirs of the Museum of Anthropology 5. Uni-
          versity of Michigan, Ann Arbor.

Krickeberg, Walter
1968 *Pre-Columbian American Religions*. Holt, Rinehart and Winston, New York.

Lagunas, Fray Juan Baptista de (1574)
1983 *Arte y dictionario con otras obras en lengua michuacana*. Edición facsimilar, edited by J. Benedict Warren. FIMAX Publicistas Editores, Morelia, Mexico.

Larsen, M. T.
1979 "The Tradition of Empire in Mesopotamia." In *Power and Propaganda: A Symposium on Ancient Empires*, edited by M. T. Larsen, pp. 75–103. Akademisk Forlag, Copenhagen.

León, Nicolás
1888 *Anales del Museo Michoacano*. Vol. 1. "Calendario de los Tarascos," pp. 33–42; "Las yácatas de Tzintzuntzan," pp. 65–70. Morelia, Mexico.
1903 *Los Tarascos*. Museo Nacional, Mexico City. Reprinted by Editorial Innovación, S.A., Mexico (1979).

León-Portilla, Miguel
1978 "Minería y metalurgia en el México antiguo." In *La Minería de México*, pp. 7–36. Universidad Nacional Autónoma de México, Mexico, D.F.

Leopold, Aldo D.
1959 *Wildlife of Mexico: The Game Birds and Mammals*. University of California Press, Berkeley.

Longacre, Robert
1967 "Systematic Comparison and Reconstruction." In *Handbook of Middle American Indians*, vol. 5, *Linguistics*, edited by N. McQuown, pp. 117–59. University of Texas Press, Austin.

López Austin, Alfredo
1976 "El fundamento mágico-religioso del poder." *Estudios de Cultura Nahuatl* 12: 197–240.

López Sarralangue, Delfina Esmeralda
1965 *La nobleza indígena de Pátzcuaro en la epoca virreinal*. Instituto de Investigaciones Historicas, Universidad Nacional Autónoma de México, Mexico.

Lumholtz, Carl
1902 *Unknown Mexico*. Charles Scribner's Sons, New York.

Lumholtz, Carl, and Ales Hrdlicka
1898 "Marked Human Bones from a Prehistoric Tarasco Burial Place in the State of Michoacán, Mexico." *Bulletin of the American Museum of Natural History* 10: 61–79.

Macías Goytia, Angelina
1988 "La arqueología en Michoacán." In *La antropología en México: Panorama histórico*, vol. 13, edited by M. Mejía Sánchez, pp. 89–132. Colección Biblioteca, INAH, Mexico.

1989    "Los entierros de un centro ceremonial tarasco." *Estudios de An-tropología Biologica* 100, pp. 531–59. UNAM, Mexico.

Macías Goytia, Angelina, and Martha Cuevas García
1988    "Rescate arqueológico de la cuenca de Cuitzeo: Copándaro." *Ar-queológia* 2: 137–54. Dirección de Monumentos Prehispánicos, INAH, Mexico.

MacNeish, Richard S., A. Nelken-Lerner, and I. W. Johnson
1967    *The Prehistory of the Tehuacan Valley*. Vol. 2. University of Texas Press, Austin.

Maldonado, Rubén
1980    *Ofrendas asociadas a entierros del infiernillo en el Balsas*. SEP-INAH Colección Científica, Mexico.

Mapes, Cristina, Gastón Guzmán, and Javier Caballero
1981    *Etnomicología purépecha*. Cuadernos de Etnobiología 2. Dirección General de Culturas Populares, SEP, Mexico.

Marquina, Ignacio
1964    *Arquitectura Prehispánica*. Second edition. INAH, Mexico.

Martínez de Lejarza, J. J.
1974    *Análisis estadístico de la provincia de Michoacán en 1822*. Fimax, Morelia, Michoacan.

Metcalfe, Sarah E., and Sarah P. Harrison
1983    "Preliminary Reconstructions of Late Quaternary Environmental Change as Recorded by Lake Margin Deposits in the Basin of Zacapu." Michoacan Tropical Paleoenvironments Research Group, School of Geography, Oxford University, Oxford. Ms.

Metcalfe, Sarah E., R. Bernard Brown, Sarah P. Harrison, F. A. Street-Perrot, and R. A. Perrot
1987    "Late Holocene Human Impact on Lake Basins in Central Mexico." Paper presented at the 12th meeting of INQUA, Ottawa.

Mexican National Census
1905    *V Censo General* (1900). Part 2, Dirección General de Estadística. Secretaría de Fomento, Mexico.
1943    *VI Censo de Población* (1940). Michoacán, Dirección General de Es-tadística. Secretaría de la Economía Nacional, Mexico.
1973    *IX Censo General de Población* (1970). Vol. 11, Dirección General de Estadística. Secretaría de Industria y Comercio, Mexico.

Michelet, Dominique
1986    "Informe preliminar general del proyecto arqueológico Michoacán, México." CEMCA, Mexico. Photocopied.
1988a   "La Ceramique de Projet Michoacán." Photocopied.
1988b   "Apuntes para el análisis de las migraciones en el México prehis-pánico." In *Movimentos de población en el occidente de México*, edited by T. Calvo and G. López, pp. 13–24. Centre d'Etudes Mexicaines et Centraméricaines and Colegio de Michoacán, México.

# BIBLIOGRAPHY

Michelet, Dominique, A. Ichon, and G. Migeon
n.d. "Residencias, barrios y sitios posclásicos en el Malpais de Zacapu." *Actas de la prima reunión sobre las sociedades prehispánicas en el Centro-Occidente de México.* Querétaro (1985).

Michelet, Dominique, M. C., Arnauld, and M-F. Fauvet Berthelot
1989 "El Proyecto del CEMCA en Michoacán. Etapa I: Un balance." *Trace* 16: 70–87.

Moedano, Hugo
1941 "Estudio preliminar de la cerámica de Tzintzuntzan. Temporada III." *Revista Mexicana de Estudios Antropológicos* 5 (1): 21–42.
1946 "La cerámica de Zinapécuaro, Michoacán." *Anales del Museo Michoacano* 2:439–49.

Moguel Cos, Ma. Antonieta
1987 "Trabajos de salvamento arqueológico en las cuencas de Cuitzeo, Pátzcuaro y Zirahuén: Un intento de interpretación cultural." Tésis para Licenciado en Arqueologia. Escuela Nacional de Antropología e Historia (ENAH), INAH, Mexico.

Moone, Jane R.
1973 *Desarrollo Tarasco: Integración nacional en el occidente de México.* Ediciones Especiales 67. Instituto Indigenista Interamericano, Mexico.

Morris, Craig
1972 "State Settlement in Tawantinsuyu: A Strategy of Compulsory Urbanism." In *Contemporary Archeology,* edited by M. Leone, pp. 393–401. Southern Illinois University Press, Carbondale.
1982 "The Infrastructure of Inka Control in the Peruvian Central Highlands." In *The Inca and Aztec States: 1400–1800,* edited by G. Collier, R. Rosaldo, and J. Wirth, pp. 153–71. Academic Press, New York.

Mountjoy, Joseph
1969 "On the Origin of West Mexican Metallurgy." *Mesoamerican Studies* 4:26–42. University Museum, Southern Illinois University, Carbondale.
1974 *Some Hypotheses Regarding the Petroglyphs of West Mexico.* Mesoamerican Studies 9. University Museum, Southern Illinois University, Carbondale.
1987 "Antiquity, Interpretation, and Stylistic Evolution of Petroglyphs." *American Antiquity* 52: 161–74.

Mountjoy, Joseph, and L. Torres M.
1985 "The Production and Use of Prehispanic Metal Artifacts in the Central Coastal Area of Jalisco, Mexico." In *The Archeology of West and Northwest Mesoamerica,* edited by M. Foster and P. Weigand, pp. 133–52. Westview Press, Boulder.

Muller, Florencia
1979 *Estudio tipologico provisional de la cerámica del Balsas Medio.* SEP-INAH Colección Científica 78. Mexico.

Murra, John V.
1982  "The Mit'a Obligations of Ethnic Groups to the Inka State." In *The Inca and Aztec States: 1400–1800*, edited by G. Collier, R. Rosaldo, and J. Wirth, pp. 237–62. Academic Press, New York.

Nansen Díaz, Eréndira
1985  *Elementos de fonología y morfología del Tarasco de San Jerónimo Purenchécuaro Michoacán.* Colección Científica 38. INAH, Departamento de Linguística, Mexico.

Nelson, Cynthia
1971  *The Waiting Village: Social Change in Rural Mexico.* Little, Brown, Boston.

Noguera, Eduardo
1931  "Exploraciones arqueológicas en las regiones de Zamora y Pátzcuaro, estado de Michoacán." *Anales del Museo Nacional de México* 4 (7): 88–104.
1944  "Exploraciones en Jiquilpan." *Anales del Museo Michoacano* 3: 37–52.
1965  *La cerámica arqueológia de Mesoamérica.* Instituto de Investigaciones Historicas 86. Universidad Nacional Autónoma de México, Mexico, D.F.

Oliveros, José Arturo
1975  "Arqueología del estado de Michoacán." In *Los pueblos y señoríos teocráticos*, Vol. 7, *México: Panorama histórico y cultural*, pp. 207–14. INAH, Mexico.

Osorio Tafall, B. F.
1944  "Biodinámica del lago de Pátzcuaro." *Revista de la Sociedad Mexicana de Historia Natural* 5 (3–4):197–227.

Palerm, Angel, and Eric Wolf
1960  "Ecological potential and cultural development in Mesoamerica." *Social Science Monographs* 3:1–37. Pan American Union, Washington, D.C.

Paredes, Carlos S.
1976  "El tributo indígena en la regíón del Lago de Pátzuaro, siglo XIV." Tésis de Licenciatura, Universidad Nacional Autónoma de México, Mexico, D.F.
1979  "El sistema tributario prehispánico entre los tarascos." Manuscript.

Paso y Troncoso, Francisco del
1888  "Calendario de los tarascos." Museo Michoacano *Anales* 1: 85–96.

Pedimento de Antonio Huit-Simíngari
1553  Archivo General de Indias (Seville), Patronato Real, legajo 60, número 2, ramos 3.

Pendergast, D. M.
1962  "Metal Artifacts in Prehispanic Mesoamerica." *American Antiquity* 27 (4): 520–44.

Piña Chan, Román
  1963  *Ciudades arqueológicas de México.* Instituto Nacional de Antropología e Historia, Mexico.
  1977  *Bitacora: Centro regional de México-Michoacán.* SEP-INAH, Mexico.
Piña Chan, Román, and Kuniaki Oí
  1982  *Exploraciones arqueológicas en Tingambato, Michoacán.* INAH, Mexico.
Plan Lerma Asistencia Técnica (PLAT)
  1968  "Operación Pátzcuaro: Información General." Photocopied.
Pollard, H. Perlstein
  1972  *Prehispanic Urbanism at Tzintzuntzan, Michoacán.* University Microfilms, Ann Arbor, Michigan.
  1977  "An Analysis of Urban Zoning and Planning in Prehispanic Tzintzuntzan." *Proceedings: American Philosophical Society* 121 (1): 46–69.
  1979  "Paleoecology of the Lake Patzcuaro Basin: Implications for the Development of the Tarascan State." Paper presented at the 43d International Congress of Americanists, Vancouver.
  1980  "Central Places and Cities: A Consideration of the Protohistoric Tarascan State." *American Antiquity* 45 (4): 677–96.
  1982a "Ecological Variation and Economic Exchange in the Tarascan State." *American Ethnologist* 9 (2): 250–68.
  1982b "Water and Politics: Paleoecology and the Centralization of the Tarascan State." Paper presented at symposium on Paleoecology and Man in Central Mexico, 44th Congress of Americanists, Manchester.
  1983  "La cuenca del lago de Pátzcuaro: Población y recursos durante el período prehispánico y comienzas del hispánico 1500–1550." *Revista de la Universidad* 2: 22–23. Universidad Michoacana, Morelia, Mexico.
  1987  "The Political Economy of Prehispanic Tarascan Metallurgy." *American Antiquity* 52 (4): 741–52.
  1988  "Irechequa Tzintzuntzan: Variation on a Mesoamerican Theme." Paper presented at symposium on Imperial Structures in Prehispanic Mesoamerica, 46th International Congress of Americanists, Amsterdam.
Pollard, H. Perlstein, and S. Gorenstein
  1978  "Development of the Prehistoric Tarascan State: A Research Strategy." Paper presented to the 43rd Annual Meeting of the Society for American Archeology, Tuscon.
  1980  "Agrarian Potential, Population and the Tarascan State." *Science* 209 (4453): 274–77.
Ponce, Alonso (1586)
  1968  *Relación breve y verdadera de algunas cosas de las muchas que sucedieron al Padre Alonso Ponce en las provincias de la Nueva España, siedo comisario general de aquellas partes.* Corresponsalia del Seminario de Cultura Mexicana, Guadalajara.

Porter, Muriel
    1948    *Pipas precortesianas*. Acta Antropológia 3, 2.
Quesada Ramírez, M. N.
    1972    *Los Matlatzincas: Epoca prehispánica y epoca colonial hasta 1650*. Serie
            Investigaciones 22. INAH, Mexico.
*Relación de Michoacán* (1541) (RM)
    1956    *Relación de las ceremonias y ritos y población y gobierno de los indios de
            la provincia de Michoacán*. Reproducción Facsimilar del Ms IV de El
            Escorial, Madrid. Aguilar Publiscistas, Madrid.
    1980    *La relación de Michoacán*. Versión Paleográfica, Separación de Textos,
            Ordenación Coloquil, Estudio Preliminar Y Notas de F. Miranda.
            Estudios Michoacanos V. Fimax, Morelia, Michoacán.
*Relación de Nuño de Guzmán*
    1526    Archivo General de Indias (Seville), Patronato Real, legajo 54, nú-
            mero 3, ramos 2.
*Relaciones geográficas* (1579–1581) (RG)
    1958    *Relaciones geográficas de la diócesis de Michoacán*. Edited by J. Corona
            Nuñez. Guadalajara.
    1985    *Relaciones y memorias de la provincia de Michoacán 1579–1581*. Edited
            by Alvaro Ochoa S. and Gerardo Sánchez D. Universidad Mich-
            oacana, Ayuntamiento de Morelia.
    1987    *Relaciones geográficas del siglo XVI: Michoacán*. Seerie Antropológica
            74. Edición de René Acuña, UNAM, Instituto de Investigaciones
            Antropológicas, Mexico.
RG (see *Relaciones Geográficas*)
RM (see *Relación de Michoacán*)
Romero, José Guadalupe
    1862    *Noticias para formar la historia y la estadística del opispado de Michoa-
            cán*. Vicente García Torres, Mexico.
Romero Flores, Jesús
    1939    *Nomenclatura geográfia de Michoacán*. Sociedad de Geografía e Histo-
            ria de Michoacán, Morelia.
Romero Molina, Javier
    1986    *Catálogo de la colección de dientes mutilados prehispánicos*. Vol. 4. Col-
            ección Fuentes, INAH, Mexico.
Ross, Virginia L.
    1939    "Some Pottery Types of the Highlands of Western Mexico." Master's
            thesis, Department of Anthropology, Yale University, New Haven.
Rouse, Irving
    1960    "The Classification of Artifacts in Archaeology," *American Antiquity*
            25 (3): 313–23.
Rowe, John H.
    1982    "Inca Policies and Institutions Relating to the Cultural Unification
            of the Empire." In *The Inca and Aztec States: 1400–1800*, edited by

G. Collier, R. Rosaldo, and J. Wirth, pp. 93–118. Academic Press, New York.

Rubín de la Borbolla, Daniel F.
1939    "Antropología Tzintzuntzan-Ihuatzio: Temporadas I y II." *Revista Mexicana de Estudios Antropológicas* 3 (2): 99–121.
1941    "Exploraciones arqueológicas en Michoacán: Tzintzuntzan Temporada III" *Revista Mexicana de Estudios Antropológicas* 5 (1): 5–20.
1944    "Orfebrería tarasca." *Cuadernos Americanos* 3: 125–38.

Sabloff, Jeremy, and Robert E. Smith
1969    "The Importance of Both Analytic and Taxonomic Classification in the Type-Variety System." *American Antiquity* 34 (3): 278–85.

Sacchetti, Alfredo
1983    *Taxa anthropológica de México en el marco mesoamericano.* Universidad Nacional Autónoma de México, Mexico.

Sahagún, Bernardino de (1569)
1950–    *Florentine Codex: General History of the Things of New Spain.* Trans-
1969    lated by A. Anderson and C. Dibble. University of Utah and School of American Research, Santa Fe and Salt Lake City.

Salmon, E. T.
1982    *The Making of Roman Italy.* Cornell University Press, Ithaca.

Sanders, William T.
1970    "The Population of the Teotihuacan Valley, the Basin of Mexico, and the Central Mexican Symbiotic Region in the Sixteenth Century." In *Teotihuacan Valley Project, Final Report.* Occasional Papers in Anthropology 3:385–457. Pennsylvania State University, University Park.

Sanders, William T., Jeffrey R. Parsons, and Robert S. Santley
1979    *The Basin of Mexico: Ecological Processes in the Evolution of a Civilization.* Academic Press, New York.

Schondube B., Otto
1987    "El occidente de México: Algunas de sus características y problemas." In *Homenaje a Román Piña Chan*, pp. 403–10. Serie Antropológica 79. Instituto de Investigaciones Antropológicas, UNAM, México.

Seler, Eduard
1908    *Gesammelte Abhandlungen zur Amerikanischen Sprach und Alterthumskunde.* Vol. 3. Behrend, Berlin.

Sepúlveda y H., María Teresa
1988    *La medicina entre los purépecha prehispánicos.* Serie Antropológica 94. UNAM, Mexico.

Simpson, Leslie Byrd
1934    "Description and Visita of the Villages of Tingambato, San Juan, Corundapan, and San Angel (1599)." Encomienda of Francisco de Villegas (AGN, Tierras, LXIV, doc. 3). In *Studies in the Administra-*

tion of the Indians of New Spain, pp. 75–78. University of California Press, Berkeley.

1950 "The Population of 22 Towns in Michoacan in 1554." *Hispanic American Historical Review* 30: 248–50.

Skylab ERTS

1973 Satellite photographs, Bands 4–7. EROS Data Center, Geological Survey, United States Department of the Interior, Sioux Falls.

Smith, Michael E.

1987 "Imperial Strategies in the Western Portion of the Aztec Empire." Paper delivered at the Annual Meeting of the American Anthropological Association, Chicago. Photocopied.

Smith, Michael E., and Kenneth G. Hirth

1988 "The Development of Prehispanic Cotton Spinning Technology in Western Morelos, Mexico." *Journal of Field Archaeology* 15 (3): 345–58.

Smith, William C.

1965 "The People of La Pacanda: Social Organization and Social Change in a Tarascan Village." Ph.D. diss., University of California, Berkeley. University Microfilms, Ann Arbor.

Stanislawski, Dan

1947 "Tarascan Political Geography." *American Anthropologist* 47: 46–55.

1950 *The Anatomy of 11 Towns in Michoacan*. Institute of Latin American Studies Publication 10. University of Texas, Austin.

Stirling, Matthew W.

1960 "The Use of the Atlatl on Lake Patzcuaro, Michoacán." Bureau of American Ethnology *Bulletin* 173, pp. 261–68, pls. 39–41. Smithsonian Institution, Washington, D.C.

Street-Perrott, F. A., R. A. Perrott, and D. Harkness

1989 "Anthropogenic Soil Erosion Around Lake Pátzcuaro, Michoacán, During the Preclassic and Late Postclassic-Hispanic Period." *American Antiquity* 54 (4): 759–65.

Suárez, Jorge A.

1983 *The Mesoamerican Indian Languages*. Cambridge University Press, Cambridge.

*Suma de visitas de pueblos* (1547–1560)

1905 *Papeles de Nueva España*. Tomo 1. F. del Paso y Troncoso, Madrid.

Swadesh, Maurecio

1969 *Elementos del tarasco antiguo*. UNAM, Instituto de Investigaciones Historicas, Mexico.

Taladoire, Eric

1989 "Las canchas de juego de pelota de Michoacán." *Trace* 16:88–99. CEMCA, Mexico.

Toledo, Victor Manuel, and Narcisco Barrera-Bassols

1984 *Ecología y desarrollo rural en Pátzcuaro*. Instituto de Biología, UNAM, Mexico.

Tolstoy, Paul
   1958   "Surface Survey of the Northern Valley of Mexico: The Classic and
          Post-Classic Periods." *Transactions of the American Philosophical Soci-
          ety* 8 (5).
   1971   "Utilitarian Artifacts of Central Mexico." In *Handbook of Middle
          American Indians*, edited by R. Wauchope, 10 (1): 270–96. University
          of Texas Press, Austin.
UNESCO
   1973   *International Classification and Mapping of Vegetation*. Ecology and
          Conservation 6. UNESCO, Paris.
USAF
   1942   Vertical and oblique aerial photographs, approximately 1:40,000.
          U.S. Army Air Force, Defense Mapping Agency, Washington, D.C.
Van Zantwijk, Rudolf A. M.
   1967   *Servants of the Saints: The Social and Cultural Identity of a Tarascan
          Community in Mexico*. Van Gorcum, Assen.
   1973   "Politics and Ethnicity in a Prehispanic Mexican State Between the
          Thirteenth and Fifteenth Centuries." *Plural Societies* 4 (2): 23–52.
Velásquez Gallardo, P.
   1978   *Diccionario de la lengua Phorhepecha: Español-Phorhepecha, Phor-
          hepecha-Español*. Fondo de Cultura Economica, Mexico, D.F.
Wachtel, Nathan
   1982   "The mitimas of the Cochabamba Valley: The Colonization Policy of
          Huayna Capac." In *The Inca and Aztec States: 1400–1800*, edited by
          G. Collier, R. Rosaldo, and J. Wirth, pp. 199–235. Academic Press,
          New York.
Warren, J. Benedict
   1963   *Vasco de Quiroga and His Pueblo-Hospitals of Santa Fe*. Academy of
          American Franciscan History, Washington, D.C.
   1968   "Minas de cobre de Michoacán, 1533." *Anales del Museo Michoacano*
          6: 35–52.
   1971   "Fray Jerónimo de Alcalá: Author of the Relación de Michoacán?"
          *The Americas* 27 (3): 307–26.
   1977   *La conquista de Michoacán 1521–1530*. Fimax Publicistas, Morelia,
          Michoacán.
   1983   "Writing the Language of Michoacan: Sixteenth Century Franciscan
          Linguistics." In *Franciscan Presence in the Americas*, edited by F. Mo-
          rales. Academy of American Franciscan History, Potomac, Maryland.
   1985   *The Conquest of Michoacán*. University of Oklahoma Press, Norman.
   1989   "Información del licenciado Vasco de Quiroga sobre el cobre de Mic-
          hoacán, 1533." *Anales del Museo Michoacano*, Tercera Epoca, pp. 30–
          52, Morelia.
Watts, W., and J. Platt Bradbury
   1982   "Paleoecological Studies at Lake Pátzucaro on the West-Central Mex-

ican Plateau and at Chalco in the Basin of Mexico." *Quaternary Research* 17: 56–70.

Weaver, Muriel Porter
  1981   *The Aztecs, Maya, and Their Predecessors: Archaeology of Mesoamerica*. Academic Press, New York.

Weigand, Phil C.
  1982a  "Introduction." *Anthropology* 6 (1–2): 1–6.
  1982b  "Mining and Mineral Trade in Prehispanic Zacatecas." *Anthropology* 6 (1–2): 87–134.
  1985   "Evidence for Complex Societies During the Western Mesoamerican Classic Period." In *The Archaeology of West and Northwest Mesoamerica*, edited by M. Foster and P. Weigand, pp. 47–91. Westview Press, Boulder.

West, Robert
  1948   *Cultural Geography of the Modern Tarascan Area*. Institute of Social Anthropology 7. Smithsonian Institution, Washington, D.C.

Wolf, Eric
  1982   *Europe and the People Without History*. University of California Press, Berkeley.
  1987   "Cultura e ideología." In *La heterodoxia recuperada en torno a Angel Palerm*, edited by Susana Glantz, pp. 582–96. Fondo de Cultura Economica, Mexico.

# INDEX

The place-names of the fifty sites in chapter 3 (table 3.2, p. 78) are not included unless they are central places; the conquests listed in chapter 4 (table 4.1, pp. 94–98) are not included in the index.